On This Day In

MEMPHIS
HISTORY

On This Day In
MEMPHIS
HISTORY

G. WAYNE DOWDY

THE
History
PRESS

Published by The History Press
Charleston, SC 29403
www.historypress.net

First published 2014

Manufactured in the United States

ISBN 978.1.62619.136.5

Library of Congress CIP data applied for.

CONTENTS

Acknowledgements 7

Introduction 9

January 11

February 42

March 74

April 107

May 138

June 172

July 203

August 235

September 267

October 297

November 328

December 360

Selected Bibliography 395

About the Author 397

ACKNOWLEDGEMENTS

This book would not have been possible without the love and support of my family. I dedicate this book to my parents, Barbara Ann Nance and Gerald McLain Dowdy; my grandparents, John McLain, Ivy Lucile Heckle Dowdy, William Herbert and Lurline Belle Griffin Nance; my brother and sister-in-law William Johnathan "Bud" and Robin Paige Clement Dowdy; my niece Britney Amber Dowdy Pierce; nephew-in-law Larry Hank Pierce and grandniece Mallorie Ann Pierce; my nephews Cody Austin Dowdy and Brandon Ryan Dowdy; Uncle J.B. and Aunt Carole Nance; Uncle Larry H. Nance, Uncle Ron G. and Aunt Donna Nance; Aunt Viola Heckle; and my cousins: Justin, Clay and Clint Nance; Lisa Nance Brooks; Mike and Forrest Brooks; Chris, Heather and Haleigh Nance; Gene and Jean Hair Miller; Laura Leigh Miller Traylor; John, Olivia Belle and Conrad Traylor; Eddie, Rachael, Alex and Stuart Miller; Lanie and Martha Miller; Faye Stabler; Kim

Hair Sox; Donald, Corey and Luke Sox; W.D. Hair; and Ann and Harold Waldon.

I also wish to thank Director of Libraries Keenon McCloy and my colleagues in the History and Social Sciences Department at the Benjamin L. Hooks Central Library—Betty Blaylock, Joan Cannon, Jeramy Clark, Gina Cordell, Laura Cunningham, Dr. Barbara D. Flanary, Sarah Frierson, Jasmine Holland, Verjeana Hunt, Dr. James R. Johnson, Thomas W. Jones, Patricia M. LaPointe, Bryan Massey, Patrick W. O'Daniel, Lanny Rodell Ross II, Belmar Toney and Marilyn Umfress—for their friendship and encouragement over the years. This also goes for Ken Kimble, Walter Hoehn, Paul Prothero, Dave "Truck" Robinson and Grant Wade. The History Press is a wonderful publisher to write for, and I thank everyone there for their support. I especially want to thank my editor Banks Smither for asking me to write this book and for his faith and kindness throughout the writing process. And last but not least my love goes to Gina Cordell, Paul Gahn, my godson Ellis Nelson Cordell Gahn and Carey, Beena, Natacha, Mischa and Dennis White.

INTRODUCTION

As a student of Memphis history, I have often uncovered fascinating stories about the Bluff City that do not fit into a larger narrative. *On This Day in Memphis History* seeks to tell these stories within the framework of a day-by-day accounting of the city's history. Above all things, Memphis is a creative town, and that is reflected in the 365 days that make up this volume. As you will see, this creativity took on many forms: in music, obviously, but also in art, barbeque cooking, entrepreneurship, literature, medicine, sports and, sadly, violent crime. The challenge in writing *On This Day in Memphis History* was to avoid the most familiar incidents in the Bluff City's history while still paying attention to the people, places and events that Memphians hold most dear. My hope is that most of the daily entries are not known to those who have studied Memphis history or even just lived here for a long period of time. Although by necessity each day's entry is short, whenever possible I have placed the story within its historical context. It would not do, I think, to introduce you to a moment in time without sharing how it all comes out. Within these pages, you will meet the prophet who vowed to sink Memphis into the Mississippi River, experience a violent Saturday night on Beale Street, watch the Tigers smash the Green Bay Packers, live through the day it rained snakes, meet the scientist who died experimenting with X-rays, smell slow-cooked pulled pork and hear the steady beat of blues, jazz and rock 'n' roll.

So let us travel back to January 1, 1950, where a New Year's celebration gets a bit out of hand.

January 1, 1950

Battle Erupts on Main Street

Hundreds of Memphians armed with firecrackers and other explosives poured onto Main Street early on this holiday morning. As the hour neared midnight, the staccato sounds of explosions filled the air as Memphians began, in the words of newspaper reporter Roy Jennings, a "prolonged bombardment with firecrackers and sidewalk torpedoes." The crowd was very large, and according to one observer, "At least half of the people on the streets [were] shooting fireworks." One zealous celebrant, John Brown of South Dunlap, temporarily lost his head and threw a large firecracker at the feet of two police officers. When it exploded, Brown immediately lost his freedom and was charged with disorderly conduct. As similar explosions rocked the downtown area, David Booker and Walter Henderson were also arrested for selling fireworks in violation of city ordinances. Police commissioner Claude Armour explained that "because Saturday night was New Year's Eve and spirit was at its highest in Memphis, our main interest was to see that no one was injured. Although the use of fireworks is a violation of the law, we didn't try to interfere unless there was an aggravated case."

January 2, 1955

Rhythm and Blues Singer Laid to Rest

The funeral for rock 'n' roll pioneer John Marshall Alexander, known to music fans as Johnny Ace, was held on this day at Clayborn Temple AME church. Known for such hits as "The Clock," "Pledging My Love" and "Never Let Me Go," Ace had begun his career as a piano player for blues performer Joe Hill Lewis. He later played with B.B. King and hosted a radio program on WDIA. On Christmas Day 1954, Ace retired to his dressing room after performing for 3,500 people at the auditorium in Houston, Texas. Ace was fiddling with a .22-caliber revolver, pointing it at those in the room with him and pulling the trigger. After singer Willie Mae "Big Mama" Thornton told him "not to snap the pistol at anybody," Ace then pointed the pistol to his head and declared, "I'll show you that it won't shoot." Unfortunately, he was mistaken. The pistol did shoot, and Ace lost his life. Attending the funeral conducted by Reverend R. McRae and disc jockey Reverend Dwight "Gatemouth" Moore were Peacock Records owner Don Robey and musicians B.B. King and Willie Mae Thornton. Pallbearers included recording artists Rosco Gordon and Little Junior Parker and jazz drummer Finas Newborn. According to historian James M. Salem, "Ace's 'Pledging My Love' will forever be *the* transitional record between rhythm and blues and rock 'n' roll, and the singer/songwriter himself will always be associated with the card still featured prominently on the cover of his only LP: Johnny Ace was, after all, the ace of hearts."

January 3, 1915

Socialists Organize for Unemployed

The *Commercial Appeal* newspaper reported on this day that the Socialist Party of Memphis met at Carpenters' Hall, where it formed an organization to demand that the government assist the jobless find meaningful work. Calling itself the Unemployed Conference, the group had earlier requested assistance from Mayor E.H. Crump, who had met with the Socialists and agreed to appoint a commission to study the unemployment problem. The conference planned to contact President Woodrow Wilson and Congress to remind them that there were four million unemployed workers in the United States. According to the reporter, the Socialists demanded "an extension of all public works and to give employment to the jobless on basis of eight-hour days and pay union wages. The government will be asked to lend money to states and municipalities without interest to carry on the public work. A demand will also be made for legislation to shorten the working day of laborers…giving each workman one and one-half days rest in each seven days. A demand also will be made to prohibit the employment of children under the age of 16 years." Little was immediately done to heed the Socialists' demands, but their call for wage and hour laws, child labor reform and federal loans for relief and expanded public works programs were adopted by the administration of Franklin D. Roosevelt in the 1930s during the Great Depression.

January 4, 1902

Buried Alive

The very much alive Carl Atheno was resurrected from a six-foot grave in which he had been buried a week earlier. Although laid out under a vacant lot at the corner of Union and Second Streets, a wooden chute connected Atheno to the surface, allowing air to flow into the grave and spectators to view him in repose. Supposedly, Atheno was hypnotized before being placed in the grave, but more likely, he was simply trained to endure the confined space. At 8:00 p.m., one thousand Memphians paid admission and crowded around the grave to witness the revival. According to a newspaper reporter, the "tall buildings around the lot cast a gloomy series of shadows over the scene—The electric lights in the streets could not reach the spot, and the chilly breezes and damp earth added to the gloom of the picture." Once workmen dug up the coffin, Atheno emerged "rigid and as stiff as a board" but soon flailed about so violently that he had to be restrained from lunging into the crowd. Fed warm milk and crackers by his wife, Atheno boarded a waiting carriage and was driven away from the astonished crowd. The stunt was organized by Memphis sports performer Christopher H. "Doc" Hottum, who once managed the prizefighter Battling Nelson, organized dance marathons and was the founder of a ten-mile swimming race on the Mississippi River that was a popular annual event for forty-five years. At a time when entertainment was confined to live theatrical performances—there were no movies, radio or television yet—Doc Hottum's stunts mystified and delighted Memphians during the first half of the twentieth century.

January 5, 1973

Patrolman's Mustache Raises Police Director's Eyebrows
Police officer Art Keene Jr. was allowed to return to work on this day after being suspended for two days for having an unauthorized mustache. Keene admitted that he was challenging the department's refusal to allow officers to grow facial hair when he reported for duty after the New Year's holiday. Ironically, police director Jay Hubbard had previously decided to allow officers to grow mustaches but had not yet informed them of that fact. Hubbard explained that the "mayor and I and Chief Price discussed the question of mustache policies some time ago. We all agreed that the prohibition of mustaches no longer made any sense. But I supported the punishment for patrolman Keene's method of raising the question." Hubbard, a retired marine corps brigadier general, assumed command of a police department battered by charges of brutality and corruption in 1972. As his handling of the mustache incident suggests, Hubbard was a strict disciplinarian who demanded much from his officers. But he was also committed to improving their working conditions, providing additional equipment and increasing their pay. Hubbard also struggled hard to create a strong relationship between police and the African American community. When he left office in February 1975, an editorial in the *Commercial Appeal* praised Hubbard: "In a little more than two years he has rebuilt public confidence in the city's police, and, equally important, has boosted police morale."

January 6, 1946

German Prisoner Flees with Another Man's Wife

Mrs. Edith Swink Rogers arrived at her parents' home on Madison Avenue after being arrested by the FBI for assisting a German prisoner of war escape from her husband's plantation in Grenada, Mississippi. Charged with "aiding in the escape and transportation of an enemy of the United States," Rogers was free on a $2,000 bond, while her lover, Luftwaffe lieutenant Helmut von der Aue, was detained by the provost marshal in Nashville. According to von der Aue, he had fallen in love with Mrs. Rogers during the four months he worked at the plantation with eighty other prisoners from POW camp McCain. After the prisoners finished their lunch on Wednesday, January 2, Rogers apparently invited von der Aue to stay behind and have a drink. The couple consumed a fifth of liquor, and when the bottle was emptied, they decided to run away together. Traveling through Memphis, they continued on to Nashville, where they were apprehended by Federal Bureau of Investigation agents. Helmut von der Aue was one of hundreds of German prisoners held in the Memphis area during World War II. One of the largest camps was located at the Army Quartermaster Depot on Airways. According to a 1944 International Red Cross report, the "inside of the camp is agreeable in aspect due to the arrangement of gardens. The day before our visit, a company of 250 men had just arrived. This increases the number of German POWs in the camp to 600." One of those prisoners was Edwin Pelz, who was so enthralled by Memphis that he returned in 1975 for a visit.

January 7, 1913

"I Have Been a Bad Girl"

Seventeen-year-old Beatrice Lauderdale was detained by police on this day during the search for a runaway teenager from Arkansas. When they got her to the station, Lauderdale told officers she had been kidnapped and sold into prostitution during a visit to Memphis in September 1912. En route from her home in Paragould, Arkansas, to visit her aunt in Chattanooga, Lauderdale had stopped in Memphis, where she planned to stay at the Hotel Gayoso overnight before boarding a train for East Tennessee. While sitting in the hotel lobby, she struck up a conversation with a young man who invited her to lunch. During the meal, Lauderdale drank enough liquor to make herself "giddy." She eventually passed out, and the following day found herself a prisoner in a house of ill fame. "I have been a bad girl," the young woman explained to the press. Beatrice Lauderdale's story was similar to those told by antiprostitution reformers when warning young girls to avoid being unaccompanied in large cities lest they be sold into "white slavery." Whether or not Lauderdale's story was true, for much of Memphis's history, organized prostitution was a common practice in the city. In 1874, for example, there were eighteen brothels in the city that contained at least ninety prostitutes, or inmates as polite society called them. Brothels remained a part of local culture until 1940, when city government permanently closed the last organized whorehouses in Memphis.

January 8, 1936

Shelby Forest Park Plan Approved

The National Park Service on this day approved the creation of a thirteen-thousand-acre park near Memphis in northern Shelby County. Named Shelby Forest, the park contained a large woodland area as well as recreational facilities that Memphians enjoyed well into the twenty-first century. The announcement was made by Conrad L. Wirth, assistant director of the National Park Service, after conferring with *Memphis Press-Scimitar* editor and member of the Shelby County Forest Committee Edward J. Meeman and other officials. According to a *Press-Scimitar* reporter, "Mr. Wirth made it clear that the project had as its purpose primarily the restoration of forest scenery and wild life for the enjoyment of present and future generations and that recreation was subordinate to this. Deer, wild turkeys and other animals and birds will roam and propagate in this area." When the park opened in 1939 it contained hiking trails, cabins, fifty acres of picnic grounds, a lake and one hundred species of trees. The driving force behind the creation of the wilderness area was Edward Meeman. In recognition of his tireless work, it was renamed Meeman-Shelby Forest in 1967.

January 9, 1940

First Lady Visits Memphis Artist

First Lady Eleanor Roosevelt visited Memphis artist Elizabeth Searcy in her studio at DuPont Circle in Washington, D.C. Born in Memphis on June 4, 1877, Searcy graduated from Miss Higbee's School and studied painting in Philadelphia. She opened a studio in New York City but returned often to paint local scenes. In 1938, she moved to Washington, where she continued to paint, and a collection of her etchings was cataloged in the Library of Congress. Mrs. Roosevelt described the visit in her popular syndicated column "My Day":

First Lady Eleanor Roosevelt praised Memphis artist Elizabeth Searcy in her syndicated newspaper column "My Day."

> *Yesterday afternoon I spent a delightful hour with Miss Elizabeth Searcy in her studio. She has painted a great deal in Newport, Rhode Island, New York City and the South. It is evident in looking at her work that she has a great feeling for her home city, Memphis, Tenn.*

In her later years, Searcy moved back to Memphis, where she died in 1969.

January 10, 1918

Memphis Equal Suffrage League Meets

Members of the Memphis Equal Suffrage league met on this day in the parlor of the Hotel Chisca to discuss several issues related to securing women the right to vote in the United States. The first order of business was a discussion of whether or not the league should merge with the statewide Tennessee Equal Suffrage Association. The group voted overwhelmingly to join with the TESA and offered its unqualified support to the current TESA president, Katherine Burch Warner of Nashville. Also adopted was the draft of a telegram to be sent to political leaders that read, "The Memphis Equal Suffrage League urges that as the national suffrage amendment is sure to pass, you ask the Tennessee delegation not to put the affront of a negative vote upon the women of Tennessee." The dedication and leadership shown by both the Memphis Equal Suffrage League and Tennessee Equal Suffrage Association led to Tennessee's being the thirty-sixth state to ratify the Nineteenth amendment on August 18, 1920.

Memphis women played an important role in the passage of the Nineteenth Amendment, which secured the right to vote for women in 1920.

January 11, 1941

War Is Declared on Gamblers and Subversives

Fire and police commissioner Joseph Boyle announced that police had under surveillance fifty or sixty gamblers who must either flee the city or give up their criminal ways: "I'm giving them 30 days in which to get jobs, go to work making an honest living, or pack their grips and get out of Memphis. These parasites contribute nothing to this community, take no part in civic work and contribute nothing except an expense to the police department which has to watch them night and day to protect the misguided suckers from their betting and stealing."

E.H. Crump, Memphis political leader, had equally harsh words for subversive elements within the city: "I am enlisting against these beastly creatures the Fifth Column in Memphis and Shelby County with an unmasked committee of loyal Americans...We must deal with those loose tongue, talking, teaching, spying lecturing traitors...These people, white and black, have just about as much love for democracy as a tramp has for soap...Who would dare carry down the main streets of Berlin or Moscow and expect police protection? They would be shot 50 times in five minutes...Free speech is a noble ideal, but not for those who wish to destroy this government."

Boyle's war on gamblers was the culmination of an anticrime offensive that began in the spring of 1940. Before the year was out, organized vice disappeared from the streets of Memphis. However, Crump's attack on so-called subversives did not yield similar results. No large groups of Communists or Nazis were ever rounded up, nor were any acts of espionage or sabotage ever uncovered.

January 12, 1960

Big Star Grocery Store Opens in Parkway Village

Raymond Robilio and Sam Sarno opened their second Big Star grocery store in the growing Parkway Village neighborhood on this day. Located at 3071 South Perkins, the 17,500-square-foot store had ample shelf space to stock customer's favorite brands of foodstuffs with thirty-eight employees on hand to provide assistance. In the words of a *Commercial Appeal* reporter, the store also boasted a snack bar "for relaxing after a hard day's shopping and so the housewife can shop through the noon hour." Robilio and Sarno had been partners since 1947, when they opened their first grocery store on Summer Avenue, and three years later, in 1950, they affiliated with the Big Star grocery chain. A native of Chicago, Sarno was stationed in Memphis during World War II and later married Robilio's sister. Sarno explained that "we offer the best national brands, quality meats and produce, recognized health and beauty aids and housewares and paper products." The partners liked being in the Parkway Village community. According to Sarno, it "is a fine place with nice people living out here." The first Big Star opened in 1949 at the Hellums Market in Whitehaven, and by 1962, there were ninety-three stores in five states. The store also inspired the name of the critically acclaimed Memphis rock 'n' roll group formed in 1971 by Alex Chilton, Chris Bell, Andy Hummell and Jody Stephens.

January 13, 1980

Paralyzed Football Player Returns from Soviet Union

Bill Crumby, paralyzed former Memphis State University football player, unexpectedly returned to Memphis from the Soviet Union on this day after deciding not to have surgery to repair his damaged spine. Crumby, the son of retired police director W.O. Crumby, broke his neck on October 29, 1977, during a football game with the University of Southern Mississippi. In late 1979, the Soviet Union's Sechenov Institute accepted his application to receive a well-regarded enzyme injection procedure designed to improve his spinal cord. "I'm not going over there with the expectation of a miracle…I don't want to expect too much, but you never want to give up on anything," he said. Funds were raised by the police department and Memphis State so his parents could travel with him, and they left on December 20, 1979. However, when they arrived, the Russian physicians told Crumby he needed surgery to remove three vertebrae to relieve pressure on the spinal cord. Reluctant to have the procedure done, Crumby decided to leave Russia when the Soviet Union invaded Afghanistan on December 24. Crumby explained that he was "too American or too redneck…but I didn't like what I was hearing." Besides, he hated the food the Russians served. "All I want right now is to get me a barbeque sandwich," he declared on his return. Bill Crumby did not regain the use of his legs, but he never lost his sunny optimism, which inspired many Memphians before his death in 2000. "I've never spent a minute getting down about my situation because I know it was something I had no control over," Crumby explained.

January 14, 1908

Lowenstein's Department Store Incorporates

On this day, the officers of B. Lowenstein and Brothers department store, located at the intersection of Main and Court Streets, announced they were incorporating the firm to make sure it would "remain a valuable asset to Memphis for many years after the founders and holders of it have passed away." Newly appointed officers of the corporation were E. Lowenstein, president; A.L. Lowenstein and L.D. Marks, vice-presidents; and J.A. Goodwin, secretary/treasurer. According to a newspaper reporter, there "is not a concern in the entire South that has been so successful as the firm of B. Lowenstein & Bros. From the time that Bernard Lowenstein began business in this city over half a century ago to the present time the motto of the firm has been 'justice' and a fair deal has been accorded all patrons and friends." The first Lowenstein store opened in 1855 at 242 North Main Street. In 1906, the store moved to the corner of Main and Court Streets, and a modern building was constructed at Monroe and Front Streets in 1924. Lowenstein's was the first major department store in Memphis to open a branch in the suburbs; in 1949, it constructed a department store at the intersection of Highland and Poplar Avenues near East Memphis.

January 15, 1877

The Day It Rained Snakes

A heavy thunderstorm slashed its way through the neighborhoods of South Memphis on this day. As the rain pelted the muddy streets, thousands of snakes suddenly appeared on the ground, which convinced many that somehow the sky had dumped reptiles on Memphis. An editor at the *Public Ledger* newspaper speculated that "it is not improbable that the water discharged from the clouds yesterday and the contents was taken up from a lake, gulf or the ocean by a waterspout thousands of miles away." In his daily report, a government weather observer wrote: "Morning opened with light rain; 10:20 a.m. began to pour down in torrents, lasting fifteen minutes, winds southwest; immediately after, the reptiles were discovered crawling on the sidewalks, in the road, gutters and yards of Vance street, between Lauderdale and Goslee streets, two blocks; careful inquiry was made to ascertain if anyone had seen them descend, but without success; neither were they found in the cisterns, on roofs, or any elevation above ground…when first seen they were a very dark brown, almost black; were very thick in some places, being tangled together like a mess of thread or yarn."

Although the incident was probably the result of nothing more than an unusually strong thunderstorm combined with high winds that forced the snakes from their natural cover, the day it rained snakes soon became one of Memphis's most persistent legends that continues to be remembered well into the twenty-first century.

January 16, 1894

Hindu Swami Visits the Bluff City

Swami Vive Kanada spoke to a large crowd of Memphians on the virtues of the Hindu religion and its relationship to Christianity. Introduced by Judge R.J. Morgan, who explained that European Americans and Indians are both members of the "Aryan" race, Swami Kanada walked on stage wearing a pink silk robe, black sash and yellow turban. According to a *Commercial Appeal* reporter, the "address might fitly be called a plea for universal tolerance illustrated by remarks concerning the religion of India." Kanada explained that the Hindu belief system is not that different from Christianity, and that Hindus feel that "all religions are embodiments of man's inspiration for holiness, and being such, all should be respected." Hindus worship the same God as Christians, the Swami declared and the "Hindu trinity of Brahma, Vishnu and Shiva is merely the embodiment of God the creator, the preserver and the destroyer." At the end of his talk, "he acknowledged his readiness to accept Christ but must also bow to Krishna and to Buddha." Although in 1894 there were few, if any, Memphis residents from the Indian subcontinent, by the beginning of the twenty-first century, there were 3,388 Memphians of Asian Indian descent living and worshipping in the Bluff City.

January 17, 1934

Central High Basketball Team Sets Scoring Record
The Central High School Warriors defeated Christian Brothers College 73–23 on this day in a hard-fought contest at the Bellevue High School gymnasium. Central quickly moved ahead, led by forwards Victor Bradford and Bill Porter, who scored 28 and 26 points respectively. Central coach Hugh Magevney took advantage of their huge lead to allow the second squad to gain some valuable experience on the court. High scorer for CBC was Pete Lenti, who made six baskets. Several other important basketball games were held across the city today. Russell Stewart of the Memphis Technical High School Yellow Jackets scored a point from the free-throw line in the final seconds of the game to beat the Messick High Panthers 19–18. The Sacred Heart Cardinals were crushed by the South Side Scrappers by 26 points, Humes High defeated Memphis University School 28–17 and the Messick Pantherettes overcame by 22 points the girls of Miss Hutchinson's School. As these contests suggest, the game of basketball was one of the city's most popular sports in the 1930s, and it only grew in the decades that followed with the success of the University of Memphis Tigers and the National Basketball Association's Memphis Grizzlies.

January 18, 1943

Memphis Nazi Blitzkriegs Beauty Shop

William Kastens, a German American who once stated that Adolph Hitler was "a wonderful man who has done great good for the German nation," was arrested for demolishing equipment in the beauty shop he once owned. Kastens settled in Memphis in 1904 and opened a popular beauty parlor. In 1939, he publicly praised both Hitler and Fritz Kuhn, head of the pro-Nazi German American Bund, and the following year, he was fined and sentenced to six months in prison for writing an obscene letter to a city official. Kastens's business declined rapidly and unable to pay his rent, Kastens's equipment was seized by the building's owners, W.P. Lowenstein and Joseph Perel. By early 1943, his anger got the better of him, and on a Sunday afternoon, he broke into the shop and smashed mirrors, slashed upholstered chairs, destroyed hairdryers, burned account books and pounded holes in the walls. Indicted for arson, malicious mischief and housebreaking, he was tried on February 8. From the witness stand, Kastens declared that he was "quite proud of my job" and explained that he had "worked like a Trojan" to destroy the equipment "to keep it out of the hands of the loan sharks." The jury deliberated a mere twenty minutes before finding him guilty, and the judge quickly sentenced him to ten years in prison. Kastens's wrath was no doubt aimed at Perel and Lowenstein, two leading members of Memphis's Jewish community. The destruction visited upon the Beauty Shop was a small reminder to Memphians of what they were fighting for in World War II.

January 19, 1921

"I Didn't Want to Live with Him"

Louise Brueley Thompson, eighteen-year-old bride of World War I veteran Louis Thompson, who resides near the city crematory at 5 Crematory Place, testified in court today that she "just decided I didn't want to live with him" when she fled to her parents' house after the wedding. The couple had wed on January 9, but the newly minted Mrs. Thompson went back to her parents' house on Faxon Avenue that evening and refused to see Mr. Thompson when he came calling. In response, Mr. Thompson petitioned probate court for a writ of habeas corpus to produce his wife, claiming she was being held against her will by her parents. According to a *News Scimitar* reporter, Mrs. Thompson testified that "she did not tell her mother about the marriage until several days later. She declared that she had changed her mind about married life and when Thompson came to the home she told him she would not return to him." Probate Judge Guthrie dismissed the habeas corpus request after he heard testimony from the girl's mother, Mrs. P. Brueley, that Mrs. Thompson was not being held against her will and that Mr. Thompson had not been kept from seeing his bride.

January 20, 1863

Mississippi River Traffic Restricted by Union Forces

On this day, Major General Ulysses S. Grant, commander of the Department of the Tennessee, issued General Orders No. 7, which stated that "all trading, trafficking, or the landing of boats at points south of Memphis other than at military posts, or points guarded by the navy, is positively prohibited." Anyone caught violating the order "will be arrested and placed in close confinement. The boats and cargoes, unless the property of the Government, will be turned over to the quartermaster's department for the benefit of the Government." In addition, the order required all officers to report violations witnessed while on board a river vessel. To make sure they remained observant, Grant issued Special Orders No. 26 on January 26, closing the bars on all government boats and "no spirituous, vinous, or malt liquors will be allowed to be sold on boats or in the camps. Card-playing and gaming is also strictly prohibited." Grant was attempting to stop the flow of supplies being smuggled to Confederate forces from the Memphis area. It was estimated that by the end of the Civil War, $20 million worth of contraband goods had been secretly transferred to Confederate forces from the Bluff City.

January 21, 1950

Memphis Symphony Conductor Acclaimed in Paris

Richard Korn, conductor of the Memphis Symphony Orchestra, tonight directed the Paris Conservatoire Orchestra at the Champs Élysées Theater in Paris, France. "Frankly, (and not just because he calls Memphis home), the program got the warmest response this correspondent has yet seen accorded an artist in Paris," wrote Martha Shaeffer of the *Commercial Appeal*. Before his performance in Paris, Korn conducted the Copenhagen Philharmonic, and after his French engagement, he was scheduled to perform in Stockholm, Oslo and London before returning to Memphis. In an interview with Shaeffer, Korn praised his fellow musicians in the Bluff City when he stated, "I sincerely believe Memphis has the best musical talent of any city its size in the country." In 1895, the Memphis Philharmonic Orchestra Association was formed by W.W. Saxby Jr., and the first Memphis Symphony Orchestra was organized in 1909 under the direction of Jacob Bloom. This orchestra remained in operation until it disbanded in 1925. The second symphony orchestra performed its first concert on March 13, 1939, and remains in operation to this day.

January 22, 1952

Prayers Sent to Stop Gambling

An interdenominational meeting of Christians was held at the newly built First Baptist Church, located at the intersection of Poplar Avenue and East Parkway, to pray that voters in West Memphis, Arkansas, reject a referendum that would allow horse race gambling directly across the Mississippi River from the Bluff City. The prayer service began at 9:00 p.m. with the ringing of a large bell imported from Holland. Each hour, a different Christian denomination led the prayer vigil, which lasted until 5:00 a.m. the following morning. *Press-Scimitar* staff writer Clark Porteous described the scene inside the sanctuary: "Some knelt in prayer, others bowed their heads reverently and continued sitting. Others stood and prayed, but there was a feeling of intense sincerity about each group. Some came richly clad, wearing fur coats. A few wore jeans and checkered shirts. Each group prayed a bit differently, yet all addressed their prayers to the same Divine Being and all opposed horse racing for Memphis vicinity." The following day, voters rejected the horse race proposal by a 173-vote majority. However, their victory over gambling was short-lived. In 1955, a dog racing track, Southland Greyhound Park, was opened across the river, and it quickly became a popular gambling destination for many Memphians.

January 23, 1925

"You Want to Send Me Back to the Asylum"

Seventy-four-year-old W.C. Hooper, armed with a shotgun and pistol, barricaded himself inside his daughter's home and refused to come out. According to his daughter, Mrs. J.C. Blancq, Hooper had been suffering from mental illness since he killed two men in Nashville in 1910 and that his mental state had been deteriorating for the past two months. This evening, Hooper came out of his room with a pistol in his hand and began threatening his daughter and son-in-law. "I know what you're talking about. You want to send me back to the asylum," he exclaimed. According to a *Commercial Appeal* reporter:

> [Hooper's] *son-in-law was in the adjoining room and rushed to telephone for police protection. When policemen arrived* [Hooper] *was locked in his room and threatening to kill the first man that entered. Police were ready for a siege and began laying plans for gassing the old man with formaldehyde. While part of the detectives were bringing the necessary chemicals Motorcycle Policeman Knox persuaded the insane man to surrender.*

Hooper was then quietly arrested and charged with insanity.

January 24, 1962

City Official Opposes Desegregation of Airport Restaurant
Mayor Henry Loeb announced on this day that he was opposed to desegregating the Dobbs House restaurant at the Memphis Airport without a court order. On January 20, Deputy Assistant Secretary of State Carl Rowan, a Tennessee-born African American serving in the administration of President John F. Kennedy, was denied service in the airport restaurant. Embarrassed by the incident, police commissioner Claude Armour stated, "I'm sure glad we didn't arrest the assistant secretary of state." Rowan filed a complaint with the Justice Department upon his return to Washington, and a suit was quickly filed with the U.S. Supreme Court. "Memphis should not voluntarily desegregate its airport restaurant to avoid a federal injunction. There is not one ounce of sincerity in Washington. This is a case of federal meddling into local affairs," said Loeb. In contrast, Commissioner Armour declared that he was "for working this out in an orderly manner, with the least possible publicity....I feel we would lose the case if it came to a federal side in this thing." James K. Dobbs Jr., president of Dobbs House, explained that "if the city commission should decide to desegregate the restaurant we would most likely abide by their decision if we were not placed in legal Jeopardy." In March 1962, the Supreme Court, in the case of *Turner v. City of Memphis*, ordered the desegregation of the airport restaurant and all other food establishments at interstate and intrastate travel facilities.

January 25, 1975

Memphians Alarmed by the Disaster Movie
The Towering Inferno

The *Commercial Appeal* reported on this day that the Memphis Fire Department and the City Complaint Center have been inundated with phone calls from nervous Memphians who have seen the Irwin Allen disaster film *The Towering Inferno* at the Crosstown Theater. According to City Complaint Center director Richard Hackett, "They all want to know if the apartment or office building they're in is safe. We're trying to get the fire department to give them the right information and the procedures to follow." The fire department distributed to concerned citizens a pamphlet entitled "Emergencies in High Rise Buildings" and offered programs on skyscraper safety to civic groups. A reporter for the *Commercial Appeal* stated that "Memphis does not have any building as tall as the fictional 136-story skyscraper depicted in the movie, but…any building taller that eight stories can have similar problems. The city's tallest ladder will reach about eight stories." Fire marshal C.E. Torian explained that "it's primarily a case of knowing the correct procedures and following them."

January 26, 1926

Boy Scout Executives Meet in Memphis

The Fifth Region of the Boy Scouts of America concluded its two-day convention in Memphis on this evening. Earlier this day, nearly every Scout in Memphis paraded by Chief Scout Executive James E. West, who addressed the young men on "The Challenge to the Future." Chief West then presented Eagle Scout badges to three young men—Jack Reynolds, Emil Tamm and James Reynolds—who had achieved Scouting's highest rank. Afterward, a meeting was held to choose officers for the upcoming year. Memphian Bolton Smith was elected vice-president of the national council; Carl Faust of Jackson, Mississippi, was selected chairman of the regional executive committee; and Chattanooga's B.E. Loveman was chosen treasurer. Bolton Smith was a very influential member of Scouting's inner circle and was instrumental in creating the National Committee on Inter-Racial Activities, which coordinated the creation of African American Boy Scout troops. Scout executives were so impressed with Memphis that in 1931 the national council held its annual conclave in Memphis. In related news, the annual meeting of the local Chickasaw Council was held on January 27 at the Peabody Hotel. John T. Morgan was elected president, and it was decided that the recently built camp in Eudora, Mississippi, would be named for Mr. and Mrs. Charles Currier.

January 27, 1955

Grain Elevator Explodes

The grain elevator located at the intersection of Lamar Avenue and Airways Boulevard suffered a grain-dust explosion at 4:43 p.m. on this day, causing injuries to nine workers and $250,000 worth of damage to the installation. Owned by Allied Mills, the elevator produced poultry and livestock grain for the brand name Wayne Feeds. A spark apparently set off a dust explosion that blew off the roof of the 125-foot building. Reporting for the *Commercial Appeal*, Warren Fosdick described the horrific scene: "One man ran from the scene with his clothes flaming. L.W. Atkins, construction foreman for a firm which was building new metal storage bins, was saved from serious injury by fellow workmen who piled sacks of grain on his body to extinguish the flames. 'When it came I was just starting work and walking down the docks between buildings. I was blown off the dock and under a railroad car. It was like a gust of wind followed by fire.'"

Nine workers were injured when the Allied Mills grain elevator on Lamar exploded.

January 28, 1967

Ku Klux Klan Rallies in Memphis

Three hundred members of the Invisible Empire met at the auditorium on this night in a quiet ceremony attended by at least two African Americans. The grand dragon of Alabama, Reverend James Speers, stated that President Lyndon Johnson is a "mad man" and reminded the audience that in his opinion "Hitler introduced the Great Society in Germany." Speers was followed by Imperial Wizard Robert M. Shelton, who explained that the "third stage in an effort by the Communist Party in the United States to break down the Republic" is the civil rights revolution then spreading across the South. "Communists found that Negroes were not gullible enough to swallow their lines…so in 1928…they changed their strategy. They began working to create a guilt complex in Christians and instill in the Negro that he was a second-class citizen and had to work to earn and demand his place as a first-class citizen." Memphians were no strangers to the activities of the KKK. The first grand wizard of the Ku Klux Klan was Memphian Nathan Bedford Forrest, and in the 1920s, the Memphis Klan elected Clifford Davis city judge and once held a rally on Beale Street, where they urged African Americans to join the KKK because "both were native born Americans and both were protestant." On January 17, 1998, the Klan again rallied in Memphis, but unlike in 1967, a counter demonstration protesting the Invisible Empire turned violent, damaging several downtown businesses.

January 29, 1946

Memphis Helps a Dutch City

Mayor Walter Chandler announced that no decision had been made regarding the suggestion that Memphis adopt the Dutch cotton mill town of Enschede devastated by World War II. The previous day, Mayor Chandler had received a transatlantic telephone call from Enschede mayor John Van Hatem asking that Memphians agree to provide food and clothing for the residents and funds to help rebuild its war-damaged infrastructure. Many in the local cotton industry were enthusiastic about the idea. Douglas Brooks, president of the Newburger cotton export company, stated, "I think the 'adoption' is a fine idea and I'm all for it. The people of Enschede, like those throughout Holland, are clean, industrious and thrifty." Working through the Memphis International Center, Memphis did agree to provide relief to the people of Enschede on May 27, 1946. As a result of this informal adoption, three thousand friendship boxes were prepared and sent to the children of Enschede by Memphis schoolchildren. In addition, ten thousand canned food tins and a large donation of clothing were also sent to the war-ravaged Dutch town. In recognition of their service, Queen Wilhelmina knighted Mayor Chandler, Memphis International Center director W.R. Herstein, Francis Hickman and Caffey Robertson with the Order of the Oranje-Nassau.

January 30, 1910

St. Louis Banker Praises Memphis

During an interview on this day with a local newspaper reporter, the president of the Mercantile Bank of St. Louis, Festus J. Wade, declared, "Memphis is the Imperial City of the South." Mr. Wade was preparing for a dinner party when the reporter arrived at his private railroad car for a scheduled interview. While adjusting his collar in front of a mirror, Wade explained, "The spirit of progressiveness manifested by your citizens is the South's tribute to the nation. The possibilities of Memphis are too vast to even think of...Memphis has been the gateway through which the larger part of the South's enormous wealth has flowed and naturally has derived great benefits. The South is becoming greater every day. It becomes richer every day, and Memphis, situated as it is, will necessarily thrive in proportion. We want to invest our money in Memphis." Wade gained this perspective earlier in the day by taking an automobile tour of the city. As the interview came to an end, Wade exclaimed, "We have visited twelve cities during our tour of the South, some of them larger and some of them smaller than this city, but we are without a dissenting voice in the opinion that Memphis is the best, most substantial, most promising and the greatest of them all."

January 31, 1929

Burglar Hides Out in Sorority House

Members of the Chi Omega Sorority at Southwestern at Memphis College discovered on this day that a criminal had been using their unoccupied clubhouse as a hideout. According to Chi Omega president Eleanor Beckham, the burglar broke out a front window and took up residence in the home. "He apparently used the place as his hotel for the past several nights, sleeping on a couch in the corner," Beckham explained. The sorority girls nicknamed the intruder the "music bandit" because it appeared he stole twenty victrola records given by a group of newly inducted members. Acting as detectives, the Chi Omega girls discovered there were ashes in the fireplace, the graphophone record player had clearly been used and, even though the house had been ransacked, the thief failed to abscond with either the silver or several expensive furnishings. Founded in Clarksville, Tennessee, in 1848, Southwestern Presbyterian University relocated to the Bluff City in 1925 and became Southwestern at Memphis. In 1984, the school was renamed Rhodes College in honor of former president Peyton Nalle Rhodes.

February 1, 1964

An Encounter with Artist Carroll Cloar

Celebrated Memphis artist Carroll Cloar sat down with *Press-Scimitar* reporter Edwin Howard today to discuss his latest painting, *Historic Encounter between E.H. Crump and W.C. Handy on Beale Street*. Howard wrote:

> *As Cloar now envisions this imaginary but plausible meeting, it occurred around 1938 to '40 in front of the ornately arched old Daisy Theater as a high-stepping Negro band marched by. On hand for the occasion, Cloar has decided, were* [Clarence] *Saunders, Sen.* [Kenneth] *McKellar,* [Shifty] *Logan, the late Arthur Halle, Sr., prominent merchant and Cotton Carnival leader, Charles Diehl, former president of Southwestern and Lt. George Washington Lee, Negro political leader.*

The painting was completed in April, and in addition to those mentioned by Howard, the work also included Mayor Watkins Overton, *Press-Scimitar* reporter Clark Porteous and news vendor Anthony "Monk" Cassata. When Cloar died, local art critic Fredric Koeppel wrote, "Cloar drew on memories of rural life to compose canvases whose realism was tempered with touches of whimsy, folklore and mystery."

February 2, 1950

Food Thieves Put on Ice

Police on this day uncovered the identity of the "produce gang," who had been stealing food from area grocery stores for the past two months. Three unemployed men—Robert Monroe Ellis, Herbert Marion Flynn and Henry Samson Looney—were arrested as they looted a local grocery store this morning. As described by *Commercial Appeal* reporter Arthur Grehan Jr., "Seven uniformed officers hid out…near the Leadway Food Store at 867 Kerr, which had previously been a victim of the gang. A delivery truck arrived about 5:30 a.m. with the trio trailing it in Ellis' auto, officers said. After the truck driver set off two cases of eggs and left, the three men took the eggs and loaded them in the auto. Then police closed in." Searching Ellis's home, police found $300 worth of produce in the attic. The perishables came from several grocery stores, including Easy Way store number twenty-four; Bet-R-Valu stores on Latham and Olive Streets; the WeOna stores at Florida, East Trigg and Getwell Streets; and Hall's Grocery on Mississippi Boulevard. Two or three times a week Ellis and his confederates peddled their stolen goods door-to-door at a discount price, undercutting legitimate grocery operators. As a result of their illegal grocery trade, Ellis, Flynn and Looney were charged with seven counts of larceny.

February 3, 1849

President-Elect Visits Memphis

Zachary Taylor, hero of the Mexican War and recently elected president of the United States, visited Memphis on his way to next month's inaugural ceremonies in the nation's capital. A cold rain fell as the steamer *Tennessee* arrived at the Memphis waterfront from New Orleans bearing the famous general and his party. A large crowd waving flags cheered the president-elect as he was officially greeted by reception committee chairman E.M. Yerger. Waiting nearby was a carriage drawn by four white horses, donated by David Cockrill, who owned a livery stable at Main and Monroe Streets. Entering the carriage, president-elect Taylor was driven to the Gayoso Hotel, where a lavish breakfast awaited him. Colonel John Pope welcomed him to the Bluff City and the president-elect followed with a short speech. When breakfast was finished, Taylor was taken to the Commercial Hotel, where a ladies' reception was held in his honor. According to a correspondent on the scene, the event was "a very pleasant occasion, for the general proved himself quite a ladies' man." Later in the day, he returned to his vessel and continued his journey to Washington, D.C. Inaugurated on March 4, 1849, Taylor died in office on July 9, 1850, shortly before passage of the controversial Compromise of 1850, which, among other things, admitted California to the Union as a free state, abolished the slave trade in the nation's capital and established a stringent Fugitive Slave Law.

February 4, 1942

Victory Book Campaign Begun in Memphis

Cossitt Library director Jesse Cunningham announced on this day a campaign to collect books for the National Victory Book Campaign, which was designed to assist the army and navy library services in providing 10 million books for America's soldiers and sailors. Cunningham, acting as state director of the campaign, outlined plans to the Business and Professional Men's Division, who offered their firms' support of the campaign. Joining Cunningham was Shelby County librarian Robert Franklin, who, as local campaign director, revealed plans to obtain donated books from the employees of area businesses. In addition to targeting local businesses, Memphis Light, Gas and Water Division sent to its customers a pamphlet requesting book donations. As explained by a *Commercial Appeal* reporter, "The 60,000 leaflets were made possible by five Memphis firms who donated the paper, typesetting and printing. The leaflets urge every Memphian who can to take at least two good books to Victory Book campaign headquarters at Cossitt Library or to any branch library, school or fire station."

February 5, 1963

New Stadium Approved for Fairgrounds

Mid-South Fair president Weldon Burrow announced on this day that the fair board would not object to the construction of a new football stadium if the city commission agreed to purchase additional land for parking.

Construction began on September 30, 1963, and was completed in time for the Tigers of Memphis State

Liberty Bowl Memorial Stadium was opened on September 18, 1965.

University to play the University of Mississippi Rebels on September 18, 1965. The structure was originally named Memphis Memorial Stadium to honor veterans. In 1975, the building was renamed Liberty Bowl Memorial Stadium in honor of the annual college football game held there.

February 6, 1916

Memphian Sent to Russia

It was announced on this day that Memphian David Bell McGowan had joined the State Department's Foreign Service as U.S. consul to Moscow. The son of the late E.L. McGowan, former executive of Toof, McGowan & Company, the new consul worked as a reporter in Memphis before moving to Europe, where he studied in Berlin. After two years as a student, McGowan covered events in Berlin, Germany, and the Russian city of St. Petersburg for several London newspapers. McGowan returned to the United States just after the Russo-Japanese War erupted in 1904, and he served as editor of the *Knoxville Sentinel* newspaper. In late 1915, he was hired by the Associated Press to serve as its foreign correspondent in St. Petersburg. McGowan, whose appointment took effect on January 1, did not have to return to Washington for training because of his intimate knowledge of Russian affairs. This knowledge served him well for he was posted to several Russian cities during his career, including Riga and Vladivostok. Retiring from the Foreign Service in 1936, McGowan settled in Lynchburg, Virginia, with his wife, Emma Woods McGowan.

February 7, 1900

Ladies' Shoe–Polishing Scheme Torments Landlord

A Memphis landlord visited the central police station asking for protection from hostile women demanding he shine their shoes. A.D. Powers of 356 Second Street recently rented a room to two young men who claimed to operate a business called the "Lady Shoe–Polishing Team." In the words of a *Commercial Appeal* reporter, the duo "proposed…to sell tickets with coupons attached, the ticket and coupon being numbered. These tickets were then sold for five cents each and were certified by the team to be 'good for one polish by the Lady Shoe–polishing Team' and also would entitle the holder to a chance on a pair of $5 lady's shoes." The two who directed this confidence racket suddenly left Powers's home on February 6, no doubt with their pockets full of loot, and hadn't been heard from since. Powers told the police that "there is a steady stream of ladies pouring into his house from morn until night, each presenting a shoe polishing ticket and insisting on the fulfillment of the contract." The correspondent concluded his report by stating that "if the police cannot give him some relief he will be compelled to polish all the shoes present in self-defense or else fly to some secluded spot whither the shoe of woman cannot follow and shoe polishing is prohibited by law."

February 8, 1974

Memphis Millionaire Plans to Buy Football Team

Edward W. "Ned" Cook, president and CEO of the international grain company Cook Industries and member of Mayor Wyeth Chandler's NFL Expansion Committee, announced today that he plans to "do every darn thing I can" to bring a National Football League team to Memphis. For nearly a decade, Memphis had attempted to land an NFL team. In 1965, Mid-South Sports Inc. was created by Mike Lynn, and earlier in 1974, Pepsico Chairman Herman Lay of Dallas announced his own plans for a Memphis team. Cook stated that he had "discussed it with Mr. Lay on a plain man-to-man basis. I don't want to get into a contest with anyone and blow us out of the tub. This gives them [the NFL] a choice. They can have an out-of-town owner or an in-town owner. It gives them a pretty good situation where they can look me over and either decide on me or the other guy. But having the NFL in Memphis is paramount." The NFL did look over both Cook and Lay but decided to award franchises to Tampa and Seattle. Later in 1974, a professional team did come to Memphis, the World Football League's Grizzlies, which played two seasons in the Bluff City. When the WFL folded in late 1975, a successful season ticket drive was orchestrated in hopes that the NFL would accept the Grizzlies, but they refused. Finally, in 1993, Memphis attempted to land a team, but the NFL again dashed the hopes of Memphians when it chose Charlotte and Jacksonville over the Bluff City.

February 9, 1965

Law School Achieves Accreditation

The American Bar Association, meeting in New Orleans on this day, approved the accreditation of the Memphis State University Law School. The school was established in September 1962 with eighty students and expanded to two hundred students in its second year of operation. According to law school dean Dr. Robert Doyle Cox, "This means that a graduate of our law school can take the bar examination in any state and that a student can transfer his credits to any other law school. Without this, a law school cannot extend its influence outside of the state in which it is recognized." University officials expressed surprise and satisfaction in achieving this distinction in such a short time. "No new school, as far as I know, has received approval within two years after it was started," Cox said. With this approval, the Memphis State University Law School became the third accredited law school in the state alongside Vanderbilt University and the University of Tennessee–Knoxville. On March 4, 1977, the Tennessee Board of Regents renamed the institution the Cecil C. Humphreys School of Law in honor of the Memphis State University president who was instrumental in establishing the school in the Bluff City.

February 10, 1919

World War I Aviator's Grave Located in Germany

Lieutenant Joseph S. Michels advised the staff of the *News Scimitar* on this day how his fellow pilot Lieutenant William A. White died during his first flight over Germany in November 1918. According to Michels, "[White] was anxious to see service before the end came and volunteered for an observation trip. He was bidden Godspeed by the boys and that was the last we ever saw of him. The intelligence department of the aero service, however, after some time ascertained that an airplane near the spot where White ascended, and of the same make, collided with a German Fokker and both crashed to the ground. The officials determined it was White's machine and have located his grave near the spot where he fell."

Before providing this account to the newspaper's staff, Michels paid a call to White's widow, Mrs. Ruth Evans White, at her home on North Claybrook Street to inform her of the news. In addition to Lieutenant White, seventy-five other men from Memphis and Shelby County gave their lives during World War I.

February 11, 1941

Radio Station Granted Power Increase

The Federal Communications Commission announced that beginning on this night, WMC, AM 780 on the radio dial, would have its nighttime broadcasting power increased from 1,000 to 5,000 watts. As a result, the radio station had 5,000 watts of signal strength throughout its broadcasting day. "We expect the new power to give WMC a much larger night audience and to provide a better service to our existing audience," explained station manager H.W. Slavick. In March 1941, the wavelength reallocation was complete, and WMC moved from its current position on the radio dial to 790 kilocycles, where it remains to this day. Programs scheduled for the first night included the news broadcast of H.V. Kaltenborn at 6:45 p.m. and the musical shows *Johnny Presents* and *Horace Hiedt* at 7:00 and 7:30 p.m. At 8:00 p.m., listeners heard the *Battle of the Sexes* quiz show followed by the comedy programs *Fibber McGee and Molly* and *Bob Hope* at 8:30 and 9:00 p.m. Owned and operated by the *Commercial Appeal*, WMC began broadcasting on January 22, 1923, and it became an affiliate of the National Broadcasting Company in 1927.

February 12, 1954

Notorious Censor Threatens Reporter

The *Press-Scimitar* reported on this day that eighty-eight-year-old Lloyd T. Binford, the irascible chairman of the Memphis Board of Censors, had twice called the police to assist him in preserving the morals of the film-going public. Described as "the most notorious censor in the world," Binford had two detectives stand guard outside the Malco Theatre during a preview of the film *The French Line*. The movie starred Jane Russell and was considered risqué by Binford and others because of the revealing costumes the actress wore on screen. The next day, Binford again called police when an Associated Press photographer attempted to snap his image outside the offices of Paramount Pictures. Binford refused the request, but AP reporter Bill Crider and photographer Gene Herrick waited outside to catch the chairman when he left. According to Herrick, when Binford saw the two loitering around the entrance he "went straight to the telephone and called the police. He stood facing the wall about 30 minutes while waiting for the police. The police came and they called us in. Mr. Binford called me a little jackass. He shook his cane at me and said 'I'd sure like to hit you with this…I wish I had my gun… .I've apprehended about 200 men and never fired a shot, but if I had my gun I'd kill you…' Mr. Binford kept saying he would have us arrested. Finally we went out onto the sidewalk and police left ahead of Binford who was in his car with his chauffeur. I took his picture sitting in the car as he was leaving."

February 13, 1872

Memphians Celebrate Mardi Gras

A loud and raucous crowd surged through the streets today in Memphis's first Mardi Gras celebration. As reported by the *Daily Appeal*, "Twenty thousand persons perambulating the streets, perhaps three thousand of them en masque. There was a complete interchange of the sexes. No such sights or sounds were ever before heard or seen in Memphis." One such sight was a Japanese visitor being accosted by a mob of women in the front of the Peabody Hotel. To escape their fervor, he jumped into the bed of an empty coal wagon, but not long after, about forty young boys jumped in with him. The driver was so startled he quickly unhitched the wagon and fled on the back of his mule as the wagon overturned, spilling the revelers onto the street. Several floats mounted on wagons were paraded down Main Street, including the one that contained the "Prince of the Carnival." The reporter noted that the prince "sat in a huge wineglass fully twenty-five feet high surrounded by Chinese lanterns and little attendants in masks and guarded by a squad of trusty knights in gorgeous apparel." Although the wildest celebrations occurred in the 1870s, Memphis continued to celebrate Mardi Gras until 1901.

The Memphis Mardi Gras parade. The city's Mardi Gras celebration was held from 1872 to 1901.

February 14, 1950

Concrete Plant Ordered Closed

Chancellor L.D. Bejach ordered the closing of the Lazarov Concrete Products Manufacturing Company, located at 1102 North Seventh Street, because of its adverse effects on nearby residents. In the summer of 1949, twenty-eight homeowners sent a petition to the city commission demanding the plant's closure because it created "a thick and gritty dust" that "constantly covered their home exteriors and porches and seeped through windows and doors." The city attorney's office filed a petition to declare the facility a nuisance that should be closed, as did Mrs. Lula Dillahunty of 1130 North Seventh Street. The plant's owner, Edward Kealensky, countered that the city had given him a license to operate the business near a residential area and that most of the dust came from the street, not his facility. In explaining his decision, as reported by the *Commercial Appeal*, "Chancellor Bejach said he did not consider the plant a 'nuisance, but obnoxious and offensive' because of the dust and 'maybe the noise.' Mr. Kealensky's contention that the city had granted him the necessary privilege license in 1946…did not affect his ruling…'The court is not bound by such action of city officials,' Chancellor Bejach said, 'and under the city ordinance the right to close the plant is granted the court.'"

February 15, 1936

Gardens Planned by Welfare Commission

The Memphis Welfare Commission announced on this day that it is creating spring gardens to supplement the food rations for unemployed Memphians on relief. The program was started by commission chairman John Ross, who donated fourteen acres on Raleigh Road that was divided into fifty-six gardens for spring cultivation. The Tennessee Emergency Relief Administration, which oversaw welfare programs across the state, provided a large supply of seeds for the spring planting. In addition to the gardens, the welfare commission used Works Progress Administration workers to operate a fully functioning farm at Park Field, the former army air corps' facility in Millington. By the year's end, "6,780 pounds of meal, 29,879 cans of vegetables, 8,742 pounds of dried beans and peas, 86,513 pounds of sweet potatoes 3,232 pounds of Irish potatoes, 8,986 cans of sorghum, and 37,946 pounds of vegetables" were grown at the Park Field farm. In addition, fourteen acres of tomatoes were grown in a garden on Chelsea Avenue. The commission also operated a cannery in the Hollywood neighborhood, which prepared 750,000 two-pound cans of food that were distributed to needy families during the winter of 1936–37.

February 16, 1964

Police Commissioner Slams Mayor

During an interview on WHBQ-TV's *Press Conference*, fire and police commissioner Claude Armour verbally attacked Mayor William B. Ingram for not working with the city commission and damaging the city's reputation. Armour began by explaining that "Mayor Ingram said it would be his policy to 'change the image of Memphis.' I can assure you it is being changed, and not for the better." The police commissioner was particularly angry that the mayor had recently purchased 1,500 tires for his department from Firestone Tire & Rubber, even though a proposal from Dunlop Tires was over $400 less than the winning bid. Claiming that this was "a decision based on purely political motives," Armour then went on to exclaim that "if we are to have a bid system of buying supplies, we ought to live by it." The commissioner concluded that he would no longer abide by Ingram's request that statements on city policy come only from the mayor's office: "Hereafter I'll make statements when I please." Armour's angry outburst was the latest in a feud that began while Ingram was judge of the city's traffic court. Judge Ingram often criticized Armour's police for not adequately enforcing traffic regulations. The sniping, which severely crippled the efficiency of local government during the mid-1960s, continued when Ingram was elected mayor in 1963 and did not end until 1967, when Armour retired and Ingram was defeated for a second term.

February 17, 1929

Drunk Drivers Lose Their Licenses

City officials on this day cracked down on Memphians who operated automobiles while intoxicated. Twelve drivers had their licenses stripped from them during a hearing of the automobile examining board at central police headquarters. Ten of the defendants—G.W. Beecher, 195 Hawthorne Place; E. Cash, 2569 Spottswood Avenue; Paul W. Hart, 1497 Rayburn Boulevard; J.R. Hill, 183 Merton Avenue; Robert Lark, 327 Decatur Street; Henry Malone, 1037 North Third; Frank C. Mason, 562 Peyton Street; Tom Patterson, 882 Orphanage Street; Walter Poole, 247 North Dunlap; and Tom Wortham, 1246 Breedlove—had their driver's licenses revoked for a year. Vincent Davis, 161 Third Street, lost his privilege to operate a motor vehicle for ninety days, and Allen Chambers, 840 Brunswick, was not able to drive for sixty days. In addition to the twelve who lost their licenses, six defendants had their cases dismissed when they pledged to drive more safely. As automobile ownership increased in the Bluff City during the twentieth century, so did drunk driving. In 1986, for example, 6,615 Memphians were arrested for driving while intoxicated and 63 people were killed in alcohol-related accidents.

February 18, 1981

Businessman Evicted from Home

Alvin Weeks, former president of Holiday Containers Inc., was evicted from the rented home on Central Avenue that he and his wife, Madelle, have been living in for the past four months. According to *Commercial Appeal* correspondent Ron Russell, "Sheriff's deputies showed up at the spacious, expensive looking house the Weekes had been renting at 3580 Central, and in minutes the couple's belongings began to be stacked on the street. The whole thing resembled some kind of sad circus." The owners of the home, Mr. and Mrs. J.D. Hibner, described the pair as "con artists. I don't know what else to call them. They flat took advantage of us. They were supposed to pay us a $700 deposit and $650 a month and all we've got to show for them living here for $4\frac{1}{2}$ months is $10." While their property was being carted out of the house, Reverend R.L. Fitts showed up to watch the eviction because, in his words, Weeks "took me too." Fitts explained that he had rented his three-bedroom home at 3847 North Watkins to the couple, who "stayed in it for five years before we finally got them out and he wound up owing me $7,100 in back rent when they left." Holiday Containers Inc. was founded in 1969 as a subsidiary of Holiday Inns of America to produce corrugated shipping containers at a plant on East Brooks Road. Holiday Inn founder and chairman Kemmons Wilson stated that the new company was "another step in our program of diversification for the service industries."

February 19, 1941

Memphis Praised for Combating Syphilis

The field director of the American Social Hygiene Association's National Anti-Syphilis Committee, Sidney Howell, spoke to a gathering of community leaders at the Peabody Hotel to discuss his group's efforts in eradicating the disease. He began his talk on this day by expressing satisfaction with the police department's campaign to suppress prostitution. Continuing his remarks, Howell declared that there was "a direct relation between accessibility and infection. If you reduce accessibility, you reduce infection. In this respect, then, it is not a question of morals but one of public administration of health." The field director then urged Memphians to combat the popular notion that "you can't eliminate prostitution by suppressing it. Such a statement is simply fifth column propaganda because it started as a whispering campaign by people who have an interest in the maintenance of organized prostitution." Howell finished his speech by explaining the moves being taken to deal with the rise of syphilis in areas near military camps: "These boys are just citizens in soldier suits. If they return home infected, they become a danger to their community. That is why this matter is a national problem." The National Anti-Syphilis Committee was not the only organization to comment on Memphis's antiprostitution offensive. The summer before Howell's appearance *Time* magazine commented, "Last week Memphis had the cold-water blues. Gone from hotel lobbies were the expectant blondes. Brothels were closed; their staffs had fled."

February 20, 1903

Segregation Law Implemented in Memphis

The Memphis Street Railway Company announced on this day that it would abide by the recently passed Hancock Law, which required segregated seating for black and white Tennesseans using public transportation. The general manager of the Memphis Street Railway Company, Frank Smith, stated that the company had actively opposed the measure "because it was believed to be impracticable and that its application here would work a hardship on many people." Despite the opposition, Smith gave orders for all cars to be altered so that separate seating could be maintained. The *Commercial Appeal* no doubt alarmed some white Memphians when it reported: "[The] part reserved for Negroes will be occupied by them and by them only. A white person being crowded from the white reservation into the Negro compartment will be made to leave and return to the part of the car reserved…for white passengers. This will be inconvenient on some lines, especially on the East End line, where at certain times during the day, few Negroes ride, but it is the law and the street car company says it is willing to do its part provided that the riding public does the same."

Whites may have been inconvenienced, but African Americans despised Jim Crow segregation and did all they could to resist it. Over the years, protests and legal challenges were mounted until the Memphis Street Railway ended segregated seating in 1960.

February 21, 1907

Memphian Becomes First Female Lawyer in Tennessee
Marion Griffin of Memphis became the first female lawyer in Tennessee when she was sworn in by deputy county court clerk James Brett on this day. A former legal stenographer for Judge Thomas M. Scruggs, Griffin studied law in her spare time, and in 1900, she was tested by two local judges who then certified her to practice law. Armed with this qualification, Griffin applied to the Tennessee Supreme Court for a license, which should have been merely a formality. However, the Supreme Court declared that state laws did not allow for a woman to be named a member of the bar. Fiercely determined to be become an attorney, Griffin enrolled in the University of Michigan's law school, where she earned a Bachelor of Laws degree in 1906. Returning to Tennessee, Griffin assiduously lobbied the General Assembly to pass a bill granting women the right to become licensed attorneys. Her efforts, combined with the support of many male lawyers, led to the adoption on February 13, 1907, of a bill granting women the right to practice law once they had passed an examination given by the state board of law examiners. Griffin quickly took and passed the test, which led to her swearing in. In 1923, Griffin became the first woman elected to the Tennessee General Assembly. Serving one term, she chaired the House Social Welfare Committee, where she worked to improve the lives of women and children in Tennessee. Griffin continued to practice law until her retirement in 1949. Marion Griffin died on January 30, 1957.

February 22, 1959

A Tour of the Luau

Press-Scimitar staff writer Mary Allie Taylor toured the Luau, a new Polynesian-themed restaurant operated by Dobbs House that opened this month at 3135 Poplar Avenue. Taylor wrote that walking into the restaurant was "like traveling to faraway places...In the entrance is a waterfall with a banyan tree rising toward the roof, dotted with coral and giant clam shells, with anthodium and birds of paradise." From the decorative entrance, she walked into the Sea Gate Room where "two 'Tikis'...stand guard. Tables are of monkey pod from Hawaii, chairs from Hong Kong, rugs from the Philippines, screens from Japan. An aisle of bamboo and tropical foliage, hung with coral, sea shells, fish and even stuffed sharks leads to the Cove and the Ravine with its trickling waterfall." Taylor then made her way into the Firefly Room, which had "tiny twinkling lights that flit on and off beneath ferns and tropical greens." The Kamahamaha Room, which contained a collection of spears, war clubs, bow and arrows and other weapons owned by Dennis Roosevelt, was also visited by the reporter. In the kitchen, Taylor found that it "takes special stoves to cook some of the Far East specialties and lots of cold storage space for fresh water chestnuts, crispy bean sprouts, snow peas, baktoy (Chinese celery), pineapples, coconuts and the like."

February 23, 1936

Memphis Baseball Player Signs with Philadelphia Phillies
Memphis Major League Baseball player Lou Chiozza agreed to sign a new contract to play second base for the Philadelphia Phillies on this day. The "Memphis Flash"—who was third in putouts for the major leagues, hit forty-seven RBI's and batted .284 during the 1935 season—refused to sign the first contract forwarded to him by team president Gerry Nugent because he was unhappy with the terms of the agreement. However, a revised contract was sent that he immediately signed and dropped in the mail to Philadelphia. Chiozza began his baseball career in 1930 with the minor league Memphis Chicks. Drafted by the Phillies in October 1933, he was the lead-off hitter during Major League Baseball's first night game in May 1935. Chiozza stayed with Philadelphia until December 1936, when he was traded to the New York Giants, which was managed by fellow Memphian Bill Terry. On July 19, 1939, Chiozza collided with another player, fracturing his left leg in three places and ending his Major League career. He remained with the Giants as an honorary coach and briefly returned to the Chicks before retiring from baseball on May 18, 1941. Lou Chiozza died on February 28, 1971.

February 24, 1927

Memphis Jug Band Records for Victor

One of the Bluff City's most popular blues acts recorded several songs for the Victor Company on this day in rooms 405 and 411 of the McCall Building. Formed by prolific songwriter Will Shade, the Memphis Jug Band performed in clubs on Beale Street as well as at political rallies and social events throughout the city. The original members included Shade on guitar and harmonica, jug player Charlie Polk, guitarist Will Weldon and Ben Ramey on kazoo with Shade, Polk and Weldon taking turns on vocals. Ralph Peer, Victor's representative in Memphis, saw the group perform and quickly signed it to a recording contract. At their first session, the men were rather nervous, so Peer passed around a bottle of whiskey; they were soon relaxed enough. Songs recorded that day were "Sun Brimmers Blues," "Memphis Jug Blues" and "Stingy Woman Blues." The recordings sold well, so Shade and the Memphis Jug Band continued to work for Victor until 1930, when the company stopped recording in Memphis. In 1928, the group was joined by guitarist Charlie Burse, who, along with Shade, honed the Memphis Jug Band style, which exploded in popularity and led to the recording of several other jug bands, most notably Gus Cannon's Jug Stompers. The music of Will Shade and Charlie Burse had a profound impact on the growth of blues music, and consequently, it influenced the development of American popular music in the twentieth century.

Jug bands in Memphis had a profound impact on the growth of blues music in the twentieth century.

February 25, 1961

Elvis Presley Day Celebrated in Tennessee

Governor Buford Ellington declared this day Elvis Presley Day in honor of the singer's effort to raise money for twenty-seven local charities. A $100-plate luncheon was held at the Hotel Claridge. Representatives of the recording industry presented Elvis with several awards for his musical accomplishments and a proclamation from Governor Ellington was read. When the ceremonies ended, Elvis signed autographs and then left for a brief rest before arriving at Ellis Auditorium to perform two shows for over five thousand screaming fans. The two concerts, with the luncheon, raised $51,607

Elvis Presley, seen here with girlfriend Barbara Hearn, raised $51,607 for several Memphis charities, including the Orange Mound Day Nursery.

for several charities, including the Orange Mound Day Nursery. During a news conference, Presley was asked if he planned to move to Hollywood because of his movie career. In reply, the King of rock 'n' roll stated, "I plan to stay right here in Memphis."

February 26, 1863

Prisoner Escapes from Civil War Prison

Union officials announced on this day that convicted murderer Lieutenant Charles Lewis, late of the Second U.S. Cavalry, had escaped from Irving Block prison. Lewis had recently been found guilty of unlawfully killing Confederate lieutenant Colonel Woods and was scheduled to be transferred to an Illinois prison, when he fled. Woods had paid Lewis to help him escape Irving Block but Lewis had the Confederate officer rearrested before he could get out of the city. Woods accused Lewis of ungentlemanly behavior, and in response, Lewis shot Woods in the head while he slept. Lewis traveled to Virginia, where he apparently changed his name to Denis Daily and joined the Confederate army. His ruse discovered, Lewis/Daily was court-martialed by the Confederate army but escaped before he was sentenced. Erected in 1859, the Irving Block was an iron-front building that was converted into a Confederate hospital. When Memphis fell to Union forces in June 1862, the hospital was converted into a prison, which remained in operation until the end of the war. In 1864, President Abraham Lincoln, hearing disturbing reports of deplorable conditions, ordered an investigation. In his report to the president, Lieutenant Colonel John F. Marsh wrote, "In a dark, wet cellar I found 28 prisoners chained to the floor where they had constantly been confined for several months, and never for a moment released." In response to this report, the president relieved the commandant and ordered conditions to be improved.

February 27, 1917

Streetcar Conductor Shoots Passengers

Streetcar conductor E.D. McRight shot two African American passengers early on this day during an argument over a transfer ticket. According to eyewitnesses, an older African American man bought a transfer ticket so he could board another car to reach his destination. Glancing at the ticket, the elderly gentleman noticed it was punched incorrectly. Taking it back to the driver, he pointed out the mistake, which quickly led to an argument. McRight then struck the man in the face with a transfer punch. When the African American kicked him in the shin, McRight pulled a pistol and fired a shot. The bullet missed its intended target and instead passed through the body of another black Memphian, Dora Perkins, piercing her left lung and nicking the arm of her nephew Lucius Granberry. Despite the serious nature of her wound, Ms. Perkins was not taken to the hospital for treatment until McRight finished the first section of his route. McRight told Emergency Officers Clark and Olive, who were investigating the incident, that he was assaulted by the elderly African American and in self-defense, he clubbed the passenger with the butt-end of the pistol and it accidently discharged. The officers did not believe McRight's version, and he was arrested and charged with carrying a pistol and shooting with intent to kill.

February 28, 1977

Memphians Protest Sex on TV

Supporting an area minister's protest against sex and violence on television, 1,379 Memphians phoned local stations and complained about what was being broadcast on their TV screens. Reverend Donald Wildmon, the minister of Southaven, Mississippi's First United Methodist Church, launched his campaign to force the heads of the ABC, NBC and CBS networks to tone down their salacious content through a boycott he called "Turn-the-Television-Off Week." As reported by *Commercial Appeal* correspondent Michael Lollar, "Switchboard operators at each of the three commercial stations in Memphis said the callers were generally 'nice,' briefly stating their cases against sex and violence. They said the callers tended to protest about programming in general, while some pointed to specific television shows, particularly *Baretta*, *Police Story*, *S.W.A.T.* and movies with sex or violence as a running theme." Lance Russell of WHBQ said that "personally and professionally, I am not at all happy about some of the material that's coming from the network." WMC general manager Mori Greiner stated that there is "no doubt a growing segment of the American public is objecting to unnecessary sex and violence." However, Greiner explained that he feels "slightly uneasy when a small segment of the public undertakes to oversee what the general public can see…I don't want to be guilty of breaking down the moral fabrics, but on the other hand, I don't want to be guilty of being a prude."

March 1, 1979

Discount Harry Checks Out of Beale Street

"Discount Harry" Leviton, owner of Harry's Discount department store, announced on this day he was closing his business, which had operated on famed Beale Street since 1927. "I've had it. I've sent everything back that the factory will take and I'm not ordering anything more. When this is gone, I'll be gone," Leviton said. Looking out his window onto an area gutted by urban renewal, Leviton reflected on Beale's storied past:

> *Peddlers walked around selling hot tamales and fish out of little carts. There were three picture shows, including one that had burlesque. There were shoeshine shops where people lined up to get a shine. There were girls from Gayoso Street and a policy numbers racket. There were knife fights, too. People would kill each other over a beer or a dime. But those fights were in the streets; never in the stores…I used to work Saturday nights until 1 or 2 in the morning and never had to worry. But I don't feel that way now.*

On October 8, 1983, the Beale Street Historic District opened and became, in a few years, one of Memphis's most popular tourist destinations.

"Discount Harry" Leviton, closed his Beale Street store after fifty years of operation.

March 2, 1928

Theater Owner Arrested

The owner of the Lincoln Theater, Fred Suzore, was arrested on this day for violating the city's fire safety ordinances. An inspection of his establishment, located at the corner of North Main Street and Market Avenue, was made by fire marshal Frank Buckalew, building inspector J.E. Hollingsworth and electrical inspector Harry L. Thomas. During the course of their inspection several violations were uncovered. Exit doors were tied up and the wiring is poor." Unlike the Lincoln, inspectors found no violations at the Pantages, Rialto and Suzore Theaters. These inspections were part of a widespread effort by city government to ensure that all public places were safe for the citizens of Memphis. Commissioner Samuel Jackson stated that every "theater and church in the city will be visited during the safety campaign. They will be followed by periodical visits at night to see that the exit doors are not locked or blocked in any way." A member of Mayor Watkins Overton's administration, Jackson was also a part of the political machine led by E.H. Crump. In 1928, the Crump political machine was determined to prove its ability to govern effectively. In addition to the safety campaign, Overton and the commission established a municipal airport and reorganized the police department.

March 3, 1961

Members-Only Department Store Opens

Dixiemart, a department store owned by the National Association of Consumer Organizations and available only to government workers, opened its doors on this day at 3645 Lamar near Knight Arnold Road. Dixiemart was the second large-scale discount department store to open in Memphis; the first was the Atlantic Thrift Center located at 2500 Lamar, which opened in 1959. As described by a *Press-Scimitar* correspondent, the first customer walked through the door and "stretched before him was 130,000 square feet of brightly-lit sales space, stocked with some 200,000 items—everything from diamond rings to 60-foot house trailers." The store had forty full-service departments, including a large, well-stocked grocery section. Don Preuss, director of member relations, explained that "membership is open to employees of city, county, state and federal governments, including retired employees, members of the armed forces, reservists, and national guardsmen." The building that housed the store was one of the largest Stran-Steel rigid frame buildings in the United States and was constructed in only five weeks by Metallic Building Company. In 1966, the store was bought by Parkview-Gem Incorporated, and in 1973, the store closed due to increased competition from national discount chains such as the Treasury and Zayre.

March 4, 1884

City Hall Salaries Revealed

City employees were paid their monthly salaries today using strict procedures to avoid the wasteful practices that had bankrupted the city and forced Memphis to surrender its charter in 1879. Becoming the Taxing District of Shelby County, the Bluff City was governed by a president and legislative council that had limited powers and could not spend money or raise taxes without the approval of the state legislature. As reported in the *Memphis Daily Appeal*, the "pay-rolls are certified and approved and checks are made by the president and signed by him and one other commissioner. These checks are given the chiefs, who draw the money from bank and are held responsible for any miscalculations. So far however, no mistakes have been made." President David Park Hadden was paid $166.67 while members of the legislative council received $41.67 per month. The salary of city engineer, Major Niles Meriwether was the same as the president and the engineering assistant was paid $115 monthly. "The pay-roll of the Board of Health includes Dr. Thornton at a salary of $150 a month, Secretary Graves at $75 a month, Health officer Jackson $60, Robert Lee, the dump boat-keeper, $50 and janitor $10, making a total of $345."

March 5, 1904

Bartender Averts Race Riot

A riot between African American and white Memphians was narrowly averted on this day thanks to the timely intervention of a bartender from nearby Horn Lake, Mississippi. According to the investigating officer, Patrolman Brittingham, two white men were driving a farm wagon on the Hernando Road, and as they passed the gates of Forest Hill Cemetery, they collided with a buggy driven by a black man. The wreck was so severe that the buggy's mule became hopelessly entangled with the wagon. Its owner offered to pay the buggy driver if he would cut the mule out of its harness so the wagon could move. The African American did so but then the white man reneged on his agreement to pay. As reported by the *Memphis Morning News*, "Other people happening along the road also took sides and at one time a battle with rocks took place between the two factions. Several people were hit by flying stones, but no one was badly hurt." Happening upon this scene was bartender I.J. Langdon, who attempted to stop the violence but soon found himself on the ground with a gushing knife wound in his chest. The sight of Langdon's crumpled body spooked the mob that quickly dispersed as an ambulance arrived to take the victim to the city hospital. Thirty-eight years before, Memphis was not so fortunate. In May 1866, a similar wagon accident sparked one of the worst racial disturbances in American history when forty-six African Americans and two white city residents were killed during three days of rioting.

March 6, 1943

War Fund Drive Begins

A mile-long parade and a visit by Hollywood stars kicked off a War Fund Drive to raise $335,000 for the activities of the American Red Cross on this day. The parade began at Poplar Avenue and then snaked onto Main Street, led by a large, white float emblazoned with the slogan "Our Wounded Can't Wait" with a crimson cross at its center. Five wounded Guadalcanal veterans sat atop the float while five thousand Red Cross volunteers, sailors, soldiers and marines followed closely behind. At 1:00 p.m., Hollywood actor Laraine Day, star of MGM's popular film series *Dr. Kildare*, and *Adventures of Sherlock Holmes* star Alan Marshal urged Memphians to give generously to the Red Cross while broadcasting over WREC radio and appearing at a luncheon at the Peabody Hotel. According to general chairman Florence Orgill O'Brian, the Red Cross had procured 1.5 million pints of blood for the military, established 150 rest centers overseas, provided twenty-eight thousand registered nurses for the armed forces and sent one million parcels to American prisoners held in German and Japanese camps. Local citizens enthusiastically supported the Red Cross's War Fund Drive and the money donated was one of many ways in which Memphians contributed to the defeat of Nazi Germany and Imperial Japan during World War II.

March 7, 1958

Women Replace Horses in Police Department

The police department announced on this day that ten young women have been hired to patrol the city's parking meters. Police chief James C. MacDonald cautioned the press to only refer to the new officers as traffic policewomen. "They're not meter maids. We hope to get away from calling them that," Chief MacDonald explained. Once they complete a two-week training course the policewomen will replace the city's mounted patrol, which consisted of five male officers and five horses. At their first briefing police commissioner Claude Armour told them that their "main job will be patrolling the meters. There will be times though when you'll be called on to direct traffic, too. For right now, none of you will try to handle violence. Your job will be to get license numbers and names of witnesses. I don't want any of you trying to apprehend dangerous criminals." The first traffic policewomen were Betty J. Coats, Lillian R. Forbes, Ossie F. Fowler, Katie Fitzhugh, Julia C. Lester, Frances Marzioli, Bernice Parish, Elsie Sanders, Rita A. Thompson and Erma Trent. These, however, were not the first women hired by the Memphis Police Department. In 1921, the Women's Protection Bureau was established to oversee female prisoners at the city jail and investigate their cases. The first policewoman hired to manage the bureau was Anna Whitmore, and Olive Marshall was the jail matron.

March 8, 1937

Dress Shop Strike Turns Violent

Women's clothes were torn on this day during a protest by Tri-State Dress Manufacturing Company workers. The protest turned violent when striking employees attacked nonstriking workers as they left the building at the end of their shifts. During the mêlée, several women's clothes were torn, a male employee was attacked after he assaulted a female bystander and four women were arrested for disturbing the peace. In response, city officials, as reported by the *Commercial Appeal*, "ordered police to block the street in front of the plant...preventing both strikers and workers from entering, and invited strike leaders and the managers of the concern to submit their controversy to Mayor [Watkins] Overton." In explaining the city's actions, Mayor Overton stated that the "City of Memphis has no sympathy with any plant which is not willing to pay its employees a living wage. We have received no assurance that this plant is paying a living wage. We intend to prevent violence because the public interest must come first." The following day, representatives of both sides met in the mayor's office and a tentative agreement was reached that led to further negotiations that ended the strike.

March 9, 1987

Record Producer Defends Former Beatle

During a press conference on this day Chips Moman, famed record producer and owner of 3 Alarm Recording Studio, lashed out at the *Commercial Appeal* for an article it published disparaging former Beatle Ringo Starr, who had been in Memphis recording an album. Written by Rheta Grimsley Johnson, the article stated that it was "hard to believe a real, live Beatle was walking the streets of Memphis and the town wasn't even in an uproar." Moman declared that the article "is a total sabotage of what we're trying to do. And to me it's a kind of tactics that a *National Enquirer* would use. I mean, this is about as cheap a shot as I've seen." In the midst of his rant, Moman ordered two *Commercial Appeal* reporters out of his studio. In the words of writer Lawrence Buser, "Shouting obscenities, Moman confronted downtown reporter John Branston, threatened him and slapped a tape recorder from Branston's hands." Later, Moman picketed outside the newspaper's offices. On April 29, Ringo hosted a lavish party aboard the *Island Queen* riverboat, where 254 guests munched on barbecue while floating down the Mississippi River. When asked about the controversy, Ringo explained that he "didn't read it…I mean all we heard about was it took a page to say I wasn't worth mentioning." The former Beatle then declared that the riverboat party was to say "thanks 'cause we've had a real good time in Memphis. Well, the people I've met—besides the one you're talking about—have all been very nice."

March 10, 1948

Drive-In Theater Washes Laundry

On this day the Memphis DriveIn movie theater, located on Lamar directly across from the Rainbow Gardens amusement center, announced it was providing "the new laundry-while-you-wait service" to its customers. According to owner Barney Woolner, the "housewife will be invited to leave her laundry with an attendant as she and the other members of her family enter the DriveIn to enjoy a movie. By the time the program is over the laundry will have been done with speedy and efficient service at a launderette conveniently nearby. We are arranging with the launderettes to pick up the bundles at regular intervals of every 15 or 20 minutes and to return them in the same fashion." Woolner also announced he had installed a new speaker system that allowed "the occupants of every car to regulate their own volume control and also eliminating the noise from the large outside speakers which has caused considerable complaint by residents." The Memphis DriveIn Theater was opened on April 30, 1940. It contained a fifty- by fifty-foot screen and was located on four and a half acres that could accommodate five hundred automobiles. On its first night, hundreds of cars lined up to see the film *Destry Rides Again*, even though a blinding rainstorm made it difficult to see the screen.

March 11, 1967

Historic Beale Street Church Struggled to Survive

Members of First Baptist Church, Beale Street discussed with *Commercial Appeal* reporter Jack Martin on this day efforts being taken to save the endangered religious institution. Completed in 1880, the Victorian Gothic building cost $100,000 and quickly became one of the most important African American institutions in Memphis. It operated a daycare that provided early childhood education to many of Memphis's poorest citizens. Although the church had a fiercely dedicated membership, by 1967, it had fallen into disrepair due to declining attendance. The Memphis Housing Authority, which oversaw the Beale Street Urban Renewal Project, required the church to make repairs in order to prevent its demolition. A widespread fundraising effort was launched that eventually raised enough money to save the church. The importance of the church can be gauged by the comments of some of its most devoted congregants: "It's the mother church of all Negro Baptist churches in the Mid-South," said Vicki Smith, a member of the youth choir. Twenty-one-year-old Harvell Cooper, a Memphis State University senior, explained that "there's so much of this turning to modern things today, you should hang on to some things from the past…To me, the church is as important as Beale Street being the birthplace of the blues." First Baptist Church, Beale Street survived until 2003, when the City of Memphis condemned the church as a fire hazard.

March 12, 1927

Memphis School Board Triumphs over Shelby County

The Tennessee Supreme Court ruled on this day that the government of Shelby County did not own a piece of land adjoining Carnes School that belonged to the Memphis Board of Education. In 1874, Shelby County purchased both pieces of land to be used for a school, but one was never actually built. Memphis annexed the tract in 1899, and the Tennessee General Assembly transferred the land to the city school board, which opened Carnes School for African Americans on that location in 1900. For over twenty years, Shelby County was allowed to operate a stable on the second parcel, but in 1926, the school board ordered the county to vacate the property for a planned school addition. In response, the county filed suit in Chancery Court, arguing that it had title to the property due to adverse possession and the school board had abrogated its right to the land because it hadn't used it in twenty-seven years. Chancellor David W. DeHaven decided that Memphis owned the land, but Shelby County appealed. The case made its way to the state Supreme Court, which ruled that "both [the] county and the board of education were state agencies in the management of the public schools and that the county could not assert any interest in school property adverse to the claim of another state agency acting under authority of a legislative act. The property was, therefore, awarded to the board of education."

March 13, 1941

Poison Milk Mystery Baffled Police

On this day, the Memphis Police Department announced there were, in the words of police chief Carrol Seabrook, "no new developments" in its investigation into the death of Spanish-American War veteran Walter Lewis Samples. As reported by the *Commercial Appeal*, "Mr. Samples, 69, a retired United States Engineers employee who lived alone, died last Thursday night at Veterans' Hospital, a day after he became sick from drinking milk from a bottle found on his porch Wednesday morning." A chemical analysis of the milk discovered it was laced with phosphorus, but police were less successful in uncovering a suspect or a motive for the crime. However, detectives did discover that Samples was a well-known womanizer who had left his entire estate to a married woman, Bertha Hamilton House. Under intense questioning, her husband, Leroy R. House, admitted to police that he had poisoned the milk and left it on Samples's porch. On April 11, 1941, the Shelby County Grand Jury indicted husband and wife for first-degree murder. Put on trial in June, Leroy and Bertha House were found guilty and sentenced to twenty years in prison. With their conviction, one of the most bizarre murder cases in Memphis history came to a close.

March 14, 1920

Noted Memphis Novelist Laid to Rest

Funeral services at Calvary Episcopal Church were held on this day for novelist Sara Beaumont Kennedy. Officiated by Reverend H.M. Dumbell, active and honorary pallbearers included *Commercial Appeal* editor C.P.J. Mooney and cartoonist J.P. Alley. Hundreds attended the funeral, including local newspaper staffs and members of the Nineteenth Century Club and Kennedy Book Club, which was named in her honor. As explained by the *Commercial Appeal*, "Few women of Memphis have so left their impress upon the community as did Mrs. Kennedy, and since the news of her death became known expressions of sorrow at her passing, and of genuine admiration for her ability as a writer, and for her sterling traits of character have been heard on all sides." Kennedy was the author of *The Wooing of Judith, Cicely, Joscelyn Cheshire: A Story of Revolutionary Days in the Carolinas* and the children's book *Told in a Little Boy's Pocket*. In a review of *Cicely*, the *Atlanta Constitution* stated that the novel was "charming; it strikes the human note and can be enjoyed by young and old alike."

March 15, 1936

WPA Band Provides Free Concert

A free concert featuring unemployed musicians was held at the Auditorium South Hall on this day in the midst of the Great Depression. As reported by the *Commercial Appeal*, the brass band was made up of "thirty Memphis musicians, many of whom were forced by the depression to mute their strings and brasses for jobs as common laborers…The program…is the most ambitious yet undertaken here since the WPA made it possible last December for talented artists to be taken from general relief rolls and welded into orchestras with more than a fair chance of becoming self-sustaining." Before the concert director Joseph Henkel stated that "all the musicians ask is that Memphians and music lovers in the surrounding territory pay them the deserved tribute of an audience. I am sure that few will be disappointed, as almost all of the musicians are men of ability, experience and understanding who are anxious to demonstrate that their talents have outlasted the dark hours of the adversity which overtook them." During the concert, the band performed several works, including *The Swan* by Saint-Saen and "Old Man River" from the musical *Showboat*. For many, the highlight of the concert was the debut of a march entitled *Memphis: Down in Dixie*, composed by assistant director Harry E. Dillman, which was dedicated to Mayor Watkins Overton, who was instrumental in securing $20,000 in federal funds to operate the band. By the end of the 1930s, the Works Progress Administration had spent $5.2 million in Memphis providing its citizens with useful employment.

March 16, 1980

Perkins Bridge Collapses

Three northbound lanes of the Perkins Street Bridge collapsed on this day, killing one person and injuring two others in perhaps the worst bridge disaster in Memphis history. As reported by the *Commercial Appeal*: "Maurice Salmon…was returning home from a date when he saw two cars…drive off the bridge…Salmon was halfway across the creek in the southbound lane when he realized the section of the bridge in the other direction was gone. 'I heard the noise of the rushing water just outside my car,' he said. 'Before I realized anything else, I saw the first car go off. I couldn't believe it was happening. Then I saw the second car go off.' Salmon stopped short, pulled his car around in front of the traffic heading for the washed-out section, blocked the road and jumped from his car waving his arms in warning."

Riding in the first car was Eleanor McCarter and Lee Gardner, who swam to safety after they plunged eighty feet into the water. Following close behind them in the second car was William L. Austin, former Memphis State University football player, who had spent the evening with McCarter and Gardner at Gaffer's Speakeasy restaurant before losing his life in the strong current of Nonconnah Creek. City officials blamed heavy rainfall and debris for the bridge collapse, but it was later determined that dredging operations for the construction of the Mall of Memphis was also a significant factor in the disaster.

March 17, 1950

Les Passes Treatment Center Opens

On this day, Les Passes Treatment Center for Cerebral Palsied Children was open at 822 Court Avenue. Four hundred people attended the opening ceremonies including the National Society for Crippled Children's director of public relations John R. Powers Jr., who stated, "We are very proud of the fine job you have done in Memphis and are especially impressed with the short space of time in which you have accomplished so much. Our society will use the work done here as a pattern for similar centers elsewhere." Sponsors contributing to the establishment of the treatment center were the University of Tennessee College of Medicine, the Cerebral Palsy Parents' Council for West Tennessee and the Shelby county chapter of the Tennessee Society for Crippled Children. Many prominent members of the city's medical community attended the festivities including dean of the University of Tennessee's College of Medicine Dr. O.W. Hyman and Dr. L.M. Graves, director of the Memphis and Shelby County Health department. Les Passes helped thousands of children suffering from cerebral palsy and other developmental diseases for forty-eight years until it merged with Le Bonheur Children's Medical center in 1997. Along with Le Bonheur and St. Jude Children's Research Hospital, Les Passes established Memphis as one of the most important centers for the treatment and cure of childhood diseases in the world and consequently saved the lives of thousands of children.

March 18, 1932

Acrimony Reigned at Republican Party Meeting

African American GOP leader Robert Church Jr. was one of the most powerful leaders in the national Republican Party during the first half of the twentieth century.

A contentious meeting of the Shelby County Republican Party was held on this day at the courthouse to plan strategy for the 1932 presidential campaign. They consented to support President Herbert Hoover's reelection bid but failed to agree on anything else. The interracial "Black and Tans" faction chose noted African American GOP leader Robert Church Jr. and bankruptcy referee C.H. King as their delegates, while the all-Caucasian "Lily Whites" chose lumber baron C. Arthur Bruce and George H. Poole to serve on the Tennessee delegation to the National Convention. Church later rose to denounce the Lily Whites, claiming they promoted a "doctrine of hate and spite" designed to remove him from the Republican Party. Bruce essentially agreed with Church's statement, declaring his desire to "break" Church's power and "bring 'the better faction' of the Republican Party into control in Shelby County."

March 19, 1911

Home for Former Slaves Proposed

A mass meeting was held on this day at metropolitan Baptist Church to raise funds for a home for former slaves living in Memphis. During the meeting a plan created by Cotton Exchange assistant secretary E.C. LaHache was adopted by the gathering. As reported by the *Commercial Appeal*, the "plan provides for the printing of a circular letter which is to be sent to all professional and business men of whatever walk of life, asking them to see that the Negroes employed by them contribute $1 each to the fund." It was also requested that the professionals contribute a dollar to the effort. The nostalgia that many white, and some black, Memphians felt for the antebellum South was in full display when the reporter wrote:

> *The sense of the white speakers was that the loyalty and fidelity of the old slaves before and during the war should interest the white people in their behalf as they become too old to support themselves. Some beautiful references were made to the trustworthiness and faithfulness of the old time Negroes, who understood the white man and is understood by him. As Rev. T.J. Searcy, the pastor of the* [African-American] *church, concisely puts it, "Those who know us love us."*

March 20, 1930

Memphis Rated Murder Capital Again

Dr. Frederick L. Hoffman, insurance statistician, issued a report on this day declaring that Memphis was the murder capital of the United States. As reported by the *Press-Scimitar*, "Dr. Hoffman gives the 1929 homicide rate for Memphis as 66.8 per 100,000 of population, the largest of all cities; Birmingham with 51.0, is second, and Atlanta, with 51.0 is third. All of the first 10 are southern cities. Chicago is way down the list with 12.7. The average for the 141 American cities considered is 10.5." Many Memphians felt that Hoffman's pronouncement unfairly stigmatized the city, and they pointed to fact that Chicago, which experienced the St. Valentine's Day Massacre and other high-profile killings during the year surveyed, was ranked much lower than the Bluff City. In explaining his report Hoffman wrote, "In response to various protests from local authorities and others, I have subjected the Memphis figures, thru co-operation of the local board of health, to a thorough examination, while I have made similar investigations for a number of other communities." In Hoffman's estimation, Memphis remained the murder capital until the 1940s, when the murder rate sharply declined.

March 21, 1960

Sit-In Demonstrators Fined

Thirty-six African American protesters and four black reporters were tried on this day for disorderly conduct because they participated in a sit-in demonstration at the Main branch of the Memphis Public Library on Saturday, March 19. The demonstrators, all students of LeMoyne College and S.A. Owen Junior College, entered the library to protest the long-standing custom of barring African Americans from all public libraries save the segregated Vance Avenue branch. Clyde Battles, a nineteen-year-old Owen Junior College sophomore, testified that he had visited the main library because it housed a book not available at his college library. LeMoyne student Gwendolyn Townsend also testified that she needed the library's materials to complete a term paper. Defense attorney Benjamin L. Hooks explained that "no amount of fines will stop occurrences such as this one…We have tried to work with the white community, but the white community takes the position that 'we are not going to move.'" Finding the defendants guilty, Judge Beverly Boushe declared that "mass demonstrations of this type can only breed contempt of the law. It is an open invitation to violence and is intended to completely disrupt the due processes of law." Sit-ins soon spread to other points across the city, which led to the desegregation of the public libraries in December 1960.

March 22, 1976

Star Trek *Fans Celebrated Defunct TV Series*

Fans of the television series *Star Trek*, which was canceled by NBC in 1969 but grew in popularity during the early 1970s, organized a weeklong celebration of the science fiction program entitled Trektennial Week. It began on this day with a birthday party for series star William Shatner at the Germantown Community Center and continued with show-related talks at several public libraries. The fan club *Star Trek* Unlimited had organized several events across the city since series creator Gene Roddenberry spoke to nine hundred "Trekkies" at Memphis State University in December 1975. One popular event was the display of *Star Trek* memorabilia at the Raleigh branch Public Library, which included a script, models and an autographed photo. Pam Ditto, president of the organization stated, "There is a tremendous amount of interest in *Star Trek* around here, you just wouldn't believe it." In June 1976, a convention was held at the Holiday Inn–Rivermont, where series stars James Doohan and George Takei appeared. In Memphis, the show was regularly broadcast on WHBQ-TV Channel 13, and its program director Lance Russell explained that fan response was "unbelievable. Trekkies have got to be the most dedicated group since the Lawrence Welk fans. I get mail from them every week, especially when we make any changes in the schedule."

March 23, 1977

Michael Jackson Fans Riot at the Southgate Shopping Center
Seven thousand fans stormed the Woolco discount department store in the Southgate Shopping Center on this day to meet and collect autographs from Michael Jackson and his four brothers, who were in town to perform a concert at the Mid-South Coliseum. The event was organized by radio station WDIA, but neither it nor the management of the department store was prepared for the onslaught that began soon after the Jacksons' arrival. Thousands of eager fans burst into the store, crushing Michael, Tito, Randy, Jack and Marlin and damaging merchandise worth several thousand dollars. Woolco and WDIA staff pulled the performers from the mob and ushered them to the roof of the store, where they dropped autographs to the crowd. No arrests were made, and no one was injured in the mêlée. In a newspaper interview later that day, the young musicians shrugged off the incident: "It's all part of the job. If you don't want to sign autographs you're in the wrong business." The brothers then discussed their upcoming television specials, although Michael pointed out that they didn't "want to be overexposed to television, because that can be harmful." Despite the altercation, Michael Jackson visited and performed in Memphis several times. In 1994 and 1995, while married to Elvis Presley's daughter, Lisa Marie, Jackson visited patients at St. Jude Children's Research Hospital and viewed the animals at the Memphis Zoo.

March 24, 1932

"The Smell of Whisky Pervaded the Entire Neighborhood"
Police on this day raided the house at 1116 Madison Avenue, once the home of former mayor Thomas Ashcroft, where they found a 7,500-gallon still, 3,000 gallons of mash and 400 gallons of liquor. Arrested at the home was J.A. Jones, an unemployed contractor from Kentucky who told police that he was "desperate" to feed his wife and two small children. After searching for six months for legitimate employment Jones gave up and turned to crime. "I had to have money so I went to work for a Memphis bootlegger" who paid him twenty dollars per week, Jones declared. The moonshining operation was discovered by the stench of liquor emanating from the stately old home. According to an *Evening Appeal* reporter, "The smell of whisky pervaded the entire neighborhood." As police dismantled the still, hundreds of area residents crowded around the yard to watch. In addition to the illegal equipment and whiskey, police found two books in the home; Thomas Dixon's novel *The Sins of the Father* and George Barr McCutcheon's *A Fool and His Money*.

March 25, 1968

Mediation Talks Resume For Striking Sanitation Workers
Hopes were raised on this day that the seven-week-old strike of the city's sanitation workers would soon end when talks resumed between union and city officials in the Adams Room of the Hotel Claridge. Frank B. Miles, industrial relations director for the E.L. Bruce Company and a former federal labor mediator, led the sessions in an attempt to end the conflict. The talks collapsed on March 23, when city representatives asked if they would be in violation of Chancellor Robert Hoffman's injunction against the strike by negotiating with union officials P.J. Ciampa, T.O. Jones and William Lucy, who had been found in contempt of the injunction. After a brief hearing in the chancellor's courtroom, the mediation continued after Hoffman ruled the talks were not in violation of his order. Events soon overtook the talks, making them pointless. On March 28, a poorly planned protest march led by Dr. Martin Luther King Jr. turned violent, and on April 4, the nonviolent leader was murdered outside his Memphis motel. The strike that had so polarized Memphis did not end until April 16, when the city finally agreed to recognize the union and increase workers' pay.

March 26, 1973

Memphis State Tigers Make First Championship Appearance
The Memphis State University Tigers men's basketball team made its first appearance in the championship game of the National Collegiate Athletic Association tournament on this day. The Tigers earned a spot in the final game by defeating the University of South Carolina, Kansas State and Providence to face the Bruins of the University of California–Los Angeles at the St. Louis Arena. In the first half, Memphis State, led by senior guard Larry Finch, who scored 29 points, played spectacularly against the nationally ranked Bruins and was able to tie the game before the first half buzzer sounded. When the second half began, the Tigers led briefly but then were stopped cold by the six-foot, eleven-inch Bill Walton, who rolled up a record-breaking 44 points to defeat Memphis State 87–66. As Memphians' hearts broke, millions of Americans watched on television when Bill Walton sprained his ankle under the Tigers' goal in the final minutes of the game. The best of Memphis was then on display when Larry Finch and teammate Billy Buford helped Walton to the UCLA bench. The next day, thousands of Memphians packed the Mid-South Coliseum to cheer Finch, Buford, Ronnie Robinson, Larry Kenon, Wes Westfall and the rest of the squad. Larry Finch thanked his fellow Memphians "for making us proud to know that we had more people pulling for us up there than any other team."

Memphis state guard Larry Finch (left), seen here with civil rights leader Maxine Smith and teammate Ronnie Robinson, scored twenty-nine points during the NCAA championship game with the University of California–Los Angeles.

March 27, 1906

Prophet Vows to Destroy the City

Mary Jones, African American street preacher, declared on this day that she would sink Memphis into the Mississippi River. She made this statement because she hoped it would frighten her wayward husband into returning to their home. As reported by the *Commercial Appeal*, "She decided to sink Memphis, and, working on the hypothesis that fear of impending death brings repentance for sin, she felt sure of the return of the errant Jones if she could get-up a decent kind of calamity with death as the long suit." Many Memphians were inclined to believe her "prophesy" because when she was arrested in 1905 for preaching loudly on the street, she promised a heavy rain would fall on the city until she was released from jail, and that is exactly what happened. Several hours before the appointed time of the sinking, a powerful thunderstorm swept through the city, causing its more superstitious citizens to flee on several outbound trains. Fortunately for Memphis, Mr. Jones returned to his wife, and Mary called off the destruction of the Bluff City.

March 28, 1959

Urban Renewal Land Cleared for Children's Hospital
Memphis Housing Authority director Walter Simmons informed the city board of commissioners on this day that the 11.57 acres in the Jackson Avenue Urban Renewal Project set aside for St. Jude's Hospital was now cleared and ready for redevelopment. As reported by *Press-Scimitar* staff writer Tom Meanley:

> *Directors say they hope to start construction this summer…Claude Coyne of the architectural firm, Paul Williams and Associates, Los Angeles, is expected in Memphis in about two weeks with preliminary final plans and specifications. Frank T. Tobey Jr., engineer son of the late mayor, has been retained to supervise construction. Bids will be taken when the final plans are approved to get a construction firm to build the hospital. The ground-breaking ceremony was held last November, with comedian Danny Thomas, whose idea it was to build the hospital, present. Thomas has led the fundraising.*

Construction began later that year, and on February 4, 1962, St. Jude Children's Research Hospital opened its doors. Since 1962, the staff at St. Jude has saved the lives of thousands of children and made many advances in the treatment of childhood diseases.

March 29, 1863

Confederate Sympathizers Exiled from Memphis

Major General S.A. Hurlbut, commander of the Sixteenth Army Corps headquartered in the Bluff City, on this day issued an order exiling several families from Memphis. Special Orders No. 52 stated: "[A] cowardly and murderous attack has been made by guerrillas on a passenger train near Moscow [Tennessee], containing women, children, and citizens, resulting in the capture of part of the passengers and the robbery of all…It is therefore ordered that Col. D.C. Anthony, provost-marshal of the District of Memphis, forthwith select, from the secessionists or rebel sympathizers within this City, the families of the greatest wealth and highest social position, and cause them to be sent south of the lines of the United States forces, not to return."

Hurlbut's predecessor, General William T. Sherman had exiled forty pro-Confederate families from Memphis in retaliation for attacks on Union gunboats, and in January 1863, Union forces issued General Orders No. 10, which stated that any guerrilla attacks occurring in or near Memphis would lead to the exiling of pro-Confederate families from the city.

March 30, 1947

USS Memphis *Docks at Pink Palace*

A ceremony was held on this day at the Pink Palace Museum to celebrate the donation of artifacts from the recently decommissioned naval cruiser USS *Memphis*. As reported by the *Commercial Appeal*'s Emory Grinnel, the donated items included "the 500-pound ship's bell," and "the magnificent, 60-piece silver service set, contributed to the ship through donations

Artifacts from the naval cruiser USS *Memphis* were donated to the Pink Palace Museum.

of Memphians." On hand for the event was Elizabeth Paine Butler, who, as a five-year-old girl, christened the vessel at a Philadelphia shipyard in 1924. Butler presented to the museum remnants of the bottle she used to christen the ship, which had been carefully preserved by her father, former mayor Rowlett Paine. The USS *Memphis* was one of the most well-known cruisers in the fleet. In 1927, it transported Charles Lindbergh back from France after his epic flight across the Atlantic, and President Franklin Roosevelt used the vessel to return from a conference at Casablanca in 1943.

March 31, 1966

Fab Four Wanted to Record in Memphis

The manager of the Beatles, Brian Epstein, recently visited Memphis to arrange a recording session at Stax Records. Staying at the Holiday Inn–Rivermont, Epstein toured the city with Estelle Axton, co-owner of Stax. According to *Press-Scimitar* staff writer Robert Johnson, the Beatles were scheduled to arrive on April 9 and begin working on an album and a single at the famous recording studio located on East McLemore Avenue in South Memphis. The plan was for co-owner Jim Stewart to oversee the session with Atlantic Records executive Tom Dowd, and Steve Cropper would act as arranger. Axton explained that the Beatles were impressed with many Stax recordings, including those by Otis Redding, Rufus Thomas and Booker T. and the MG's. Arrangements for the Beatles security was a challenge, and Axton declared, "They want a house and a suitable one is hard to find. We're not used to something like this in a town this size." Unfortunately for Stax and the legion of Beatles fans residing in the Bluff City, the Fab Four did not arrive in Memphis on April 9, nor did they record an album here. They did perform two concerts at the Mid-South Coliseum in August 1966. During a press conference the Beatles were asked why they didn't record in Memphis. "Little things kept getting in the way…we wanted to come. A couple of tracks [on their album *Revolver*, released August 1] would have been much better if we had come. We wanted Steve Cropper, a guitarist for Booker T. and the MG's to A&R [direct] the session. He's the best we've heard."

April 1, 1945

Ellendale Tank Driver Liberated German Town

On this day African American tank driver William "Bill" Hart Jr. was leading a column of tanks down a road heading to the German village of Untermassfeld. As he approached the town he saw a slim, young woman wearing a Red Cross nurse's uniform blocking the road. The young woman, Marliese Farish, had been ordered to surrender the village by the mayor. When he stuck his head out of the turret, she was startled to see that he was black. In the words of *Commercial Appeal* reporter Lela Garlington, "When she reached into the tank, Marliese closed her eyes and waited for him to shoot her. But no shots rang out. Hart had radioed his commanding officer. Minutes later, an officer drove up in a jeep and pointed a gun at her, warning her that if anyone attempted to shoot his men, she would be the first to die." The surrender was affected peacefully, and Hart soon returned home and later moved to the Shelby County community of Ellendale near Memphis. Marliese married an American soldier and moved to the United States. In 1987, with her second husband, John Farish, she moved to Ellendale on a piece of property that bordered Hart's land. The two families became close friends, but it took over five years from their first meeting for Bill and Marliese to realize they had met briefly once before on a road outside a small village in Germany.

April 2, 1886

Memphis Browns Play National League Champions

Seven hundred Memphis baseball fans watched a fascinating exhibition of horsehide skill when the Chicago Whitestockings played the Memphis Browns on this day at newly constructed Citizens' Park. The Browns scored one run in the first inning, taking an early lead that they maintained until the third, when Chicago tied the score. As reported by the *Daily Avalanche*:

> [In the] *fourth by good batting and daring base running the Chicagos added three more runs and "chic-goed" the locale...The ninth proved to be the most interesting and exciting inning of the entire game. The Chicagos went to bat first and made one run, placing the score eight to one in their favor. The Memphis boys then went in and to the amazement and delight of every one pounced on the great* [Whitestockings right-handed pitcher John Gibson] *Clarkson all over the field, rattling him considerably, making four runs and having all the bases filled when* [Browns player John] *Lavin came to the bat and made his second and the third out, ending the finest game...ever seen in this city.*

Professional baseball was first played in Memphis in the spring of 1877, when the Memphis Reds club was organized. Although the Reds lasted but one season, they did establish a fan base in the city, which was exploited when the Browns were formed in 1885.

April 3, 1918

Loafers Threatened with Jail

Police chief J.B Burney and Shelby County sheriff Mike Tate announced on this day that all unemployed men must find a job immediately or be sent to jail. The ultimatum was delivered because local businessmen and the chamber of commerce have reported that hundreds of men are roaming the streets without gainful employment while they suffer from a labor shortage because of World War I. As reported by the *Commercial Appeal*, "In most cases this condition arises from disinclination to work and efforts directed by the loafers to subsist either by underhand methods or through a hand-to-mouth existence by working a few days on one job and then laying off until they are broke." Police officers and sheriff's deputies were ordered to round up these men and charge them with loitering and vagrancy. Once they were hauled into court, city judge L.T. Fitzhugh explained what happened next: "Every man arrested who cannot show me that he is working on a steady job will be fined $50. This fine will be held up providing he reports to work the following morning on which he is arraigned in court to a place assigned by me. Business men who need labor can receive this service by furnishing me with their names. The officer who makes the arrest is instructed to watch his prisoner and if he is found loitering again to take him into custody and he will be sent to the workhouse and forced to work where no remuneration will be forthcoming. The man who is guilty of a breach of this kind will be subject to arrest immediately."

April 4, 1925

Ford Plant Hires More Workers

W.K. Edmonds, manager of the South Memphis Ford Motor Company plant, announced on this day the hiring of an additional 250 employees. The men were hired in response to increased demand in the Memphis territory for Ford automobiles. According to a company official, "thirty-two percent more cars were sold in this territory during January, February and March than were sold in the corresponding three months of last year and 62 percent more trucks than the same time last year." Because of these additional sales, the production goals for the South Memphis plant were increased to 288 cars per day, up from the previous goal of 188 per day. The Ford Motor Company opened its first assembly line at 495 Union Avenue on July 10, 1912, and the South Memphis plant, located on thirty-eight acres just north of Riverside Park, began operations in September 1924. As described by the *Memphis Chamber of Commerce Journal*, the plant consisted of "240,000 square feet of floor space, without a single pillar to obscure the view or obstruct free movement throughout the entire building. Here all departments are ideally located on the same floor, which enables the superintendent to have in sight and under his direction constantly the work in each department."

April 5, 1982

Television Star Taken to Hospital

Andy Kaufman, costar of the hit ABC TV show *Taxi*, was supposedly injured on this day at the Mid-South Coliseum during a professional wrestling match with Jerry "the King" Lawler. The comedian suffered a "sprained cervical spine" when Lawler lifted him in the air and slammed his head into the ring floor. Known as a pile driver, the move is considered illegal, but that meant little to the eight thousand screaming fans gathered to watch Kaufman's humiliation. As reported by the *Commercial Appeal*, "Kaufman lay sprawled in the ring as Lawler pranced about and spectators cheered." The crowd was so pleased to see Kaufman writhe in pain because he had said such stinging comments as: "You're from May'm-fuss, Tennessee. All's we do is plow the fields and farm the farm. Is that how you talk in May'm-fuss, Tennessee, Mr. Lawler? Duhhh." An ambulance was called and the TV star was taken to St. Francis Hospital in East Memphis, where doctors allegedly put him in traction. Lawler declared to the press, "I went into it with the idea of hurting him, and I'm not sorry for it a bit." From his hospital bed, Kaufman declared he was through with wrestling and would stick to comedy, saying, "Before the match, I thought wrestling was phony, I guess I learned different…after something like this, I can't believe it's phony…or as phony as I used to think it was."

April 6, 1950

Fishing in Exclusive Neighborhood Proposed

Three representatives of the West Tennessee Sportsman's Club met on this day with the Memphis Park Commission to request that it open the lake in the exclusive Chickasaw Gardens neighborhood for children's fishing. Earlier in the year, the park commission voted not to restock the lake with fish because neighbors had complained that having children playing in their neighborhood was a nuisance. According to the residents, children often left trash in their yards and annoyed them with requests to use their telephones and bathrooms. Club president Gilbert Wilson countered that "if you put in toilet facilities out there, the biggest part of the annoyance will be done away with. I think there would be more recreation per acre in that lake than you could get out of 10 times as many acres for any other sport. As it is the recreational value of that lake is now useless." Commissioners consulted records from 1926 which revealed that twenty acres, including those the lake occupied, within Chickasaw Gardens were deeded to the city to be used for recreational purposes. Curtis Turner, maintenance superintendent, reported that the lake and property were being kept up with city funds, and general park superintendent H.S. Lewis explained that there were no recreational activities being offered at the Chickasaw Gardens Lake. As reported by the *Commercial Appeal*, the "Park Commission sidestepped giving the sportsmen an answer and suggested they confer further with Chickasaw Gardens residents."

April 7, 1931

Livestock Trading Expands in Memphis

On this day, the Dixie National Stockyards, located on Warford Street, announced it was expanding its market despite the economic ravages of the Great Depression. According to president and general manager C.M. Raffety, the stockyards "are transacting a regular commission business in cattle, sheep and hogs…We are drawing cattle to Memphis from many sections and shipping them to all parts of the surrounding five states. At our plant…we are handling hundreds of head weekly and we have facilities for handling hundreds of carloads." Next door was the Abraham brothers packing plant, which made it more economical for farmers to sell their livestock in Memphis. As reported by the *Commercial Appeal*, the "Dixie yards were built as a civic movement here by a group of public-spirited men who thought that by their establishment they could help promote agricultural diversification by providing a steady market for cattle. Diversification was seen as a possible aid to the solution of the Mid-South's one-crop ills."

April 8, 1980

Prince Mongo Is Crazy

Federal judge Harry W. Wellford ruled on this day that Robert Hodges, better known as Prince Mongo, suffered from a "mental disease" and was entitled to receive $2,000 per month from an insurance policy he took out in 1971. Hodges filed a claim in 1976 with the Springfield Insurance Company, which paid him $34,000 over 17 months. However when Hodges/Mongo ran for mayor of Shelby County in 1978, the company filed suit requesting the court declare him ineligible for disability payments because of his business and political interests. Prince Mongo claimed to be a 334-year-old refugee from the planet Zambodia. Known for his outrageous behavior, Mongo appeared in Wellford's courtroom in bare feet, wearing only a knee-length fur coat and, during the proceedings, frequently sprinkled a white powder on the floor to ward off evil spirits. Judge Wellford admitted that Hodge's behavior was "bizarre and unusual" and that it was clear that "although the defendant may have a considerable degree of native intelligence, he suffers from a mental disease or disorder or psychosis, and that this condition has apparently worsened since 1976." In response to the verdict, Hodges explained that he'd "never said I'm crazy, but I'll tell you this. I don't know many people who are sane." He also expressed satisfaction in the judge's decision: "This is a victory for the people. We're tired of being pushed and pulled by the superpowers here on Earth." Prince Mongo continued to run for public office and also shock, amuse and anger Memphians well into the twenty-first century.

April 9, 1969

Civil Rights Leader Honored by Catholic Church

The Memphis Catholic Council on Human Relations honored Reverend James M. Lawson, pastor of Centenary Methodist Church, with its annual award at a testimonial dinner on this day. Lawson was presented with the council's award for "increasing understanding among all people." Lawson was one of the founders of the Student Nonviolent Coordinating Committee (SNCC), and he participated in

James Lawson (far left) leads a civil rights march down Main Street in the late 1960s.

many of the significant civil rights initiatives of the 1960s, including the Nashville sit-ins, the Freedom Rides and the Memphis Sanitation Workers' Strike. When police attacked workers and strike supporters on February 23, 1968, Lawson and other leaders formed the Committee on the Move to Equality (COME), which organized many protests and invited Dr. Martin Luther King Jr. to the Bluff City. Lawson continued his civil rights work in Memphis until he moved to Los Angeles in 1974 to pastor Holman United Methodist Church.

April 10, 1952

Senator Runs for Reelection

U.S. senator Kenneth McKellar, a Democrat from Memphis, announced on this day that, despite rumors of the opposite, he would run for a seventh term: "I want to make the unequivocal statement that I am a candidate…and I have no intentions whatever of withdrawing. Some wishful thinkers have been spreading false reports that I was considering withdrawing. I want to brand that as an absolute falsehood…In checking over my record, I find that I have a lot of unfinished business that I do not believe a green hand could bring to fruition." The "green hand" McKellar was referring to was Congressman Albert Gore, who was running against the aging senator. McKellar pledged to secure legislation to develop the Cumberland River, reduce federal taxes and expenditures, support Korean War veterans and improve education. Despite McKellar's many accomplishments and the support of Memphis political boss E.H. Crump, McKellar was defeated by Gore, who served in that seat until he, too, was defeated in 1970.

April 11, 1894

Dynamite Nearly Blows Up Memphis

A railroad car filled with 30,000 pounds of stick dynamite slammed into a railroad yard at Union and Gayoso Streets on this day, wrecking the engine and many railroad cars. Engineer J. Bruso and fireman J.A. Holt were guiding Newport News & Mississippi Valley Railroad Engine No. 529 into the yard and switching freight cars when they became distracted by a gang of workmen and accidentally entered an open switch. Both Bruso and Holt escaped injury by jumping from the engine before impact. As reported by the *Commercial Appeal*, "So complete was the wreck that the sills of the dynamite car were broken and the trucks knocked off, the car itself being thrown over on its side across the track. The dynamite was packed in boxes of 50 pounds each, many of them being broken open by the force of the shock." Had the dynamite exploded, hundreds of lives almost certainly would have been lost and most of downtown would have been destroyed. Fortunately for Memphis, that disaster was averted.

April 12, 1931

Westinghouse Saluted Memphis

The NBC radio network on this day broadcast the Westinghouse Salute to Memphis. The program, sponsored by Westinghouse Electric and Manufacturing Company, was created to pay tribute to "the cities and industries that make America great." Westinghouse and NBC worked closely with Hal W. Mott, chairman of the Memphis Chamber of Commerce's publicity committee in preparing the script. The program opened with narrator Frederick G. Rodgers describing the early history of Memphis, from Hernando Desoto's expedition to the founding of the city in 1819. When Rodgers explained that Memphis was named for the ancient Egyptian city on the Nile, the orchestra played Strauss's *Egyptian March*. As reported by the *Commercial Appeal*, the program then traced "[The] progress of waterway transportation that first brought Memphis to note as a distributing center, re-born in co-ordination with railroad transportation as Memphis became the South's leading railroad center, with 17 radiating lines in nine systems. How coal, electric power and natural gas have joined the major factors of transportation to build business and industry in Memphis, will follow with [an] announcement devoted to the cotton market, the cottonseed products industry, the Memphis Cotton Carnival, held March 2–5, Memphis' fast-growing industry of steel distribution, the hardwood and woodworking industries."

It was estimated that 14 million radio listeners across the nation heard the broadcast.

April 13, 1964

President Appoints Memphian His Personal Representative

A. Maceo Walker (far left), seen here with the executive board of Universal Life Insurance Company, was appointed the personal representative of President Lyndon Johnson to a trade show in Africa.

A. Maceo Walker, president of Universal Life Insurance Company, was appointed on this day to be the personal representative of President Lyndon Johnson to the American Industrial Exposition in the Republic of Mali. Well known in Democratic Party circles, the head of one of the nation's largest black-owned businesses was once honored by President Harry Truman "for significant leadership in the war on inflation." As soon as the appointment was announced, Walker flew to Washington to be briefed by Commerce Secretary Luther Hodges. The industrial exposition was designed to show citizens of the African nation examples of small industries that could be developed in Mali. At the exposition, Walker met with Malian leaders and made the opening address on behalf of President Johnson."

April 14, 1967

"Soul Finger" Released

Stax Records released the single "Soul Finger" by the Bar-Kays on this day. Originally known as the Imperials, the group changed its name to the Bar-Kays after keyboardist Ronnie Caldwell, guitarist Jimmy King, Bassist James Alexander, trumpet player Ben Cauley, drummer Carl Cunningham and saxophonist Phalon Jones saw a billboard advertising Bacardi Rum as they passed through the intersection of E.H. Crump Boulevard and Georgia Avenue. At first, Stax was not interested in signing the Bar-Kays, but cofounder Jim Stewart invited them to record on March 13, 1967. While working on the song "You Can't Sit Down," the group began to play around with an ad-libbed riff they had been working on since October 1966. Impressed with what he heard, Stewart abandoned the other song and began recording the number. The songwriting duo of Isaac Hayes and David Porter suggested the title, and according to historian Rob Bowman, "Porter came up with the idea of bringing in a bunch of local children who were hanging around outside the studio to shout the song's title and to carry on as if there was a party ensuing while the record was being made." "Soul Finger" made it to number seventeen on the *Billboard* pop chart and number three on the rhythm and blues chart. They had little time to enjoy their success, however, for on December 10, 1967, Caldwell, King, Alexander, Cunningham and Jones died in a plane crash with Stax singer Otis Redding. Although tragedy ended the original Bar-Kays, their recording of "Soul Finger" made a lasting contribution to Memphis soul music.

April 15, 1940

Memphis Wins Public Health Award

Dr. L.M. Graves, superintendent of the Memphis Health Department, announced on this day that the American Public Health Association and the U.S. Chamber of Commerce had presented Memphis with its 1939 Health Conservation Award. The award was given to "communities meeting health problems in the most competent manner" and recognized the Bluff City as the healthiest city with a population of 250,000 to 500,000. Memphis was cited for implementing several innovative public health programs during 1939. These included providing free drugs to private physicians treating syphilis patients, operating three tuberculosis clinics, twenty-three child welfare clinics and four maternity clinics in health centers, libraries and schools and supervising 375 local dairies. In the words of a *Commercial Appeal* reporter, "Less than 75 years ago people fled a town of mud streets and saloons when yellow fever struck a frantic citizenry. That and similar health blights in the past temporarily stunted the growth of the 'Friendly City.'" Dr. Graves explained that the improvements in public health since those days was due to "community co-operation in a good health program."

April 16, 1937

Chicks Lose Season Opener to Birmingham

On this day, 7,002 fans packed Rickwood Park in Birmingham to watch the Memphis Chickasaws take the field against the Barons in the opening game of the 1937 Southern League season. In the early innings, the Chicks held the lead but their luck ran out in the eighth when pitcher Dell Wetherell gave up a hit to Barons catcher Red Sueme. As reported by the *Commercial Appeal*:

> [Chicks center fielder Coaker] *Triplett got in front of the ball and it hit his big glove with a plop and with the same kind of dull thud, hit the ground. Red reached second and Red should have been the third out. Wetherell served a fat pitch to Elmer Trapp and Trapp smacked the ball between left and center. Triplett made a desperate effort for this one, dived, got his hands on the ball and couldn't quite hold it. This one went for a two-base hit and Sueme galloped home…The Chicks outdid the Barons in everything but run-making which counts most. They got 11 hits off Roy Joiner, the ace left-hander of the Barons, and the right-handed Jones while Birmingham was gleaning nine off Wetherell. The Tribesmen stole two bases that turned into runs. They smacked the ball to all corners of the field, compiling three triples and a double, and made only one error to the Barons two. But the Chicks' error was the big one.*

April 17, 1973

FedEx Begins Overnight Delivery Service

Federal Express launched its overnight package delivery service on this day at the Memphis International Airport. Founded by Frederick W. Smith in Little Rock, Arkansas, in June 1972, the company relocated to take advantage of the Bluff City's central location and superior airport facilities. Employing 389 workers and fourteen Dassault Falcon jets, the company delivered 186 packages to twenty-five cities during its first night of operation. A month later, Federal Express purchased eighteen additional aircraft, and in August, it began a $2.9 million construction project to build aircraft hangers, a package-sorting facility and permanent headquarters at the airport. As explained by *Commercial Appeal* reporter Bruce Sankey: "Each night, when the system becomes fully operational early in 1974, Federal Express' jet fleet will pick up packages at more than 100 cities across the country and fly them into Memphis to the central sorting facility. There a computer-controlled apparatus will sort the packages at the rate of 10,000 per hour. Seventy minutes after arriving, all packages can be enroute to the destination city aboard the same planes that brought them to Memphis. At the destination city, the packages will be picked up by courier truck and delivered to consignees."

FedEx's daily operation remains in the twenty-first century much as it did when Sankey described it in 1973 with one major exception: the company now employs thirty thousand Memphians, who deliver packages to nearly every nation in the world.

April 18, 1902

Chinese Hop Joint Raided by Police

An opium den was uncovered by police on this day at Kee Sing's laundry, located at 178 Beale Street next door to property owned by African American saloon owner and real estate baron Robert R. Church Sr. Detectives Lawless and Wolff, assisted by patrolmen Carter, Crenshaw, Crouch, Matthews, Meskel and Soefker, raided the establishment, where they found "a wagonload of paraphernalia" and several men and women smoking opium. Arrested were eight Chinese patrons, including Jim Loy, Wing Sing and Sam Kee; Harry Behr and five other young white men; and two African American women. As reported by the *Commercial Appeal*: "[An] assorted lot of dope furniture was hauled in with the gang, an inventory of which showed nine large opium pipes, a fine nickel-plated water pipe for smoking tobacco, two lacquered Chinese pillows, several pound packages of opium fresh from China, the date, 'San Francisco, March 16,' appearing on one of them, a half dozen glass lamps, several tin trays, lighters, a box of Chinese dominoes and a lot of other stuff made up this curious assortment of a pipe-hitter's outfit."

Opium smoking was rampant in Memphis during the late nineteenth and early twentieth centuries, so much so that on June 28, 1879, it became illegal to "keep for sale, give away, or have or loan or loan for use, with or without hire or reward, any opium or deleterious drug, to be smoked, inhaled or otherwise used."

April 19, 1976

City Angry over Survey Results

The Council on Municipal Performance, a national watchdog group that monitored the activities of city governments, on this day released a report criticizing Memphis's government for being, in the words of the *Press-Scimitar*, "one of the poorest in the nation in responding to citizen complaints." The report was taken from a survey sent to twenty local civic groups in the city that asked several questions, including, "How responsive is your city to your group?" and "How much encouragement does your city give to local groups to participate in decision-making?" According to the council's executive director Dr. John T. Marlin, the organization also contacted Clay Huddleston, the city's chief administrative officer, for information regarding the process for handling citizen complaints. However Huddleston's assistant Leola Hansen replied that "at this time we don't feel we can respond to your request for information." When Mayor Wyeth Chandler learned of the report he phoned Marlin and told him that "we don't cater to organizations in Memphis, we deal with citizens."

April 20, 1955

Memphis National Guard Units Activated

National guardsmen from Memphis on this day participated in Operation Minuteman, the first nationwide alert of guard units in U.S. history. The surprise alert began at 5:30 p.m., and within an hour, the majority of guardsmen had reported for duty. According to Louis Silver of the *Commercial Appeal*, a "chain of swift telephone calls spread the alert to ground force units totaling 800 here…Into action went the 215th Medical Battalion…the 196th Armored Field Artillery Battalion…and the 130th Armored Military Police Company." The medical unit set up four hospital tents on the grounds of the National Guard Armory at 2525 Central Avenue and ambulances shuttled make-believe casualties from the imaginary front lines near the Mississippi River. Soldiers from the military police company guarded bridges, a water plant and television facilities while five B-26 planes patrolled the skies between Memphis and Helena, Arkansas.

Dedicated on September 7, 1943, the Tennessee National Guard Armory was located at 2525 Central Avenue until 1983.

April 21, 1960

Politicians Skewered at Gridiron Show

The Memphis Press Club held the Gridiron Show on this day at the Hotel Claridge to make fun of political leaders and raise money to establish a scholarship fund at Memphis State University. An overflow crowd of over four hundred people watched as newspaper reporters and editors portrayed local politicians in a series of skits that lampooned their careers. According to *Commercial Appeal* reporter Reese Wells, Arkansas "gov. Orval Faubus laughed as uproariously as a man can while watching himself on a bicycle built for two, with [civil rights activist] Mrs. Daisy Bates, and singing: 'Daisy, Daisy, give me your little hand. I'm half crazy to be the king of the land. I'll gladly support the sit-ins…And you'll look grand shaking the hand of the president of the land.'" In other skits, Memphis congressman Clifford Davis was portrayed as a doddering geriatric who urged his constituents to "Remember the *Maine*," and later, the newsman imitating Tennessee senator Albert Gore sang about his frustration over the 1960 Civil Rights Bill: "Well I never felt more like singing the Blues because I never thought that I'd ever lose in the Senate. Why do they do me this way?"

April 22, 1864

Health Officer Appointed by Union Army during Civil War
Union military commanders on this day appointed Dr. F. Noel Burke as health officer for the City of Memphis. Burke's appointment gave him full authority to direct the "sanitary arrangements of the city." As reported by the *Memphis Bulletin*:

> *This is an office which has already been too long vacant, and now that it is filled by the appointment of Surgeon Burke, this competent gentleman will doubtless find many duties to perform, which have arisen from past neglect, and rendered more difficult by an over laxity in the municipal regulations heretofore. All the difficulties, however, we trust will soon be overcome, and the condition of our city materially improved. Dr. Burke is a gentleman who we deem fully sufficient for the labors of the responsible position to which he has been assigned, and we trust he may be abetting in these labors not only by the authorities, but by every good citizen of the community, as it is a matter in which we all have an interest.*

Despite the hopes of the *Bulletin*, the streets of Memphis remained in a filthy state long after the Civil War ended. In the words of one historian, "Dead animals, rotting food and other refuse were casually thrown into Memphis's alleys and gutters, while stagnant water collected in every crevice and pothole in the city." It was not until after the yellow fever epidemic of 1878 that Memphis cleaned its streets and constructed a modern sanitary sewer system.

April 23, 1970

Republicans Meet to Choose Governor

The Shelby County Republican Party met on this day to choose a chairman and endorse a gubernatorial candidate. Alex Dann, Shelby County election commissioner and supporter of Memphis dentist Winfield Dunn for governor, was elected chairman over his opponent, state election commissioner James E. Harpster. According to *Press-Scimitar* politics editor Null Adams, "Dunn had a big evening, being the only one of four GOP candidates for governor who attended. He received a 20-minute demonstration when introduced, was led to the platform as a band and a group of 'Dunn Dolls,' pretty young girls in costumes, paraded all over the Auditorium of East High School. All other GOP candidates sent excuses." Dunn forces also secured a majority on the party's steering committee, as well as key endorsements from city council member Robert James and Congressman Dan Kuykendall. Winfield Dunn secured the Republican nomination, and in November 1970, he defeated Democrat John J. Hooker to become governor of Tennessee. Serving until 1974, Dunn, in the words of historian Michael Rogers, "developed a statewide kindergarten program, pushed highway construction legislation to an all-time high, reorganized major branches of the state government, and created the Department of Economic and Community development."

April 24, 1939

Maid of Cotton Wowed Nation

Alice Louise Hall, the National Cotton Council's first Maid of Cotton, on this day appeared in Buffalo, New York, as part of a tour promoting the virtues of the South's agricultural staple and the Memphis Cotton Carnival. As reported by the *Press-Scimitar*, "Miss Hall was selected in a contest sponsored by the *Press-Scimitar* and the Cotton Carnival. On her coast to coast air trip, she is carrying a message of greater use of cotton, particularly in women's clothes, and is inviting dignitaries to the Cotton Carnival, May 9–14. She is also boosting National Cotton Week, May 22–27." During the East Coast leg of her journey, Hall, a Tech High School senior, appeared on the front page of hundreds of newspapers when she kissed New York mayor Fiorello H. LaGuardia while visiting Manhattan. On the West Coast, Hall appeared on Bing Crosby's radio show, met Hollywood stars Jack Benny, Humphrey Bogart, Edgar Bergen and Dorothy Lamour and was presented with a white, fluffy puppy by comedian Bob Hope. Hall returned to Memphis, graduated from high school and became a teacher. She later married Van Smith and had a son and daughter, Van Jr. and Phyllis. In addition to raising her children, Hall worked as a bookkeeper and was active in Women in Construction and the DeMolay Mothers Club until her death in 1991.

April 25, 1975

Memphian Honored for Courageous Fight against Cancer
Mitchell Road High School graduate Robert Johnson, the first African American captain of West Point's varsity football team, was honored on this day for his courageous battle with cancer. During an event at the Hilton Inn, Johnson received awards from city government and Congressman Harold Ford for bravely dealing with a cancerous arm that prevented him from playing football during the 1974 season. Although unable to play, Johnson's teammates elected him captain, and he was able to lead the team from the sidelines. On March 26, President Gerald R. Ford and actress Raquel Welch presented Johnson with the American Cancer Society's Courage Award in a ceremony at the White House attended by First Lady Betty Ford and the West Point cadet's mother, Mary Ann Johnson. The text of the plaque presented Johnson read, "The American Cancer Society salutes a courageous young man, Cadet Robert E. Johnson, for his bravery in his battle against cancer; and for the hope and inspiration he has given all Americans in the fight for life and health." During the ceremony, which also launched the American Cancer Society's 1975 fundraising crusade, the president said of Johnson, "Your courage is an inspiration to all Americans."

April 26, 1977

Vietnamese Refugees Settle in Memphis

Vietnamese refugee Nguyen Van Trieu and his family celebrated their second year of settling in Memphis after fleeing the Communist takeover of South Vietnam. Trieu, a former South Vietnamese army radio operator, arrived in the Bluff City in the spring of 1975, when he went to work for the Catholic Charities' resettlement program. In that position, he assisted 296 Cambodian, Laotian and Vietnamese families adjust to life in the United States. One such family was Nguyen Thanh Duong and his wife, Tai Chi. Because of Trieu's efforts, Duong found work as a paint mixer at McDowell Industries, and Tai Chi worked at Memphis Furniture Manufacturing Company as a seamstress. When their son, Thanh, was born, the birth certificate mistakenly listed his name as "Ann" so Trieu had the document corrected. For his advocacy, Trieu was elected chairman of the Vietnamese Friendship Association. Reflecting on his changed circumstances, Trieu stated that "we come from a little village… everybody knows your name. We walk around the village and visit everyone…In America you live more private. You do not know your neighbors. You close your door and watch television."

April 27, 1865

Sultana Leaves Memphis Harbor

The steamboat *Sultana*, carrying around 2,400 former Union prisoners of war, lurched out of the Memphis Harbor at 1:00 a.m. on this day. The boat slowly made its way upstream, but then suddenly, an hour and a half after leaving Memphis, its boilers exploded and the ship began to sink into the muddy waters of the Mississippi River. At 3:30 a.m., two men in a wharf boat patrolling the Memphis Harbor came across the half-naked Private Wesley Lee of the 102nd Ohio, desperately clinging to a pine board. Hauling him ashore, they learned of the *Sultana*'s destruction, which they immediately reported to river transportation master Captain John Curtis. Every available boat was ordered to search for survivors, and Curtis took personal command of the steamboat *Jenny Lind*, the military packet *Pocahontas* and the ferry *Rosadella* and soon arrived at the scene of the explosion. According to historian Perre Magness, the "first gray light revealed a horrible sight; the river was clogged with swimmers, many of them scalded and badly injured, clinging to any bits of debris that floated. Soon a dozen or more steamboats and skiffs were plying back and forth to pull the bodies out of the water. The groans and cries of the injured came from all across the broad expanse of swollen river." When the dead were tallied, it was discovered that 1,647 people died in the explosion and sinking, making the *Sultana* incident the worst maritime disaster in American history.

April 28, 1933

Former Slave Remembers Slave Market

Former slave Mary Herndon shared on this day what life was like in Memphis during the 1850s and 1860s with *Commercial Appeal* reporter J.H. Curtis. Herndon was bought by Nathan Bedford Forrest, slave trader, politician and future Confederate general, in Springfield, Missouri, where she, along with one hundred others, was "loaded into wagons and taken to St. Louis. We come on a steamboat from St. Louis to Memphis." Herndon arrived in Memphis during a raucous Independence Day celebration. She continued: "I saw lots of white men, all drunk, some fightin' and some standin' about in front of saloons…Main Street was just a mud hole with empty wagons pulled by two and three yokes of oxen…We was all taken to the…house, a long shed, divided and built on each side of a big yard. There we was kept until in the late fall, when I was sold to Louis Fortner, a rich planter with a big place near where Mason, Tenn., is. For a while, I nursed in the family, but next summer I was put to work in the field. I had never done field work in my life, but I soon learned. I chopped cotton, plowed it and did everything any other slave done."

She remained at the Fortner plantation until Union forces occupied West Tennessee during the Civil War. Herndon recalled that once she learned of emancipation, "next mornin' I specks I wanted to get a little uppish with ole' mistus and when she ordered me to do something I remarked I was free. 'You are not free. You get that hoe and go to the field,' she said. I sassed her again and she up with the hoe and hit me on the head."

April 29, 1949

Commercial Appeal Wins Award

The University of Missouri's Columbia School of Journalism announced on this day that Memphis's "old reliable" newspaper, the *Commercial Appeal*, was being presented with its Honor Award for Distinguished Service in Journalism. The dean of the school, Dr. Frank Luther Mott, explained that the newspaper was being recognized for its "long and proud history as a courageous newspaper, from the days of its founders, through the heroic episode of B.F. Dill's 'Moving Appeal' during the Civil War to its present fearless management. It's notable record of public service in its 'Plant to Prosper' campaign, and in many other projects of wide public benefit and its greatest achievement—that of being, day in and day out a good newspaper." Editor Frank Ahlgren stated that he was "especially pleased with that part of the award which says the *Commercial Appeal*'s greatest achievement has been that of being a good newspaper day in and day out." This was not the first time the *Commercial Appeal* was honored by the journalism profession. In 1923, the newspaper received the Pulitzer Prize for its editorial campaign against the Ku Klux Klan.

April 30, 1975

A Visit to the Cotton Exchange

On this day, *Press-Scimitar* staff writer Jess Bunn visited the Memphis Cotton Exchange, 65 Union Avenue, where he found that members "continue to conduct business much the same as when the exchange was formed in 1873…The organization still functions as it was designed to do when cotton merchants in the city decided an agency was needed for them to keep abreast of events in their sector of the economy more than 100 years ago." Secretary of the exchange Melvon W. Swett toured Bunn around the exchange and explained the inner-workings of the venerable Memphis institution. According to Swett, "Buying and selling firms gather in an individual firm's office and determine the price to be paid for the cotton based on samples drawn from the bales. Once a price is agreed on, both men regard the verbal agreement as if it were a legal contract. A man's word is strictly his bond. There are no contracts signed." On the floor of the cotton exchange, the membership, who pay $1,000 to join the organization and $400 per year in dues, meet to discuss the industry, play dominoes, smoke cigars and watch price quotations and other statistics being written on a large board. The Cotton Exchange remained at its Union Avenue location until 2005, when it moved out east and the trading floor became the Cotton Museum at the Memphis Cotton Exchange.

May 1, 1979

Columnist Strolls Away

Newspaper readers across the mid-South on this day mourned the death of Eldon Roark, beloved columnist for the *Memphis Press-Scimitar*. Roark began writing his popular "Strolling" column for the *Press-Scimitar* in 1933. A well-respected journalist, Roark received the National Headliners Club Medal in 1947 for writing the best newspaper feature column in the United States, and in 1954, he won the Ernie Pyle Memorial Award. A collection of his columns was published in 1945 by McGraw-Hill entitled

Eldon Roark began writing his popular Strolling column for the *Press-Scimitar* in 1933 and continued until his death in 1979.

Memphis Bragabouts. A writer for the *Saturday Review of Literature* described the volume as an "amusing little book about curious and nice people, it will tell you more about the South than a dozen novels about Marse Henry and the old plantation." In its obituary of Roark, the *Commercial Appeal* reported: "[He was a] man with a gentle good humor and a deep understanding of human nature."

May 2, 1933

Teachers Give Up Salary to Avoid Lay-Offs

During a meeting of the Memphis Teacher's Association at the county courthouse on this day, the teachers voted to forfeit a week's pay in order to make up a deficit in the school's budget, which would then prevent teacher lay-offs. As reported by the *Commercial Appeal*:

> [The action] *will be forwarded to the city school board in the form of a resolution drafted by Miss Grace Mauzy, corresponding secretary, that reads as follows: "In order to avoid the dismissal of 25 or more classroom teachers to make up an anticipated deficit of $40,000 in school board revenue for the 1933–34 year, we, the members of the Memphis Teacher's Association go on record as willing to forfeit another week's salary, if necessary, to retain the said teachers."*

Due to the economic ravages of the Great Depression, the school system was nearly bankrupt in 1932, which led to teachers having their pay cut by one-sixth, the slashing of kindergarten programs and the elimination of 107 classroom positions.

May 3, 1940

WeOna Stores Celebrate Ten-Year Anniversary

Memphis's largest independent grocery store chain, the WeOna Food Stores, celebrated its tenth anniversary on this day. Established by ten independent stores, it was designed to give local merchants the means to compete with the large national grocery store chains. The WeOna Food Stores not only provided foodstuffs for thousands of Memphians but also was one of the most significant contributions the Italian immigrant community made to the economic development of the Bluff City in the twentieth century.

The WeOna Food Stores, like this one at 1714 Netherwood, was Memphis's largest independent grocery store chain during the 1940s.

May 4, 1917

Memphis Greeks Support American War Effort

The Greek American community of Memphis on this day pledged its unwavering support for President Woodrow Wilson's recent declaration of war against Germany. Calling itself the Liberal League, it adopted a resolution that stated, "We the Greeks of the City of Memphis support the American cause...The twentieth century is the time to support civilization against the despotic rulers." Officers of the league included president Speros Vryonis, treasurer O.D. Nicholas and secretary V. Velissaratos. Members of the Liberal League were followers of former Greek prime minister Eleutherios Venizelos, who supported the Allies and led an armed revolt against the pro-German Greek monarchy. In response to the Memphis league's activities, Venizelos sent them a telegram that stated, "I congratulate you on your resolve to devote all your strength to the noble task undertaken by the United States...I am convinced that the Greeks of the United States...will succeed in winning the active and highly valued sympathy of the great American nation."

May 5, 1947

Bellhops Fingered in Vice Probe

Twenty-two-year-old prostitute Rose Marie Galvin declared that several local bellhops had assisted her in securing assignations with hotel guests. Identified in court were Hotel Chisca employee Louis Waddington and Chester Taylor of the William Len Hotel. The two, along with nine other bellhops, were charged with aiding and abetting prostitution, disorderly conduct and soliciting males. As reported by the *Press-Scimitar*, "Eleven of the hotel bellhops paid fines and forfeits totaling $1,683 in city court today. Each of the 11 was fined $51 on each of the charges." Galvin, according to purity squad lieutenant R.E. Crawford, came to Memphis several months before with Paul Pablovich, who moved her from one hotel to another and split the earnings with her. The two were apparently successful until Galvin learned that Pablovich had secretly married another woman in Mississippi. Hungry for revenge, Galvin told her story to police. Pablovich was bound over to a federal court, which charged him with violating the Mann Act, which prohibited the transportation of women across state lines for immoral purposes.

May 6, 1960

Censor Board Sued

The producer of the Warner Brothers film *This Rebel Breed* filed suit in federal court on this day to block the banning of the movie by the Memphis Board of Censors. Attorney H.T. Lockard made the complaint on behalf of Los Angeles film producer William Rowland, who argued that "to deny exhibition of the film is unlawful and is a violation of Constitutional rights of free speech and due process of the law in that no hearing was held before the censor board." However, board chair Mrs. J. Judson McKellar said that she had "reviewed the movie Feb. 10 and I thought it was obscene and racially objectionable, but it has not yet been banned." As reported by *Commercial Appeal* reporter Richard Connelly, "Mrs. McKellar saw the movie with board member Fred M. Morton who was completely opposed to the picture's being shown here. She explained it is often board policy for two members to see several movies and hold for official action those movies they think objectionable...According to Mrs. McKellar the film shows 'a girl almost stripped,' teenagers 'selling drugs' and unfavorably portraying white, Negro and Mexican races." In July 1965, federal judge Bailey Brown ruled that the ordinances and statutes that created the Memphis Board of Censors were unconstitutional.

May 7, 1977

Waitress Hob-Nobs with Celebrities

Catherine Reynolds, waitress at the Memphis International Airport's Dobbs House Coffee Shop, sat down with *Press-Scimitar* staff writer Charles Goodman to tell him of the many celebrities she had served over the years. The waitress, who apparently talked as fast as she poured a hot cup of coffee, recounted that when "Chuck Conners walked in—you know, *The Rifleman*—he's really tall so I asked him, 'When are you going to grow up?' And he smiled and said, 'Gimme a little time.' He slid in a chair and I said, 'How come you're so ugly?' and he laughed and said, 'Here I was, thinking you were so pretty.'" Reynolds explained that most of the celebrities she met were kind and down-to-earth like Conners. When she served singer Dale Evans and her husband, cowboy star Roy Rogers, Ms. Evans asked Reynolds how Dobbs House made its turkey dressing and they exchanged favorite recipes. She also described the day TV star Eddie Albert "was in that booth over there. And I said to a lady at another table. 'Do you see Eddie Albert, the *Green Acres* man, around here anywhere?' Well, she ran over to see him and he stood up and kissed her hand right there." Not all of her interactions were pleasant, however. Reynolds said she once waited on the founder of Kentucky Fried Chicken, Colonel Harland Sanders and his wife. "When he got up to go pay, he left four quarters on the table. His wife stayed behind to fix her lips and makeup. And she picked up two of the quarters and put them in her purse. I'll never get over that."

May 8, 1940

Federal Cotton Program Launched in Memphis

An experimental national welfare program was implemented on this day in Memphis by the Federal Surplus Commodities Corporation. As reported by the *Commercial Appeal*: "Needy families eligible for Federal stamps redeemable in cotton goods thronged the Cotton Stamp offices at the Auditorium yesterday to receive approximately $3000 worth of the stamps...launched Tuesday morning as the result of combined efforts of the Department of Agriculture, the city and Shelby County, the cotton stamp plan can provide more than 12,000 needy families here with stamps for redemption. Thus the nation's surplus of cotton is expected to be reduced through a revival of the domestic demand and, at the same time, thousands of needy will be aided."

Those who received the stamps included those enrolled in the aid-to-dependent-children program and Work Projects Administration workers. Around 1,150 received the stamps and many flocked to downtown department stores, which reported selling between $300 and $500 worth of cotton goods such as stockings, dresses and underwear. The project was considered so important that *Life* magazine sent one of its most experienced photographers, Eliot Elisofon, to Memphis to record the scene. Unfortunately, Memphis's cotton stamp experiment was not implemented nationwide because the Federal Surplus Commodities Corporation was abolished later in 1940.

May 9, 1980

Memphian Becomes Federal Judge

The U.S. Senate on this day confirmed Memphian Odell Horton Jr. as the first African American federal district judge for the Western District of Tennessee. In 1962, Horton was appointed assistant U.S. attorney by President John F. Kennedy, and he remained in this post until 1969, when he became a criminal court judge. Later, he was appointed a federal bankruptcy judge in 1976, after having served as president of LeMoyne-Owen College. Horton was sworn-

in at the Clifford Davis Federal Building on May 16 where family members and local dignitaries crowded into a courtroom to watch him take the oath of office. Horton remained on the bench

Odell Horton Jr. was the first African American federal district judge for the Western District of Tennessee.

until his retirement in 1997. He died on February 22, 2006, and the building where his court was located was renamed the Clifford Davis-Odell Horton Jr. Federal Building on May 3, 2007.

May 10, 1864

Trade and Travel in Memphis Restricted by

Major General C.C. Washburn, commander of the Union army's District of West Tennessee, ordered that "the lines of the army at Memphis be closed, and no person will be permitted to leave the city, except by river, without a special pass from these headquarters." Those who wanted to travel to Memphis were allowed to do so but were prevented from leaving the city by the major general's order. Washburn was attempting to cut off the illegal flow of goods and money from Memphis to the Confederate army, which was hampering Union efforts to pacify West Tennessee. In his order, the major general stated: "Memphis has been of more value to the Southern Confederacy since it fell into Federal hands than Nassau. To take cotton belonging to the rebel government to Nassau, or any foreign port, is a hazardous proceeding. To take it to Memphis and convert it into supplies and greenbacks and return to the lines of the enemy, or place the proceeds to the credit of the rebel government in Europe, without passing again into rebel lines, is safe and easy…The past and present system of trade…has invited the enemy to hover around Memphis as his base of supply, when otherwise he would have abandoned the country…It opens our lines to the spies of the enemy, and renders it next to impossible to execute any military plan without its becoming known to him long enough in advance for him to prepare for it."

May 11, 1898

Memphians Enlist to Fight for Cuba

On this day young, able-bodied men were being recruited by representatives of the Second Regiment, Tennessee Volunteers, to fight in Cuba against the Spanish Empire. Lieutenant Colonel T.E. Patterson and several other officers from Nashville set up a recruiting station at the Neely Zouaves Armory, where many young men enthusiastically volunteered to serve. According to the *Commercial Appeal*, "The boys in West Tennessee do not care to see the Second made up of men from other sections of the state, and it is believed by the officers who left Memphis about two weeks ago that it will be an easy matter to get all the men needed from home." Not all the men from home were able to join, however, due to their poor health. Regimental Surgeon George Seay reported that many men begged to be let in, but he could not overlook the health regulations. As the Second Regiment was being filled, two companies of African American soldiers were organized. One of the companies was led by R.T. Brown, who was the first African American officer in the Tennessee National Guard and formerly was the commander of the Bluff City Guards. During the Spanish-American War, five full companies of the Second Tennessee Volunteer Infantry were organized in Memphis.

May 12, 1966

Beale Street Designated a Historic Site

U.S. secretary of the interior Stewart Udall announced from his office in Washington, D.C., that Beale Street, famous for its contributions to American popular music, had been added to the Register of National Historic Landmarks. The action came after Congressman George W. Grider requested the designation and a survey was completed by National Park Service historian Horace J. Sheely. According to *Commercial Appeal* reporter Louis Silver, "Memphis' world-famed Beale Street achieved national landmark status yesterday with a bow to W.C. Handy, who created his Memphis Blues there more than 50 years ago…In Yonkers, N.Y. the widow of Mr. Handy, whose statue stands in the Beale Street park bearing his name, applauded the move as making the street 'a fine tourist attraction.'" Memphis Housing Authority director Walter Simmons echoed Mrs. Handy's sentiment when he explained that the national landmark designation would "lend impetus to the over-all project for redevelopment and restoration of historic Beale that will make it well worth visiting." The clarinet player from New Orleans's Preservation Hall Jazz Band, George Lewis, stated that "as long as there is Memphis and as long as we have Beale Street, there'll always be the good blues music. Handy's music is not ever going to die."

May 13, 1967

The Air Age of Medicine comes to Memphis

A neurosurgeon who holds a fixed-wing pilot's license announced on this day he planned to use Methodist Hospital's Heliport in his practice. Dr. Joseph Miller explained that helicopters are vital tools in treating many emergency cases. For example, he described a recent automobile accident in rural West Tennessee in which the victim died after waiting two hours for an ambulance. Dr. Miller contrasted this with the use of helicopters in Vietnam to immediately treat wounded soldiers. Three days before Dr. Miller's pronouncement, the Federal Aviation Administration gave its approval for Methodist Hospital to build a heliport atop its roof to receive critically ill patients. According to hospital public relations director Las Savell, "As far as civilian hospitals are concerned, it will be the first in the nation." *Press-Scimitar* staff writer Wayne Chastain explained that the "value of the heliport would be to save time in transferring patients from aircraft at the airport to motor vehicles for the long ride to town. Instead, helicopters can fly the patients from unloading aircraft at the airport directly to the hospital."

May 14, 1939

Memphian Publishes History of the Bluff City

Gerald Capers wrote the book
*Biography of a River Town:
Memphis, Its Heroic Age.*

The University of North Carolina Press on this day published the first history of Memphis written by a trained historian. Entitled *Biography of a River Town: Memphis, Its Heroic Age*, the book was composed by former Memphian Gerald M. Capers Jr. *Biography of a River Town* traced the history of Memphis from its founding in 1819 to 1900. The author was born in Memphis, and after graduating from Southwestern at Memphis, he earned a PhD in history at Yale University. Capers taught briefly at Yale before joining the faculty of Tulane University. *Biography of a River Town* is recognized by many as a pioneering work in the field of local history and remains perhaps the best single volume ever written on the Bluff City.

May 15, 1952

Welcome Wagon Drives to New Headquarters

On this day, Welcome Wagon Inc., the Memphis-based company that provided information and gift baskets filled with local goods to new residents, announced it was moving its headquarters to the old *Commercial Appeal* building at Court and Second Streets. Founded by Memphian Thomas W. Briggs in 1928, Welcome Wagon was described by its founder as "more than a business—it is almost a religion." As reported by the *Commercial Appeal*, the company "sends 4,000 hostesses in 1,100 cities in the United States and Canada to call on newcomers, women about to be married and new mothers…Nowadays the Welcome Wagon distributes gifts from local merchants…to acquaint newcomers with local firms. It also distributes leaflets on civic projects, such as the City Beautiful Commission and the Chamber of Commerce." Briggs died in 1964, and four years later, his company was sold to Famous Artists Schools Inc., headquartered in Westport, Connecticut. The company remained in operation until 1998. When Welcome Wagon folded, a company spokesman stated, "It's just become increasingly difficult to greet new movers door to door."

May 16, 1919

Grand Jury Declared Memphis a Lawless Town

The Shelby County Grand Jury, which served for four months and handed down 547 indictments, concluded its session on this day with a scathing report criticizing the city's unwillingness to enforce its own statutes and calling upon citizens to take the law into their own hands. Signed by Foreman F.A. Curtius and secretary W.S. Lawo, the report stated:

> [The] *grand jury is made up largely of business men who until this service had no great knowledge of the roguery that exists in this county, and so has been appalled by the number of cases of murder, carrying concealed weapons, violation of liquor laws, theft, etc., that have been presented to it. Is the human mind becoming more and more perverted? Or is this sad condition the result of lax enforcement of the law. This jury is firmly of the opinion that there is laxity in law enforcement. Whether this be due to the size or the incompetency of the police authorities remains, of course, to be seen…We believe public-spirited citizens…should take such action as is necessary to form a research or vigilance committee that will arrest the continuance of the deplorable conditions now existing, unless the constituted authorities put a stop to these at once, at the same time co-operating with the authorities. To see a proper enforcement of the criminal laws in this county would be not only an event but an emotion.*

May 17, 1972

Protesters Condemn School Busing

Today, 1,200 members of Citizens Against Busing marched from the Poplar Plaza shopping center to the board of education building to protest the April 20 decision by federal judge Robert McRae to integrate public schools by transferring students across the district. Speaking before the protest began, CAB president Ken Keele called on his members to "send a message to the judge, the school board, and liberals everywhere that this community is not going to have busing…We have had only one champion for what we stand for. He is now lying in a hospital bed for what he believes." Keele then asked for a moment of silence to pray for Alabama governor George Wallace, who had been shot two days before during a presidential campaign rally. Several of those who bowed their heads carried signs with Wallace's picture on them along with the slogan "Send them a message. Stop busing." According to *Press-Scimitar* staff reporter Jerry Robbins, during "the march, bystanders supporting the CAB protest gave the marchers ice cream and soft drinks. One used-car dealer on Poplar opened up his drink-vending machine and passed out all the drinks in stock." Despite their protests, busing was implemented in the Memphis City schools on January 24, 1973.

May 18, 1937

Goldsmith's Department Store Cooled Off

Memphians who suffered from the spring and summer heat rejoiced to learn on this day that Goldsmith's department store had begun installing air-conditioning equipment in its Main Street store. Fred Goldsmith, president of the store, stated that by "installing an air conditioning system of such magnitude and completeness Goldsmith gives Memphis and the South its largest and first all-the-year-round air conditioning department store, thus fulfilling its obligation of being 'Memphis'

Opened in 1902, the Goldsmith's department store at Main and Gayoso Streets was a popular shopping destination in Memphis until it closed in 1990.

Greatest Department Store.'" Two shifts of workers from York Ice Machinery Company labored to install enough refrigeration equipment to cool the entire store. As Fred Goldsmith explained, the air cooling system "will furnish refrigeration to cool 1,036,800 gallons of water each eight-hour day to a temperature of 45 degrees." Opened in 1902, the Goldsmith's department store at Main and Gayoso Streets remained an important shopping destination for Memphians until it closed in 1990.

May 19, 1942

War Powers Conferred on Mayor

The city commission on this day granted Mayor Walter Chandler extraordinary war powers to defend Memphis in case of an emergency. As reported by the *Press-Scimitar*: "Under the ordinance, the mayor may… appoint volunteer policemen, firemen, air raid wardens, fire wardens and other volunteer personnel of every kind. The mayor would be given the power to confer full police powers upon private citizens in emergencies and 'could call upon any inhabitant or any organization at any time to aid in enforcement of rules and regulations [and defend the city]."

Specifically the measure gave the city's executive power to enforce blackout regulations. The Office of Civil Defense recommended the ordinance be passed in time for the city's first blackout drill on June 9. At 9:00 p.m. on that date, the mayor's war powers were put into effect when a total blackout was implemented across Memphis. As reported by Robert Talley of the *Commercial Appeal*: "The signal in Memphis was the turning off of the city's 7,716 street lights promptly at 9 p.m. Almost immediately lights in thousands of homes went out. Towering office buildings dissolved into the pitch-black skies. Store windows darkened, advertising signs faded from view… Uniformed policemen and State guardsmen…were shadowy figures in the ghostly darkness as they patrolled each block and alley in the business district."

May 20, 1978

Soccer Team Scores First Win

Over eight thousand newly minted soccer fans cheered as the Memphis Rogues scored their first ever win at the Liberty Bowl Memorial Stadium. Owned by Memphian Avron Fogleman, the North American Soccer League's Memphis franchise opened its inaugural season on April 1 but remained winless until it defeated the Dallas Tornados on this day in 1978. Despite their popularity, Fogleman sold the Rogues in 1980 to a Canadian millionaire, who relocated the team to Calgary.

The Memphis Rogues professional soccer team played in the Bluff City from 1978 to 1980.

May 21, 1973

Gunman Kills Five on Kansas Street

David Sanders, a mentally ill ex-convict, murdered five people and wounded four others during a shooting rampage on Kansas Street. About 2:40 in the afternoon, fifty-one-year-old Jesse Dooley pulled his truck into the parking lot of the Kansas Package Store, 1721 Kansas Street. Walking past was Sanders, armed with a .30-06 shotgun; suddenly, he pointed the weapon and, in rapid succession, shot retired railroad worker William Farmer, candy store employee Henrietta Watson Jones and Dooley. A few minutes later, he killed handyman John Aldridge, who was standing next to his tool cart. Sanders then began shooting at passing cars as Patrolman David Clark and his partner, J.L. Cottingham, arrived on the scene. Clark was shot in the head as Sanders fled into a home at 1760 Kansas that contained four children, who hid under a bed during the confrontation. As reported by the *Commercial Appeal*, "Police pumped tear gas into the house, Sanders ran out the front door, his rifle at the ready, perhaps shooting. He was mowed down by waiting policemen, themselves armed with rifles and shotguns. Reports said Sanders was shot about 30 times. Sanders was shot at 3:09 p.m., only 29 minutes after he began the terror on Kansas Street."

May 22, 1925

President Honors Memphis Hero

Tom Lee, a Memphis African American who pulled a large group of drowning people from the Mississippi River, met with President Calvin Coolidge at the White House on this day. Introduced by *Memphis News-Scimitar* president Paul Block, Coolidge warmly shook Lee's hand and declared him to be an "outstanding marine hero." After meeting with the president, Lee was taken on a sightseeing tour of the nation's capital and was the guest of honor at a reception hosted by the Colored Tennessee Society of Washington. While returning from Helena, Arkansas in his small motorboat, *The Zev*, Lee spied the steamboat *M.E. Norman* listing badly in the water. As Lee later explained, "I turned the prow of my boat around and started for her just as fast as I could go…Just as I got there the hull went out of sight and I could see the heads of people bobbing up all around me. I began grabbing them right and left on both sides of the boat. I got all she'd hold, 'bout eight." Lee made several trips between the shore and wreckage, ultimately rescuing thirty-eight people. In addition to his trip to Washington, the citizens of Memphis donated thousands of dollars to build Lee a new home, and he went to work with the city's sanitation department. Shortly after his death in 1952, Tom Lee Park was constructed on the riverfront, and a monument was dedicated in his honor.

May 23, 1968

Black Power Group Organized at Carver High School

The Invaders, a group of young African Americans who advocated the militant philosophy of black power, presented a list of demands to parents and school officials during a meeting at Carver High School on this day. A series of disturbances at the school, where Invaders John B. Smith and John H. Ferguson were arrested for disorderly conduct, prompted the formation of a fifteen-member committee to listen to the Invaders' concerns. As reported by the *Commercial Appeal*, the "Invaders at Wednesday's meeting demanded a place on the campus as an organization and complained of overcrowded conditions, inadequate facilities, high cafeteria prices and absence of Negro history and Negro art courses. They also wanted students to be allowed to wear 'natural' haircuts (Afro style) and black power amulets." Coming less than two months after the murder of Dr. Martin Luther King Jr. and the conclusion of the sanitation strike, the Invaders' agitation at Carver High School was one of several civil rights actions that occurred in Memphis during the late 1960s and early 1970s.

May 24, 1959

Hollywood Actress's Parents Arrested

In the midst of a bitter feud with her ex-husband over custody of their son, former Memphian and Hollywood movie star Stella Stevens violated a court order by taking her son and fleeing to California. In response, circuit judge Greenfield Q. Polk issued arrest warrants for her parents, Thomas E. and Estelle Caro Eggleston, who were detained on this day for fear they were planning to join their daughter and grandson in Hollywood. At age sixteen, Estelle Eggleston married Herman Stephens, and they had one son, Andrew, before divorcing in 1956. The court gave her custody of Andrew, but when she adopted the stage name Stella Stevens and moved to Hollywood, Judge Polk gave the youngster to his father. In April 1960, Herman Stephens flew to Los Angeles and stole Andrew back, but Stella regained custody of her son in August 1961. Stella Stevens had a long career in Hollywood, starring in such films as *Say One for Me*, *Lil' Abner*, *The Ballad of Cable Hogue* and *The Poseidon Adventure*.

May 25, 1973

CB Radio Operators Terrorize Whitehaven

For more than six months in 1973, several operators of Citizen's Band radios had aggravated residents of the Whitehaven neighborhood. Using the aliases "Pistol Pete," "Red Dog Charlie" and "Wild Man," the CB broadcasters were supposed to use only five watts of power but instead used between five hundred and one thousand watts, which jammed the signals of many Whitehaven residents' radios and televisions. As reported by *Press-Scimitar* staff writer Forrest Laws: "Pistol Pete's signals filter into the audio of TV sets and drown out the regular program in a way that has his listeners almost at their wit's end. 'When we set our radio for an hour of music at bed-time we have to listen to him,' says Mrs. Billy Jean Evans. 'When the alarm goes off on our clock radio at 6 a.m. he comes on.' Pistol Pete's signal knocks off the color on Channel 5 on her TV set, she said. 'You can turn the volume to the lowest setting, but he still comes through strong,' she said. 'It drives you straight up the wall.'"

Citizen's Band radio stations were first licensed in 1947, and by the early 1970s, hundreds of Memphians were buying CB radios and using "Lester 'Roadhog Dees' Convoy Code: a Quick Reference Guide to C.B. Jargon," which was distributed by Scott Appliance Stores and radio station WMPS.

May 26, 1989

Noted Jazz Performer Dies

Jazz pianist Phineas Newborn Jr. was found dead on his front porch at 5:30 in the morning on this day in 1989. Newborn's friend and agent Irvin Salky explained to the press that physicians had recently found a growth on Newborn's lung that he refused to treat. In April, Newborn had performed "The Lord's Prayer" at the Overton Park Shell, and Salky believed that signaled Newborn's acceptance of his mortality: "I think he knew what was happening and he just didn't want to have to stay in the hospital. He wanted to be free to walk around and talk with his friends and enjoy the music up to the end." In the 1950s, Newborn released a series of groundbreaking jazz albums, including *A World of Piano* and *The Newborn Touch*, which led critic Leonard Feather to declare that "in his prime, he was one of the three greatest Jazz pianists of all time, right up there with Bud Powell and Art Tatum." Despite suffering from occasional bouts of mental illness, Newborn continued to compose music; in 1975, he received a Grammy nomination for his album *Solo Piano*. Fellow jazz pianist James Williams summed up Newborn's career when he stated, "People just don't know how great he was and what a genius he was."

May 27, 1909

Committee Formed to Secure Normal School

In response to the passage of a bill by the Tennessee General Assembly authorizing the creation of teacher colleges in the state's three grand divisions, a committee of business and educational leaders met at the Goodwyn Institute on this day to discuss ways of securing the West Tennessee School for Memphis. The new organization called upon the City of Memphis and the Shelby County Quarterly Court to jointly issue bonds totaling $100,000 to build the school and create

The West Tennessee Normal School opened in 1912, and the school became the University of Memphis in 1994.

an endowment to supplement operating funds supplied by the state. Plans were also laid to raise at least $75,000 from private donors. The West Tennessee Normal School opened in 1912, and twenty-nine years later, it became Memphis State College. In 1957, the school achieved university status, and on July 1, 1994, its name was changed to the University of Memphis.

May 28, 1877

Confederate War Dead Honored

A large group of Memphians visited Elmwood Cemetery on this day to decorate the graves of fallen Confederate soldiers. As reported by the *Daily Memphis Avalanche*:

> *In the quiet of the Sabbath…the people of Memphis assembled in groups, or singly, all unostentatiously to lay their tribute of flowers upon the little turf-covered mounds that marked the eternal sleeping place of the soldiers of the Lost Cause…No parade, no pomp, or sound of drum or fife, no orator with set speech to tell the glorious life and death of the brave sleeping in the silent city of the dead…The heavy crepe of mother, or sister, or widow was more fitting tribute to the dead…Quietly only a sob breaking the silence…thus in reverence and respect, they came with their pure offerings to the valor, patriotism and nobility of the dead.*

Veterans of the Bluff City Grays placed flowers on the graves of their fallen while the Chickasaw Guards decorated the resting place of their comrade Emmet Cochran. The veneration of the Lost Cause reached its zenith in Memphis and across the South between the years 1890 and 1910, when a grand monument was erected to Confederate general Nathan Bedford Forrest and African Americans were rigidly segregated from the white population.

May 29, 1977

Furry Lewis Sings the Sizzling Blues

Eighty-four-year-old bluesman Walter "Furry" Lewis collapsed on this day while performing at the Cotton Pickin' Country Music and Crafts Jubilee. Lewis was taken by ambulance to city hospital where he was treated for heat exhaustion and later released. The temperature rose to a scorching ninety-six degrees, which tied the record set in 1879. Born in Greenwood, Mississippi, on March 6, 1893, Lewis moved to Memphis when he was six, and by the time he turned thirteen, he was playing guitar and learning the blues from W.C. Handy's band. In the 1920s, he recorded for the Vocalion and Victor recording companies but then faded into obscurity as he made a living as a street sweeper. Furry was rediscovered in the 1960s, when he performed at blues festivals across the country. In 1975, he appeared in the Burt Reynolds film *W.W. and the Dixie Dancekings* and also performed with the Rolling Stones during their appearance at Liberty Bowl Memorial Stadium. The following year, singer Joni Mitchell composed *Furry Sings the Blues* in his honor, and in 1977, he appeared on the *Tonight Show* starring Johnny Carson. Reflecting on his early days as an itinerant bluesman, Furry, who died on September 14, 1981, explained that "them days were real hard times, but the music helped a whole lot."

May 30, 1955

City-County Consolidation Studied

Edmund Orgill, executive board chairman of the Civic Research Committee, announced that a subcommittee had been formed to study "consolidating duplicate services of the city and county governments." Named to head the committee was attorney Leo R. Burson, who explained that it was his "considered opinion that both the governments of Memphis and Shelby County can be greatly simplified by consolidating overlapping functioning units of the city and county. This action would bring about a more modern and efficient administration of affairs, thereby causing a tremendous savings in operating costs which in turn would relieve the tax burden of our citizenry." The Civic Research Committee was formed in 1949, and it had much to do with Memphis adopting the mayor/city council form of government in 1967. Consolidation, however, did not fare so well. Three times, in 1962, 1971 and 2010, voters in Memphis and Shelby County rejected efforts to merge their dual governments.

May 31, 1926

Plough Chemical Issues Dividend Checks

As the third quarter of 1926 began, the Plough Chemical Company issued dividend checks to its shareholders on this day. In the words of the *Commercial Appeal*, "Since the Plough Chemical Company adopted the policy of dividing their profits with dealers all over the country who handle their products, sales of the Black and White Beauty Creations and St. Joseph's Family Medicines have grown to the overwhelming volume of more than 30 million packages a year." In 1908, sixteen-year-old Abe Plough borrowed $125 to establish a manufacturing plant above his father's furniture store on North Second Street. His first product was Plough's Antiseptic Healing Oil, and from that modest beginning, Plough built a worldwide pharmaceutical empire that manufactured many well-known items, including St. Joseph Aspirin, Coppertone Suntan Lotion and Solarcaine burn ointment. The company acquired Maybelline cosmetics in 1967, and four years later, it merged with New Jersey pharmaceutical giant Schering Corporation. Schering-Plough remained one of Memphis's most important chemical manufacturing concerns well into the twenty-first century. In 2009, 101 years after its founding, Plough was absorbed by Merck and Company Inc.

June 1, 1940

Chinese Aviator Takes Poison

Shu Wong, former Chinese army aviator and son of convicted narcotics peddler Wong Kop, attempted to commit suicide with his wife, Mabel, in their room at 378 South Main on this day. In a report filed by Patrolmen Hillin and Moloughney, it was stated that "his wife took poison because her husband took it, and Wong took poison because he was despondent at not being able to get a job." Born in China, Shu settled in Memphis with his father in 1922. While his father ran the popular Mandarin Inn, Shu learned to fly airplanes from noted aviator Vernon Omlie. In 1932, he returned to China, where he flew for the Chinese air force. He left China in 1936 but returned a year later when Imperial Japan invaded. While Shu was flying for his homeland, his father, Wong Kop, was convicted of peddling narcotics and sentenced to ten years in federal prison. As reported by the *Press-Scimitar*, the Chinese aviator "was sitting on the bed with his wife…Shu first drank from the bottle, then his wife drank some…Condition of both was reported 'fair…They were given antidotes promptly at the rooming house…Mrs. M.J. Smith, Shu's landlady, said the couple married only recently, but had been keeping the marriage secret from Shu's uncle because the girl is an American." Reporters were allowed to visit Shu, but he refused to explain his actions. When asked if he still liked to fly, Shu replied, "I'll keep flying even after I'm dead."

June 2, 1943

Crop Corps Helps Farmer

Farmer D.R. Stanford of the Woodstock community faced a dire situation in June 1943. He had a mature berry crop in the field but no farm hands to pick them. So he turned to the local Boy Scout office that had recently implemented the national Scout Crop Corps program in Memphis. According to Chickasaw Council Scout executive Gordon Morris,

> *Our boys will help out any time they are needed. Scouts all over the Nation are doing much to relieve the farm labor shortage. In several states, groups of older boys are attending Scout operated farm schools where they learn to drive tractors and handle other farm implements. In other sections, younger lads are being organized for "day haul" and week-end work. They are also laboring on the home front, promoting Victory Gardens, poultry and small stock projects.*

Sixty Memphis Boy Scouts volunteered to work at Stanford's farm for six weeks until all his berries were picked and ready to ship to market. The young men worked every day from 7:30 a.m. to 12:30 p.m. and proved a valuable service not only to Stanford but also to America's war effort during World War II.

June 3, 1932

Bonus Army Pulled into Memphis

Three hundred threadbare World War I veterans arrived in Memphis from Little Rock, Arkansas. The unemployed former soldiers were en route to join the Bonus Army encamped in Washington, D.C., where they had gathered to demand Congress pay them a promised bonus for their military service. Deposited by train at the fairgrounds, the hungry veterans were fed by a joint committee established by the American Legion, Veterans of Foreign Wars and Disabled Veterans. When the Southern Railroad refused to take the former soldiers any farther, police commissioner Clifford Davis was faced with a serious problem. As reported by the *Evening Appeal*, "Railroad property was under heavy guard this afternoon as the bonus army of 500 ex-service men threatened to seize a train to continue their journey to Washington. Police were ordered by Commissioner Davis not to interfere." With the railroad refusing to transport them for free, Davis and the American Legion gathered a fleet of trucks and transported the veterans to the city limits of Nashville. Undoubtedly, many of those who passed through the Bluff City made it to the Washington encampment. On July 28, frustrated with the 200,000 veterans congregating in the capital, President Herbert Hoover called out the army to forcibly remove them. In the ensuing mêlée, the veterans were routed, but Hoover secured his defeat in the 1932 presidential election.

June 4, 1973

Paid Concerts Banned at Overton Park Shell

The Memphis Park Commission on this day ended commercial rock concerts at the Overton Park Shell after complaints that attendees engaged in criminal activities while listening to the music. As reported by *Press-Scimitar* staff writer Orville Hancock, "Special police had to be hired to control crowds which at various times smoked marijuana, drank alcoholic beverages, took drugs and openly participated in love-making." On April 13, the park commission board voted to end paid concerts and remove the fence surrounding the shell after an event scheduled for June 3. This did not end concerts in Overton Park, for thirty free events were also approved by the board. According to Hancock, "Types of entertainment for the free concerts include jazz, band music, ballet, gospel singing, Dixieland, choral, classical music, opera singing, dance revues, rock music, amateur talent, an arts and crafts show, choir singing and barbershop quartet singing." On the day of the final commercial show five thousand people listened to the Marshall Tucker Band, Hydra, Gabriel and Trapeze. During the middle of Trapeze's performance, two thousand people who didn't have tickets crashed through the fence and rushed the stage, essentially doing the park commission's work for them. Built in 1936, the Overton Park Shell continues to host outdoor performances in Memphis, and it remains one of the city's most popular attractions during the spring and summer months.

June 5, 1955

Irish Travelers Lose Their Memphis Base

A group of nomads who called themselves the Mississippi Travelers and used Memphis as their winter headquarters learned they no longer have a place to reside in the Bluff City. For decades, they stayed at a trailer park known as "the Hill," located at 2544 Hernando Road. The owner, Mrs. Eva McGuire, wanted to rent the property to more permanent tenants. *Commercial Appeal* reporter William Sorrels spoke to one of the Mississippi Travelers, Eddie Costello, who had "turned from mule trading to house and barn painting…There are several traveling groups, all descendants of the fabled Irish tinkers of the old country…During World War II, Memphis was the year-round headquarters of the Mississippi group. In all their travels, the men say, they have been unable to find a city with better Catholic churches, parochial schools and hospitals." Costello emphatically declared to Sorrels "how much we think of Memphis. If one gets sick—even 400 or 500 miles away—we'll put him in a car and bring him to Memphis…we're going to have to find a place to stay but we're going to come back to Memphis."

June 6, 1932

Memphis Author Travels on a Flying Carpet

Richard Halliburton, noted author and explorer, returned home to Memphis on this day to briefly visit his parents, Wesley and Nelle Halliburton, before traveling to New York to confer with his publisher. Halliburton recently completed a flight around the world in his plane, the Flying Carpet. As reported by the *Commercial Appeal*'s George Morris Jr., "Completion of his flight set an all-time record for the 'slowest round the world flight ever attempted,' he said. Haliburton and his pilot, Moye Stephens, left Hollywood, Cal., Dec. 20, 1930, and returned June 3, 1932, after having spent 400 hours in the air and riding the Flying Carpet more than 40,000 miles." During their flight, Halliburton and Stephens traveled first to London and then to Morocco. Crossing the Sahara Desert, they then flew to Switzerland, Turkey, Palestine, Borneo and the Philippines. Halliburton finished writing the account of his journey while staying with his parents in Memphis, and it was published in 1932 as *The Flying Carpet*. In the early 1920s, Halliburton traveled across Asia and Africa, which he described in his first book, *The Royal Road to Romance*. He continued to embark on adventures and write bestselling books about them until he disappeared on March 24, 1939, while piloting a Chinese junk through the Pacific Ocean near Midway Island.

June 7, 1963

Anti-U.N. Protesters Interrupt Airport Dedication

A small group of anti–United Nations protesters mingled with a large crowd attending the dedication of a new, modern terminal at Memphis Metropolitan Airport on this day. Led by the pastor of Tabernacle Baptist Church, Reverend J.H. Melton, the thirty men and women came to the airport because U.S. ambassador to the United Nations Adlai Stevenson was the dedication speaker. Many in the group were members of the right-wing John Birch Society, including its Memphis coordinator Mrs. W.M. Chamber. The protesters carried signs that declared, "Get U.S. Out of the U.N.," "Surrender Now—Avoid the Rush" and "Adlai anti-American." "We're not interested in agitating. We just want people to know…the United Nations has usurped the sovereignty of our country," said protester Joseph Cavallo. According to *Commercial Appeal* reporter Louis Silver, "Jeers from the pickets contrasted with cheers from the bleachers when Mr. Stevenson said, 'To those Americans, therefore, who ascribe to the United Nations not benefit but malign danger to our country, I would ask if they also question the principles of our Declaration of Independence and Constitution.'" The terminal, which still stands today, was designed by architect Roy Harrover and was constructed at a cost of over $5 million.

June 8, 1910

Crook Turns Himself In

Much to the dismay of police captain John Couch, confessed gangster James J. Drury walked into central police headquarters and declared on this day he was through with the criminal life. According to Drury, he was an important figure in the underworld until a drug habit led to his downfall. Forced to seek treatment in a Jacksonville, Illinois hospital, Drury spent several months recuperating only to find his position within the criminal hierarchy eroded beyond repair. Drury explained to the police:

> I tried to connect with some of my erstwhile yegg friends, but they turned me down with the word 'dope' and a significant tap on the head. Then I wandered down here, and under the busy lights of this city I resolved to be once more an honest man, like I was born...I want honest work and will do anything from scrubbing up the floor to keeping the books of the police department. I am sick and tired of it all. I have been disowned by my family and given the hot end of it for the last few years by my pals and associates and now I am going to shame the devil by being honest and earning an honest living.

Captain Couch, somewhat suspicious of his story, locked him up until his information could be verified.

June 9, 1951

Singer Makes Memphis Mad

When Memphis Technical High School graduate Kathryn Starks appeared on the Ed Sullivan Show, she was asked where she was born, and she replied Oklahoma. "They're mad at me in Memphis," the singer, better known by her stage name Kay Starr, told reporter Rhea Talley. "When I went back to Memphis to sing…they said, 'Why didn't you say Memphis?' But I had to tell the truth." Despite where she was born, Starr began her musical career by singing in the Bellevue Junior High glee club and later performed with local swing bands and on WMPS radio while a student at Tech. In the summer of 1938, the sixteen-year-old was discovered by bandleader Joe Venuti, who signed Starr to sing with his orchestra during a summer tour. She later sang with the Bob Crosby Orchestra on the Camel Caravan radio show. Returning to Memphis, she continued to sing on WMPS while she finished high school. After graduation, she reunited with Venuti and then launched a successful solo career. In the early 1950s, Starr had several hit records including the million sellers *Wheel of Fortune* and *Rock and Roll Waltz*. Whatever animosity some Memphians may have felt over her Ed Sullivan appearance was quickly forgotten. In May 1974, the city celebrated Kay Starr Day, on which the Memphis Federation of Musicians presented her with a bronze plaque in honor of her contributions to American music, and in 1988, Starr was given Memphis State University's Distinguished Achievement Award.

June 10, 1962

Dissident Baptists Hold Church Service

Discontented parishioners of the 9,400-member Bellevue Baptist Church held services at the Crosstown Theatre on this day because they were not receiving "the spiritual food" they needed from Pastor Ramsey Pollard. Incorporating themselves as Loyal Bellevue Members, the dissident group stopped tithing to the church in December 1961 when it failed to oust Pollard from his pulpit for "being dictatorial, neglecting his duties and not properly administering the church budget." According to vice-president Eugene D. Rutland, the organization "decided to start these separate services a week ago after Dr. Pollard was so vicious in a sermon about people who no longer contribute tithes to Bellevue. These new services are temporary but we will continue until the situation at Bellevue has been corrected." Rutland went on to explain that Loyal Bellevue Members Inc. had a great deal of financial leverage, which it hoped would eventually lead to a settlement of grievances. "It is estimated that those who belong to our organization used to contribute about $150,000 a year to the Bellevue budget, which is about $525,000." Despite its best efforts Ramsey Pollard remained pastor of Bellevue Baptist Church until his retirement on June 1, 1972.

June 11, 1977

Young Republican Convention Meets in Memphis

The Young Republican National Federation met in Memphis on this day to choose a chairman and rebuild the GOP after its defeat in the 1976 presidential election. During a bitter floor fight at the Holiday Inn–Rivermont, the federation chose Roger Stone as chairman over Rich Evans. The highlight of the convention was the appearance of former California governor Ronald Reagan, who spoke after Stone's victory. Reagan declared that "adhering to the GOP platform of Kansas City is the only way the party will broaden its base. We stand for something with that platform. It declares to the American people principles by which they will know exactly where we stand. I believe the majority of American people, if they knew what our platform is, would agree with the policies we adopted. But, we have done a lousy job in communicating our platform principles to the people." According to *Press-Scimitar* staff writer Clark Porteous: "Reagan was critical of the proposed [President Jimmy] Carter election reform program. He called it 'an election fraud program. I am opposed to the public financing of federal elections,' Reagan said. 'It is an incumbent's guarantee program. The reason so many people are not voting is not because the election laws are too stringent, but because they have lost faith in government.' Reagan declined to say whether he will seek the GOP presidential nomination in 1980, saying it is 'still too early to say.'"

June 12, 1912

Elephant Eats Girl's Clothes

At the Overton Park swimming pool on this day, a twelve-year-old girl was wading in the cool liquid when a group of rowdy boys splashed her with water. The soggy girl hurried to the nearby Memphis Zoo, where she hid in the Elephant House to dry her clothes. Meanwhile, her sister rushed home and quickly brought dry garments for her shivering kin. While taking off her wet garments,

Located in the Overton Park Zoo, the Elephant House was built in 1909.

the elephant lumbered in and made a quick meal of her dry clothes. The Overton Park Zoo was opened in 1906, and the Elephant House was built in 1909. The zoo's first elephant was named Margaret and lived in Memphis until 1926, when she was traded for two Asian elephants called Alice and Florence. Two years later, in 1928, the two pachyderms broke through a fence and wandered through the campus of Rhodes College before being caught.

June 13, 1862

Martial Law Declared in Memphis

One week after Union forces took possession of Memphis during the Civil War, Special Orders No. 1 was issued declaring martial law within the limits of the Bluff City. As reported in the *Memphis Union Appeal*, the order stated:

> *All persons leaving the city by any public conveyance, or to travel beyond the picket lines by any road leading into the country, shall first procure, from the Provost Marshal, a pass, and the Provost Marshal is hereby instructed not to grant passes to anyone except in cases of urgent necessity, and requiring of persons receiving passes to take the oath of allegiance; and all persons violating this order shall be promptly arrested and detained for future trial and punishment.*

The order also required that

> *all officers and soldiers of this command to see that the public peace is maintained; that the rights of persons and property under the Constitution of the United States are protected; that the blessing of the Government of our fathers shall be restored to all its pristine vigor and beauty; and as so far as can be done, consistent with military rule, no one shall be disturbed in the pursuit of his legitimate business; and all officers and soldiers violating this order shall be severely punished.*

June 14, 1944

Street Railway Hires Female Drivers

In response to the loss of 120 male employees to the armed forces and the refusal of drivers to work overtime until the War Labor Board approved a five-cent wage increase, the Memphis Street Railway began training four women to drive streetcars and buses. The first woman to be hired was Shirley Kenny, who wrote on her application that she had "two people dependent upon me for support and I've always wanted to be a street car operator. I feel that if I make a success of this work I will have a permanent job." Emma Jeanne Cable, Opey Mae Goss and Ada S. Garner also began their training on June 14. According to the *Commercial Appeal*, "For the next two or three weeks they will receive instructions on buses and street cars, minus passengers, during the dull hours of the forenoon and afternoon, and after that they will be full-fledged operators at the same pay as men."

June 15, 1995

Barbecue Pizza Invented in Memphis

Horest and Jerry Coletta, the third-generation owners of Coletta's Italian Restaurant, sat down on this day with John Semien of the *Commercial Appeal* to discuss the history of the popular seventy-year-old eatery. The business was started by his grandfather Emil Coletta in 1922 as the Suburban Ice Cream Company at their present location at 1063 South Parkway East. "He had sandwiches and spaghetti back then, and he had an ice cream wagon drawn by a horse. But the main attraction was restaurant-made ice cream," Jerry Coletta explained. In 1951, the business was expanded and the name changed to Coletta's Italian Restaurant to meet the growing demand for pizza among the large number of sailors stationed at Memphis Naval Air Station. According to Emil's son Horest, the sailors "had come from the east where they had pizzas, but pizzas weren't available in Memphis, so I asked my father to show me how to make pizzas, and we started. It took a while because for local people, we had to sell it by the slice." To entice Memphians to try the food, Horest created a barbecue pizza, which soon became a local sensation. Elvis Presley loved eating barbecue pizza, and in the early twenty-first century, Coletta's and its famous creation were featured on the Food Network's *FoodNation* television program.

June 16, 1940

Italian Truck Farmers Refuse to Support Mussolini

Meeting at the Italian Hall, 450 members of the Shelby County Growers' Association and the Italian Gardeners' Society adopted a resolution on this day pledging their loyalty to democratic ideals and the United States of America. The meeting was in response to their mother country's declaration of war against France and England on June 10. The resolution declared:

> *Whereas, the Italian farmer of this community believes in the ideals of democracy, and desires that such ideals remain in force throughout the ages as the greatest benefit to the human race, and that civilization may endure. Therefore be it resolved by the Shelby County Growers Association and the Italian Gardeners Society, in joint session...at a time when a great crisis confronts the world, that we again pledge our allegiance and reaffirm our loyalty to the United States of America, that great bulwark of democracy, and stand ready to give our lives if necessary that said country, its ideals and institutions may be maintained for posterity.*

During World War II, many Memphians of Italian descent served in the armed forces, including Staff Sergeant Julius C. Galliani, who was killed during the invasion of Germany in November 1944.

June 17, 1901

Pastor's Finger Bitten Off

After two days of testimony, Zach Claxton was found guilty on this day of committing mayhem against the pastor of Beale Street Baptist Church. As a result, Claxton was fined $200 and ordered to serve a six-month stretch in the county workhouse. Claxton was the leader of a church faction working to oust Pastor Clemmons from the pulpit. In April 1901, the group sued to have him removed, but its lawsuit failed. In addition, contempt charges were subsequently filed against Claxton for not obeying the orders of the court. As reported by the *Commercial Appeal*, the day after the contempt order was handed down, "Claxton and Clemmons met…near the corner of Beale and DeSoto streets and an ugly scrimmage followed." Claxton struck his pastor in the face several times, kicked him "and then chewed off the end of one of his fingers." During the trial, Claxton admitted the assault and claimed he bit off Clemmons's digit because he "had assumed a threatening attitude with an uplifted stick."

June 18, 1929

South Memphis Political Operative Arrested

Police announced on this day the arrest of former patrolman, South Memphis politician and owner of the Stock Yards Hotel E.A. Laughter for owning a still that exploded, causing a large fire that damaged several homes on McLemore Avenue in the gas house district. Laughter served in the police department from 1909 to 1915 and then became a minor political operative within the political machine controlled by E.H. Crump. In the mid-1920s, Laughter broke with the Crump machine and drifted into bootlegging. Police chief Will D. Lee explained that the former political leader "was arrested because we learned he had rented four houses on McLemore Avenue and was paying rent on them. Two of the homes he rented housed the distillery." Despite this evidence, Laughter beat the bootlegging rap only to be convicted of income tax evasion in 1944. Paroled in 1947, Laughter returned to Memphis only to be thrown in jail and told to get out of town. Police commissioner Joseph Boyle declared that "we're not going to allow Laughter or his kind to hang around Memphis. We just don't intend to allow ex-convicts to congregate here."

June 19, 1949

Memphis Golfer Ties Tournament

Memphis dentist Carey Middlecoff, the National Open Champion who was golf's top money winner in 1949, found himself in an eleven-hole "sudden death" playoff on this day during the final round of the Motor City Open Golf Tournament in Detroit. After playing fifty-four holes, Middlecoff and Lloyd Mangrum, 1949's third-highest money winner, both scored a 69, 2 under par. As reported by Associated Press staff writer Charles C. Cain, "After a brief rest, they set out on their playoff and at the end of the first nine each had a 35, even par. Playing steady and conservative golf, they had matched seven pars, one birdie and one bogie. After consulting with tournament

Memphis dentist Carey Middlecoff was golf's top money winner in 1949.

sponsors and P.G.A. officials, Middlecoff and Mangrum decided to play two more holes in the hopes of breaking the deadlock but they parred each hole." Carey Middlecoff was the most successful professional golfer to come from Memphis. In addition to the National Open, he also won the Master's Tournament in 1955.

June 20, 1862

Union Forces Seize Second Presbyterian Church during the Civil War

Union general Lew Wallace, author of the novel *Ben Hur*, seized control of Second Presbyterian Church, located at the corner of Main and Beale Streets, on this day to prevent pro-Confederate sermons and prayers. An army chaplain was installed to lead services, but the congregation bitterly resented this interference with their worship service. When General Ulysses S. Grant arrived in Memphis on June 23, he offered to return church property if members would agree to install a pro-Union pastor. The congregation refused to accept this condition, and the church remained in Union hands for two more years. In early 1864, members of the Second Presbyterian Church sent a petition to President Abraham Lincoln requesting the return of church property. On March 4, 1864, the president read the petition and sent a firm message to the Union military commander of Memphis, General C.C. Washburne:

> *I have written before and I now repeat: the U.S. Government must not undertake to run the churches. When an individual, in a church or out of it, becomes dangerous to the public interest, he must be checked; but the churches as such, must take care of themselves. It will not do for the U.S. to appoint Trustees, Supervisors or other agents for the churches. I add, if the military have military need for the church building let them keep it; otherwise let them get out of it, and leave it and its owners alone.*

June 21, 1968

Mahalia Jackson Visits African American Business

Famed Gospel singer Mahalia Jackson visited Memphis on this day to promote a chain of fried chicken restaurants named in her honor. Established two months after the assassination of Dr. Martin Luther King, Jr., the restaurant chain was started by A.W. Willis and Benjamin L. Hooks. The restaurant chain was created to provide African Americans with opportunities to own and operate their own businesses in black neighborhoods. The company partnered with Minnie Pearl Fried Chicken Inc., a white-owned company named for the famed country music comedian, in order to "set an example of racial partnership." The restaurant chain did not quite achieve what Hooks and Willis hoped it would, but it did provide economic opportunity to some African Americans while showing that black and white Memphians could work together even during the difficult year of 1968.

Named for famed gospel singer Mahalia Jackson (far right), the Mahalia Jackson Chicken Restaurants were established by state representative A.W. Willis and criminal court judge Benjamin L. Hooks in 1968.

June 22, 1919

Memphis Doughboy Barely Survives Hun Captivity

Sergeant William A. Montgomery arrived back home from Europe on this day after spending several months recuperating from severe wounds and poor medical care he received while a prisoner of the Germans. Montgomery, a former employee of the Bannon Coal and Ice Company, entered the army on May 12, 1918. Assigned to Company M, 326th Infantry, 82nd Division, the sergeant arrived in France on August 12 and participated in many combat missions on the Verdun front. On October 24, he was leading a day patrol near the German lines when a sniper opened fire, inflicting six wounds in Montgomery's leg. As he lay bleeding on the battlefield, the sergeant was captured by elements of the German army. In the words of a *Commercial Appeal* reporter, "His leg was dressed with a plain bandage, this being the only first aid rendered. He was subjected to rigid questioning by the Germans despite the agonizing suffering which he was undergoing. For 11 days the dressing was not changed. His caretakers did not deign to administer one dose of anti-tetanus serum." Because of this neglect, German surgeons were forced to amputate his wounded leg. Sergeant Montgomery was then moved from one hospital to another as the enemy lines shrunk from Allied pressure. On Thanksgiving Day, he was liberated by American forces, and after many months of treatment, he finally was reunited with his family in Memphis.

June 23, 1932

Food Committee Formed to Help the Needy

To combat the human misery wrought by the Great Depression, the city commission on this day formed a committee to, in the words of the *Commercial Appeal*, "supervise the expenditure of $10,000 appropriated by the city for the purchase of surplus foodstuffs at low prices for canning and storage in preparation for another winter of unemployment, privation and want." Chairman of the Food Conservation Committee was John Ross. Ross had retired in the 1920s as president of Otto Schwill and Sons Seed Company before devoting himself to civic affairs. During the 1927 Mississippi River flood, Ross supervised a refugee camp at the fairgrounds and he distributed medical supplies during an influenza epidemic. Because of his skill and compassion, Mayor Watkins Overton appointed Ross to head the Mayor's Commission on Employment and Relief. According to the *Commercial Appeal*, Ross was "the directing force in the collection and disbursement of $176,000 in cash and as much more in clothing and merchandise…. At one time, his committee was caring for 3,500 families and more than 8,000 families have received assistance…In 1931 the committee handled 22,368 orders for fuel, food, clothing and medical supplies." Although modest in scope, both the Food Conservation Committee and the Mayor's Commission on Employment and Relief did provide assistance to those most in need during the Great Depression.

June 24, 1955

Memphis Baseball Legend Retires

Frank Longinotti, longtime vice-president of the Memphis Chicks baseball club, announced his retirement along with President Ed Barry. Longinotti literally grew up in Memphis baseball. His brother John served as secretary to the Chicks until his death in 1918. The club's owner, Tom Watkins, asked Longinotti to take his brother's place, in which role, in addition to his other duties, he supervised the construction of $50,000 of new bleachers at Russwood Park in 1922. When a bank in 1940 attempted to seize control of the team from Watkins, Longinotti bought the team with Barry and Joe Verret. In 1942, Thompson "Doc" Prothro bought an interest in the club, and they continued to operate the Chicks franchise until they sold their controlling interest to the Chicago White Sox. Despite the sale, Barry and Longinotti remained president and vice-president until the White Sox announced they wanted to sell the team. The two baseball executives declined to repurchase the club and resigned instead. On December 6, 1975, Longinotti was crossing Park Avenue after attending Mass at Holy Rosary Catholic Church when he was struck and killed by a passing motorist. According to old friend George Bugby, Frank Longinotti "knew every phase of baseball. He was honest and had great integrity."

June 25, 1895

Reformers Condemn Gambling in Memphis

The Good Government Club met on this day to hear a report compiled by Secretary J.H. Barnum detailing the organization's effort to curb gambling in the Bluff City. Barnum began his investigation by meeting with Mayor W. L. Clapp and police chief Davis. According to the secretary, Clapp said: "[that] the law gave the police commissioners power to 'regulate or suppress gambling' and that his predecessors in office, and he himself, during his first term had adopted the policy of regulating gambling by a sort of quasi license making gamblers pay certain sums of money and nominally conform to certain rules, and he thought that the best way, but that the newspapers jumped on him so heavy for it, during the last campaign for election, that he had to give up the plan of regulating; and they adopted the plan of suppressing, and so gave a positive order to the chief of police to suppress gambling." Barnum pointed out during the exchange that games of chance had not been eliminated by police, and Davis replied that he was not receiving any support from either the courts or the police commission. Barnum wrote that "it was well understood at police headquarters that gambling houses…were not to be interfered with; in fact their official position depended on their not seeing this business." Barnum's report to the Good Government Club provides a fascinating glimpse into the operation of illegal gaming and how local government let it flourish in Memphis at the end of the nineteenth century.

June 26, 1917

City Declares War on Mosquitoes

A widespread program to combat malaria was announced on this day by Streets Commissioner George C. Love. According to the commissioner, a nine-man work crew completely drained the bayou on Waldron Street and the portion of the Sophia Spring Bayou running between Wentworth Street and Union Avenue in order to eliminate breeding areas for mosquitoes. The *Commercial Appeal* reported that Love declared: "[The] work of draining and oiling should easily be completed before the first of August, and thoroughly appreciates the interest of the public in the campaign and the assistance citizens are rendering by the cleaning up of their own premises. Particular attention is called by the commissioner to the accumulation existing under many of the houses not having cellars. Often, he states, there exists in such places rubbish sufficient to fill a large cart, and usually this damp, rotting material proves a favorite breeding ground for mosquitoes."

The antimalarial campaign launched in 1917 largely eradicated the disease in Memphis. The director of the health department's laboratories, Dr. William G. Krauss, stated in the 1920s that "malaria in Memphis has been reduced to such an extent we are finding it difficult to train laboratory technicians to diagnose the disease because we cannot get specimens for them to work on." Because of Memphis's great success in combating the disease, the headquarters of United States Public Health Service Malaria Investigation Division was moved to Memphis in 1941.

June 27, 1948

Orange Mound Nursery Dedicated

The first permanent structure for the seven-year-old Orange Mound Nursery was dedicated on this day in that historic African American neighborhood. Costing $9,000, the renovated three-room home at 640 Grand Avenue provided childcare for working mothers who otherwise had to leave their children unattended during the workday. The nursery was founded in 1941, and until the home was renovated, it was forced to operate at several locations, including Melrose School and the basement of Beulah Baptist Church. As reported by the *Press-Scimitar*, the "nursery, with 40 children registered and an average attendance of 30, is the fulfillment of a two-year dream of the 32 directors, including 16 whites and 16 Negroes. Mrs. Shubael T. Beasley…is chairman of the board. The nursery has new swings and other playground equipment, but still needs a piano and a sand box." In 1971, the Orange Mound Day Nursery moved to a newly constructed facility at 2415 Saratoga, which was paid for by businessman Nat Buring. The facility was later renamed the Nat Buring Orange Mound Day Nursery & Learning Center, and in 1987, it became the first daycare center in Memphis to receive accreditation from the National Association for the Education of Young Children. Named for a hedge of Osage orange bushes owned by John George Deaderick, Orange Mound was the first subdivision in Memphis marketed exclusively to African Americans. As the nursery suggests, it remains one of the most important neighborhoods in the Bluff City.

June 28, 1925

Memphis Boys Travel to the Foothills of the Ozarks

The summer camp of the Memphis Boy Scout council, Kamp Kia Kima began its first full day of activities after a contingent of Scouts arrived on the day before. Located on the Spring River in the foothills of the Ozarks three miles from Hardy, Arkansas, the 1925 camping season was directed by Charles Craig, a Memphis Eagle Scout and Harvard University student. Associate director was Eagle Scout Jack Hale of the University of Arkansas. A typical day at Kia Kima in the 1920s began at 7:00 a.m. with reveille followed by breakfast, medical and lodge inspections, Scouting instruction and a morning swim. In the afternoon, Scouts participated in "games, stunts and hikes" before an afternoon swim and a campfire after supper. As reported by the *Commercial Appeal*, "Extensive replacements have been made in the camp equipment. Six new stone lodges have been constructed to take the place of the wooden buildings. Two new canoes will be put into service. Dr. J.C. Ayres, chairman of the camping commission and Byron O. Lutman, Scout executive, recently inspected the grounds and buildings and were highly pleased with conditions." Kia Kima was donated to the Chickasaw Council in 1916 by investment banker Bolton Smith, and it remained at its original location until 1964, when the camp moved to a larger location between Hardy and Ash Flat, Arkansas. Now called Kia Kima Scout Reservation, the summer camp continues in operation to the present day.

June 29, 1933

Explosion Rocks Memphis Waterfront

Captain Charles Hutchings, pilot of the $42,000 cruiser *Cher Ami* owned by B.F. McCreery, walked into the vessel's engine room, where he smelled fumes. When Hutchings switched on the exhaust fan, a short circuit ignited gas vapors emanating from two three-hundred-gallon tanks, which caused an explosion and fire on this day. "There was a terrific explosion and flames shot all around me," Hutchings explained to reporters. Quickly jumping into the water, he was rescued by his brother, Walter Hutchings, who happened to be working at the Kate Adams wharf. The captain was rushed to St. Joseph Hospital with severe burns. Meanwhile the fire that erupted on the *Cher Ami* soon spread to the craft's boathouse and other nearby vessels, including the speedboat *Rascal* owned by Welcome Wagon founder Thomas W. Briggs. In all, two boathouses and ten vessels were destroyed in the explosion and fire, which was estimated to have caused $60,000 in damages.

June 30, 1946

Army Hospital Transferred to Veteran's Administration

Kennedy Army Hospital, named for Brigadier General James M. Kennedy and built in 1942, was on this day rechristened a Veterans' Administration medical center. During transfer ceremonies, Dr. Paul R. Hawley, chief medical director of the VA, stated that the "army has set high standards here at Kennedy and we pledge ourselves to meet these standards. We of the Veterans' Administration propose to make the great institution an ideal and a model for veterans' hospitals everywhere." Colonel Albert E. McEvers, the former army commander of Kennedy, praised Memphis for its long-standing support of the institution. Echoing the colonel was Mayor Walter Chandler, who stated that the "people of Memphis accept this great hospital as a solemn trust and as a hearty complement to the hospitality of our city and the spirit of the people here." During World War II, Kennedy Army Hospital had a staff of six hundred that treated over twenty-four thousand combat casualties; in 1952, the name was officially changed to Veterans' Administration Medical Teaching Group Hospital, but nearly everyone in Memphis continued to call it Kennedy until a modern facility was built in the medical center in 1967.

July 1, 1978

Memphis Burns as Firefighters Watch

Memphis firefighters walked off the job, sparking a large number of fires that gutted parts of the city during the three-day strike. By late morning, dispatchers began receiving an alarming number of calls reporting fires. At first, the majority of fires erupted in abandoned or out-of-the-way parts of the city, including several vacant lots and warehouses, but by late evening, they had spread to more populated parts of the city. At the Audubon Square Townhouses, four units were blazing out of control when District Chief Charles Jurden and Captain James O. Wimberley arrived on the scene. Organizing residents and other volunteers into a makeshift engine company, they fought the blaze for forty-five minutes before they extinguished the fire. As the smoke began to clear, Jurden and Wimberley collapsed from heat exhaustion and were hospitalized. Meanwhile, across town at Vance and Lauderdale, a vacant two-story apartment complex burst into flames and spread to the nearby Vance Avenue branch of the public library. Nearly five hundred residents of the historic Vance-Lauderdale neighborhood poured into the streets to watch the inferno, while a group of striking firefighters laughed and taunted their former supervisors. "Hey captain, that's not the way to lay a line. You'll never get the fire out that way," one striker yelled as another shouted, "Let it burn!" Three fire units combated the blaze, but they were unable to save either the apartments or the library. Twenty-two thousand books were lost in what library director Lamar Wallis aptly called "a horrible waste to the community."

July 2, 1864

Civil Government Dissolved in Memphis

Major General C.C. Washburne suspended Memphis government on this day when he issued Special Orders No. 70. Wasburne declared:

> [The] *utter failure of municipal government of Memphis for the past two years to discharge its proper functions, the disloyal character of that government, its want of sympathy for the government of the United States, and its indisposition to co-operate with the military authorities, have long been felt as evils which the public welfare require to be abated...the City of Memphis is under martial law, and the municipal government existing since the armed traitors were driven from the city has been only by sufferance of the Military authorities.*

Washburne appointed Lieutenant Colonel Thomas H. Harris acting mayor along with a group of loyal civilians who "constitute a board, which shall discharge the duties heretofore devolving upon the board of aldermen." Harris remained acting mayor until civil government was restored with an election held on June 29, 1865. John Park, who had been city executive when local government was dissolved, was reelected mayor and served until October 1866.

July 3, 1983

Mud Island Reborn

A park containing a carved model of the Mississippi River, a monorail and museum was opened on this day on Mud Island, the peninsula located on the mainland of Memphis near the mouth of the Wolf River. As described by the *Commercial Appeal*'s Deborah M. Clubb, three thousand Memphians "came quickly, by monorail, walkway and ferry, to ring the stage in the center courtyard. Many had criticized the cost of this downtown redevelopment project at a time when few Memphians ventured into the heart of the city, but that was not in evidence on this warm summer day. Several speakers praised the effort, including Mayor Wyeth Chandler, who stated that the "road has not been easy…but Memphis has kept the pace. Memphis would not settle for second best…We must honor our past, honor our roots, honor our heritage and go forward with a new confidence in ourselves and turn to an even brighter tomorrow for ourselves." Mud Island board chairman Avron Fogelman boasted that it would "change the image of Memphis. It will make Memphis a destination point." Mud Island did not exactly live up to Fogelman's promise, but it did make a contribution to the redevelopment of downtown along with the Memphis in May International Festival, construction of the River Row Condominiums and the renovations of the Orpheum Theatre and the Peabody Hotel.

July 4, 1976

Bicentennial Celebrated at the Fairgrounds

On the Bicentennial of America's independence, many Memphians celebrated by attending the opening ceremonies of the city's Libertyland Amusement Park. Located on the site of the old Fairgrounds Amusement Park, the theme park was founded by Jack Morris III, who served as its first board chairman. According to Morris, Libertyland was "filled with rides, adventure, experiences, nostalgia, illusion, music, color and fanfare." The park was divided into three parts, Colonial Land, Turn-of-the Century Land and Pioneer Land, which contained such popular rides as the log flume and the Zippin Pippin roller coaster. In addition, musical revues such as the Memphis Hit Parade and the American Spirit were performed daily in the Handy Theatre. On opening day, 13,500 Memphians poured into the park to hear Congressman Harold Ford Sr. speak and watch the great-great-great-great-granddaughter of second president John Adams, Barbara Bonifield, ring a replica of the Liberty Bell. By the end of its first season, 322,000 people had visited Libertyland, and it remained a popular attraction until it closed on November 4, 2005.

July 5, 1945

Memphis Gestapo Agent Grills Soldier

Staff Sergeant Herman L. Duncan returned home after six months in German prison camps, and on this day, he sat down with *Press-Scimitar* staff writer Catherine Meacham and described his experiences as a prisoner of war. On Christmas Eve 1944, Duncan, a member of the 106th Infantry Division, was shot in the ankle as his position was being overrun by elements of the German army. Captured, Duncan was marched one hundred miles to an enemy Stalag. Shortly after his arrival, Duncan was escorted into a room occupied by a man in civilian clothes who spoke perfect English. The man, identified as a Gestapo agent, asked Duncan where he was from and when he replied, the "man smiled slightly and replied that he had lived in Memphis for many years. The agent said he formerly worked for a Cotton company on Front Street. He asked about [E.H.] Crump and if [Walter] Chandler was still mayor." At first, the sergeant refused to believe him but changed his mind when the Nazi opened his coat, which had a "Phil A. Halle Men's Store, Memphis" tag sewn in the lining. Duncan wasn't the only Memphian to have such an experience in World War II. In 1945, Technical Sergeant Edward Pearson was interrogated by a Nazi who had been a newspaperman in Iowa before the war. To the sergeant's dismay, the German told him all about Memphis and the Pearson family.

July 6, 1973

Memphis Radio Show Reaches the Zero Hour

Radio announcers Fred Cook and John Powell completed on this day their final broadcast of *The Zero Hour* on WREC-AM. The duo, known for their witty banter, was forced to end the popular show because Powell had recently been named news director for WREC-TV and no longer had time for the program, which broadcast from 12:30 to 2:00 p.m. every weekday. According to the *Commercial Appeal*, the show's cancellation "meant an end to daily diversions with such characters as Freemont Filligree, the effeminate poet, or Leonard Leap, the fellow who attempted to leap across the Mississippi River on a pogo stick, or to the comments from the wise old Park Bench Philosopher." Cook remembered that in 1953, a fire erupted in the building that housed the WREC studios: "We lost all our power here and John and I were compelled to stay on the air with our not having any turntables. It was pitch dark and all we could do was talk. I later thought we might sustain a regular talk show. In September of 1964 we began an hour-long show and later expanded it to an hour-and-a half." Even though *The Zero Hour* has been off the air for forty years, the wit and charm of Fred Cook and John Powell is still remembered by many Memphians.

July 7, 1895

Streetcar Smashes Buggy

A box buggy being driven by Henry and Ophelia Willis was destroyed on this day when it crossed paths with an electric streetcar. The brother and sister had just left church when they drove into the path of the Raleigh Springs line's streetcar No. 70 as they crossed the intersection of Lane and Manassas Streets. According to the *Commercial Appeal*, "Just as they were crossing the track the car came upon them very rapidly…striking the buggy broadside. The vehicle did not turn over, but…the buggy was pushed along about thirty feet by the car and smashed into smithereens against a telegraph post." Nearby residents rushed to the scene and pulled the unfortunate couple from the buggy rubble. Ophelia Willis was not harmed, but brother Henry suffered severe injuries and was not expected to live. The streetcar motorman, Thomas Clay, was arrested by police officer Franklin and charged with "recklessly running an electric car." Franklin was an eyewitness to the accident, and he explained that the crash "was due to the narrow streets and down-grade, where the outgoing cars move swiftly along without the necessity of having the electric current turned on. Scarcely any noise is made as the car rolls along as smoothly as a bicycle…." On October 5, 1890, electric streetcars debuted in Memphis, and they remained a major part of the city's public transportation system until they were abandoned in 1947. Memphis remained without streetcars until they were reintroduced in 1993.

July 8, 1979

MagicLand Broadcasts 700th Episode

At 10:00 a.m. on this day, thousands of Memphis children turned their television dials to WMC-TV channel 5 to watch the 700th *MagicLand* program hosted by magician and TV weatherman Dick "Mr. Magic" Williams. The show debuted in 1966, and according to its first producer, Jay Perkins, *MagicLand* "got some good response right away. But it was a pretty shaky first two years. We had some definite, positive help from Saul Kaplan of McDonald's, our first sponsor…we sort of happened together at the right time. All of us were interested in magic and wanted to do a show, and along comes Kaplan wanting to present a family show. So we were started." Despite its "shaky" start, the show became very popular, garnering 70 percent of the local Sunday morning TV audience, and reservations for the studio audience were always filled three months in advance. In addition to Williams performing tricks and showing cartoons, on the 700th episode, Miss Tennessee Terry Alden appeared as Wonder Woman while magician Janie Pardue also performed. *MagicLand* remained on the air until 1989 and still holds the Guinness World Record for being the longest-running magic program in television history.

July 9, 1862

Discipline Tightened for Union Troops during the Civil War
Special Orders No. 133 was issued on this day by the
commander of the Military District of West Tennessee,
Major General U.S. Grant. The order was designed to
improve discipline among the Union troops occupying
Memphis. Grant declared: "Officers, non-commissioned
officers, soldiers and persons in the service of the United
States are forbidden to trespass upon the orchards,
gardens, or private grounds of any person or persons,
or in any manner whatever to interfere with the same,
without proper written authority to do so. Marauding,
pilfering, and any unauthorized and unnecessary seizure
or destruction of private property is prohibited…and will
be punished with the extreme penalty imposed by the laws
of war, which is death."

Grant's directive prohibited all commissioned officers
from leaving their campgrounds without written permission
and noncommissioned officers and soldiers were not
allowed to pass beyond camp lines at all. The order also
provided that "military police, patrols, and picket guards
will arrest all persons found violating any of the provisions
of this order, either by trespassing upon the…grounds
herein mentioned, or seizure or destruction of private
property, or being outside of camp lines or straggling from
their guard stations without proper authority."

July 10, 1900

Beale Street Bursts into Flames

A can of gasoline stored in a grocery at 148 Beale Street near DeSoto exploded around 6:30 in the evening on this day. The explosion caused a fire that severely damaged the store owned by Morris Myers and Jesse Dehart's barbershop. Fire Department Engines Nos. 2 and 3, along with chemical engine No. 1, responded quickly to the blaze, which prevented the fire's spreading beyond the grocery and barbershop. As reported by the *Commercial Appeal*:

> *Blazing fluid was scattered through the interior, instantly igniting everything it touched. Flames and smoke burst from front and rear of the store. A partition divided the rear into family apartments, where Myers, his wife and several children lived. The stock of groceries in the front, valued at $500 was entirely destroyed. All of Myer's [sic] household effects were ruined by fire and water. The interior of the store room was gutted by the flames. Jesse Dehart removed a portion of his property, but was damaged to the extent of $50.*

July 11, 1915

African American Nuns Visit Memphis

Two African American Roman Catholic nuns visited St. Anthony of Padua Church on this day, six years after the first African American Catholic church was built in Memphis. Construction began on October 12, 1908, at the corner of Hill and Concord Streets, and the building was completed in late summer 1909. Less than a year after the cornerstone was laid, the church was dedicated by Bishop Thomas Byrne on June 13, 1909, the feast day of St. Anthony. Father Joseph Dube was appointed the church's first pastor, and in September, a school was established by the Sisters of Charity of Mount St. Joseph in Ohio. Originally offering classes up to the eighth grade, a high school was added in 1940. Two years later, in 1942, a new building was constructed at the same site. According to the *Commercial Appeal*, the new church was "built of Tishomingo stone, the church is gothic in design." In the early 1960s, St. Anthony's property was taken for the interstate highway system and the building of St. Jude Children's Research Hospital. The parish moved to a new location on Vollentine Avenue, but declining membership forced St. Anthony of Padua Church to close its doors in 1968.

July 12, 1974

Mister Sam Creates a Restaurant Empire

Local businessman "Mister Sam" Bomarito informed *Press-Scimitar* columnist Eldon Roark that he had purchased the faltering restaurant the Embers, which was located across the street from his popular eatery Pete & Sam's, 3886 Park Avenue. The purchase was the latest acquisition made by Bomarito, who had recently bought a nightclub at 3523 Lamar called the Travelin' Fox and the Knights Out lounge located at 851 Loeb. Bomarito also owned a second Pete & Sam's location in the Trave-Lodge near the International Airport. According to Roark, "Watching over this 'empire' of restaurants and night spots is, needless to say, a full-time task for Bomarito, whose days start at 10 a.m. and go into the wee hours…In all, his restaurants can seat over 1,000 patrons…Pete & Sam's on Park has 275 seats and, as regulars well know, these 275 seats are usually full all the time." After service in World War II, Bomarito opened his first restaurant in 1948 with his cousin Pete Romeo at the corner of Alcy Road and Airways Boulevard. In 1961, he relocated to Park Avenue, where it remains one of the city's most popular eating establishments. Sam Bomarito eventually sold his other locations but continued to operate Pete & Sam's until his death on March 17, 2012.

July 13, 1973

FCC Forces Captain Bill Off TV

Bill Killebrew, known to legions of Memphis children as "Cap'n Bill," was forced to stop hosting his early morning cartoon show on WHBQ-TV Channel 13 because of a ruling by the FCC. Bowing to parental pressure, the Federal Communications Commission ruled that the hosts of children's programs could not also present live commercials. Cap'n Bill, who is also the advertising director for Hart's Bread, which sponsored his show, explained to *Press-Scimitar* TV columnist Mary Ann Lee that "they say you aren't supposed to exert your influence on the children. Well I spent 23 years building that influence and now they tell me I'm not supposed to use it." According to Lee, Killebrew "has been a familiar figure to Memphis televiewers, especially the younger viewers, since 1949, when he went on TV for the first time at WMC-TV," where he appeared on the show *Spinning Images.* "I'd draw cartoons while music played," he explained. Moving to WHBQ in 1955, he appeared in several shows before becoming the host of *Hartoon Time with Cap'n Bill.*

July 14, 1912

Ice War Freezes Memphis

Bayliss G. Lee, president of the Bohlen-Huse Ice Company announced on this day a significant decrease in the cost of ice for the Memphis market. To the dismay of its competitors and the delight of consumers, Bohlen-Huse lowered its price from 35 cents per hundred pounds to 10 cents per hundred. Lee stated that the purpose of the decrease was to force the setting of a standard price of "30 cents per hundred on coupon books and 20 cents per hundred to dealers." This explanation was disputed by the larger ice companies in the city. According to the *Commercial Appeal*, "William W. Johnson, secretary and treasurer of the Tennessee Ice and Storage Company, said: 'It's a freeze-out game—that's all.'"

The Bohlen-Huse Ice Company undercut its competitors during the ice war of 1912.

July 15, 1934

Memphis Author Honored by Book of the Month Club

Beale Street: Where the Blues Began, written by Memphian George W. Lee, was selected by the Book of the Month Club as its alternate choice for the month of July. According to the *Press-Scimitar*: "[The] saga of Beale Street, the smell of frying catfish and wood-smoke under barbequed beef, the night cries of happy cornfield Negroes from Mississippi coupled with the shrill laughter of high-browns—all this, along with the historic significance of Memphis' most widely known thoroughfare is contained in the pages...of 'Beale Street.' Lee...has written the story of Beale Street, as W.C. Handy once set its life to music, with sympathy and a feeling for the dramatic."

George W. Lee's book *Beale Street: Where the Blues Began* was selected by the Book of the Month Club as its alternate choice for July 1934.

Local newspapers and the Book of the Month Club were not the only ones impressed with Lee's narrative. The *New York Times* wrote that "tucked away in his pages are many authentic contributions to Americana."

July 16, 1959

Ronco Foods Plant Reopens

Ronco Foods reopened its factory on this day after being closed for a two-week vacation. The sixty-four-thousand-square-foot facility produced thirty different types of pasta,

including spaghetti, vermicelli and macaroni, which made Ronco one of the largest manufacturers of pasta in the United States. Ronco, named for its founders John S. Robilio Sr. and Thomas Cuneo, began making pasta in 1929. By the 1970s, the company was manufacturing thirteen thousand tons of macaroni and spaghetti per year, with annual sales totaling $186.7 million.

Founded in Memphis by John S. Robilio Sr. and Thomas Cuneo in 1929, Ronco Foods was one of the largest manufacturers of pasta in the United States.

July 17, 1955

Crippled Adults' Hospital Expanded

The Rotary Club's Tri-States Association for Cripples Inc. announced on this day that the Hospital for Crippled Adults, which provided free orthopedic care to adults in Arkansas, Mississippi and Tennessee, would expand its services to parts of Kentucky, Louisiana and Missouri. The expansion was due to the generous support of Rotarians who, over the years, donated thousands of dollars to maintain the hospital. In 1936, for example, it took a mere twenty minutes for Memphis Rotary members to raise $10,100. As explained by the *Commercial Appeal*, the "idea for the institution was conceived by Dr. Willis C. Campbell, who was a Rotary leader. In 1923 the hospital...opened at the old Alabama Street Presbyterian Hospital. The present 56-bed hospital was made possible in 1927 when the late Bernard Bryan Jones of Kosciusko, Miss, who made a fortune in the Oklahoma Oil Fields, donated $200,000 for a building." The hospital's executive secretary, Truman S. Lewis, reported that 865 patients were treated by the institution in 1954. The Hospital for Crippled Adults closed in July 1970, leaving behind many midsoutherners who, in the words of one Rotarian, "came in unable to walk. Some could not talk, yet they left here in perfect health."

July 18, 1967

Civil Rights Demonstrators Protest Feed Mill

Twenty civil rights demonstrators, led by Centenary Methodist Church pastor James Lawson, marched in front of the entrance to the Mid-South Milling Company at 1229 Kansas to protest the foul stench that emanated from the facility. Located in South Memphis on a site that once housed mule barns, Mid-South Milling manufactured animal feed by using the smelly process of grinding meat and bone together to make its product. "It's just unbearable, night or day," explained Ida Lewis who as president of the Utah Avenue War on Poverty project helped coordinate the direct action. According to J.L. Petty, president of the firm, "You can't have any kind of feed mill without odors…and…odor control has improved. People from the health department came out and gave us a clean bill of health." This statement was disputed by the health department's director of sanitary engineering Everett C. Handorf, who felt that the civil rights demonstration was "justified. We are on record as saying we think existing operations need cleaning up and we oppose further expansion." Despite the protest march, Mid-South Milling continued to make feed until 1974, when the company bought Valley Mills in Mississippi and converted the Memphis plant into a feed distribution center. The feed mill protest, although small in and of itself, was part of a larger effort to expand the Memphis civil rights movement into areas of economic justice and quality of life that reached its fruition seven months later during the 1968 sanitation strike.

July 19, 1884

A Typical Saturday in Memphis

Police suffered on this day through another raucous Saturday as criminality flared in several parts of the city. The trouble began in the morning when river worker Henry Wilson got into an argument with a "disreputable woman" called Annie Kelly. They were standing near the Bayou Gayoso, and when Wilson slashed Kelly with a knife, she jumped into the filthy water to escape being murdered. Early in the afternoon, police broke up a confidence racket operating on Front Street.

That evening E.M. Allen, John Dougal and Tom Honan visited the brothel located at 67 Jefferson. In addition to sampling the inmates' wares, they also blew out gas lamps, kicked in doors and caused other property damage before they were picked up by Officer Baker. The typical Saturday night ended with a shootout between Bob Kiles and Frank Lambeth at the corner of LaRose and Georgia Streets. Although neither man was seriously injured in the fracas, both were thrown in the jug by Patrolman Overton.

July 20, 1973

Elvis Records at Stax

The Beatles wanted to record at Stax, but Elvis Presley actually did on this day. In the summer of 1973, Presley needed to record a new album for RCA-Victor but didn't want to leave Memphis and his daughter, Lisa Marie. So he called music producer Marty Lacker, who arranged for Elvis to record at the legendary Stax recording studio in South Memphis. Conducted over three days, the first sessions were uninspired, largely because Elvis was in the midst of a painful divorce from his wife, Priscilla. According to music historian Robert Gordon, Presley's work with Stax "was a period of great opportunity but it was also a bad time in his life." As reported by *Commercial Appeal* reporter James Kingsley, the "Stax session marked the first time Elvis has recorded in Memphis since 1969, when he recorded four million-selling singles and two million-dollar albums at American Studios." Despite the disappointment some felt, the July recordings, along with sessions in December, led to three top-twenty hits for the King of rock 'n' roll, including the song "Promised Land." The last time Elvis recorded in Memphis was in 1976, when he made several records at Graceland in the Jungle Room.

July 21, 1940

Mister Crump Returns from Chicago

Memphis political leader E.H. Crump returned from the Chicago Democratic Convention on this day with a message for Memphians. At the convention, Crump successfully supported the renomination of President Franklin D. Roosevelt and was reelected to the Democratic National Committee. In a prepared statement, he praised FDR and bitterly denounced both the Republican nominee Wendell Willkie and the local newspapers: "I hope Memphians in all walks will stop, look and listen and not permit newspaper propaganda to influence them unduly for there will be story after story boosting Willkie and belittling Roosevelt—expect this, it's coming…Willkie is just another Hoover-product of the hard boiled money changing crowd of Wall Street. That cold-blooded Wall Street outfit dreams of nothing but money." Crump then lauded Roosevelt who, in his words, "has done more for the South than any president—aid to the farmers, public works, TVA…The South owes a debt of gratitude to Franklin D. Roosevelt. He has been their friend. David and Jonathan, Damon and Pythias were no closer—no more devoted than Roosevelt has been to the South, and if nothing else he has given Memphis and all Tennesseans TVA—cheaper electricity."

July 22, 1906

Women Held Up on Raleigh Road

Frankie Hern and May Goodwin made the mistake of visiting the roadhouse owned by notorious gangster Mike Shanley, for they were relieved of their valuables shortly after leaving. In the early evening of this day, the two young women took a buggy ride to Overton Park and then decided to go to Shanley's place on the Old Raleigh Road. While drinking with Shanley, the women apparently showed off the expensive diamonds and jewelry they were wearing as well as where they kept their money. Leaving the roadhouse around 10:00 p.m., Hern and Goodwin were quietly driving in their buggy when they were set upon by two bandits. One grabbed the reins while the other highwayman fired two warning shots, which quickly got their attention. As reported by the *Commercial Appeal*, "The man at the buggy then secured $117 in cash from the stockings of the Hern woman and $90 from the hose of the Goodwin woman." In addition to the money, the well-heeled highwaymen stole $2,300 worth of diamonds and jewelry from the frightened pair. When finished, the bandits fired two rounds and ordered the women to drive as fast as their horse could carry them. Hern and Goodwin rushed to the subdivision of Binghamton, where they phoned central police headquarters and reported the incident.

July 23, 1970

Otis Higgs Appointed Judge

Otis Higgs was appointed judge of the Shelby County Criminal Court Division Four by Tennessee governor Buford Ellington.

Civil rights attorney W. Otis Higgs Jr. on this day was appointed judge of the Shelby County Criminal Court Fourth Division by Tennessee governor Buford Ellington. Higgs replaced Judge Odell Horton, who resigned to become president of LeMoyne-Owen College. According to *Commercial Appeal* reporter Michael Lollar, Higgs rose to prominence when he "waged a campaign in March as a private attorney in behalf of residents of 12 substandard apartments in the city to order the premises repaired to conform to city building codes." Higgs was the third African American—Benjamin L. Hooks and Horton were the others—to serve on the Fourth Division bench and was the first University of Memphis Law School graduate to secure a judicial appointment. He served until 1975, and in 1990, Higgs became the first African American Shelby County sheriff. Elected criminal court judge in 1998, he served until his death in 2013.

July 24, 1928

Glenview Celebrates Litty Day

Hundreds of Glenview neighborhood residents flocked to Litty Park to celebrate Harry H. Litty, who donated the parkland for his neighbors' enjoyment in 1922. The program was organized by the Park Commission's recreation department and the Glenview Home Improvement Club. The celebration began at 3:00 p.m. with games and contests for the children, who each received a lollypop from Litty himself. Commenting on the festivities, Litty said, "I love the out-of-doors. I fear I could not sit still long enough to see a movie…Seeing young people enjoy themselves outdoors is the kind of movie I like." Adults were not ignored; from 5:00 to 6:00 p.m., games for men and women were offered, and at 7:00 p.m., a picnic supper was available for the hungry participants. The evening ended with a concert provided by the City of Memphis Band. Born in Waterville, Ohio, in 1862, Litty worked for the Kansas City, Memphis and Birmingham Railroad until he resigned to practice law in the Bluff City. From 1896 to 1900, he served on the city's legislative council and was mayor from August 1917 to August 1918. Litty died on November 15, 1929, and was mourned by many Memphis children who remembered his smiling face as they played on Litty Day.

July 25, 1995

Soulful Country Music Legend Dies

Entertainer Charlie Rich had many country music hits in the 1970s.

Songwriter Charlie Rich, who recorded at Sun Studios in the 1950s and scored a string of country music hits in the 1970s, passed away on this day while sleeping in a Holiday Inn during a family vacation in Hammond, Louisiana. Born in Colt Arkansas, Rich moved to Memphis to record with legendary music producer Sam Phillips. According to Sam's son Kox, Rich was "probably the most talented guy that ever came through the Sun Music Company, and he was probably the most talented guy in country music." Larry Nager, *Commercial Appeal* music reporter, wrote that "Rich…is remembered for bringing elements of jazz and R&B into country music in the '70s." During that decade, he released a series of hit records, including *Behind Closed Doors*, and in 1974, he was honored by the Country Music Association with its Entertainer of the Year Award.

July 26, 1922

City Pool So Popular It Has to Close

Opened on June 21, the city's first public swimming pool was ordered closed on this day by the Park Commission to repair damage due to the large number of people seeking liquid relief from the sweltering summer heat. In its first five weeks, 82,094 Memphians swam in the pool located at the fairgrounds, so many that the concrete posts, which held ropes dividing the pool's sections, cracked and had to be repaired. As reported by the *Commercial Appeal*: "Persistent rumors that disease and vermin are to be found in the water are again vigorously denied by the commissioners. Two tests are being made daily for all kinds of foreign bacteria… in addition the two pump engines sterilize 60,000 gallons of water per hour, which takes care of the entire 1,250,000 gallons per day."

Unsanitary water was but one concern for some Memphians. The Park Commission, nervous about the interactions between male and female swimmers, passed a resolution requiring women's bathing suits to be made in "somber colors, with sleeves sewn in and with skirts of the prescribed length." According to historian Paul Coppock, restrictions on women's bathing suits were not enough for the Shelby County Baptist Association, which "adopted a resolution calling on the city to close the pool. It was called 'a veritable hell hole' because women in 'tight-fitting, immodest suits' were bathing at the same time as men."

July 27, 1933

Movie Theaters Bombed

Work crews spent this day cleaning the Memphian and Linden Circle movie theaters after unknown assailants set off stink bombs at both locations. Owner M.A. Lightman believed the attacks were related to labor troubles he was having at his Princess movie house. "It is very strange that we never had such an outrage in one of our theaters until we were forced to employ non-union movie operators at the Princess Theater." The Malco Theater chain began during World War I when Lightman opened the Liberty Theater in Muscle Shoals, Alabama. He later owned a theater in Little Rock, Arkansas, and in 1929, he came to Memphis. Malco Theatres Inc. now owns more than three hundred movie screens across the mid-South and is one of Memphis's most important businesses.

Labor agitators set off a stink bomb in the Linden Circle movie theater owned by M.A. Lightman.

July 28, 1982

Wrestler Slaps Comedian on National TV

The feud between wrestler Jerry "the King" Lawler and Hollywood comedian Andy Kaufman continued on this day when both men appeared on NBC's *Late Night with David Letterman*. The feud began in April, when Kaufman disparaged the people of Memphis, and Lawler slammed the comedian's head into the ring floor during a match at the Mid-South Coliseum. Kaufman, who allegedly wanted an apology from the wrestler, still wore a neck brace when he walked out on stage and sat down with Lawler and Letterman. "Is that a neck brace or a flea collar? I can't believe it's a neck brace. I've known people in automobile accidents who didn't have to wear their braces as long as you've worn this one," the King said to the comedian. According to *Press-Scimitar* writer Jack Brennan, the verbal abuse continued until Lawler "rose from his chair and appeared to slap Kaufman, knocking him to the floor. Kaufman responded by cursing and throwing coffee on Lawler, and left the stage threatening to sue the wrestler 'for everything you've got.'" In later years, Lawler admitted that he and Kaufman had choreographed the feud, wrestling match and slap to build excitement for Memphis-style wrestling. This mattered little to the many Memphians who remember when they squealed with delight as a hometown boy avenged the ridicule of a smart-aleck Hollywood actor.

July 29, 1964

First Memphis Casualty of the Vietnam War Honored

Girl Scout Deborah Gray, wearing her full dress uniform, on this day stood silently at attention as her father was honored for his service in Vietnam. Five hundred Memphians joined the eleven-year-old, her mother, the mayor of Memphis and the governor of Tennessee in paying tribute to the first Memphian killed in the Vietnam War, Sergeant First Class Jesse Alexander Gray of the U.S. Army Special Forces, who died during a Viet Cong ambush in South Vietnam. The crowd standing in Court Square watched respectfully as an Oak Leaf Cluster to the Purple Heart was presented to Deborah in recognition of her father's sacrifice. As the citation was presented to Deborah, Major General Howard Snyder Jr. stated, "It gives us great pride to know that men such as your father serve so bravely." Mayor William Ingram proclaimed July 29 "Sergeant Gray Day," and Governor Frank G. Clement said, "If men like Sergeant Gray are willing to spill blood, if they are willing to die for their flag, it does appear that we can live by the same principles." In addition to Sergeant Gray, 214 other warriors from Memphis and Shelby County gave their lives during the Vietnam War.

July 30, 1945

Victory Garden Sprouts Loco Weed

Acting on an anonymous tip, police officials announced on this day that they had discovered marijuana plants growing in a victory garden on West McLemore. Victory gardens were supposed to make up for the widespread rationing of processed foods, but this particular garden had a much different purpose. According to the *Press-Scimitar*, the "harmless looking 'loco weed' was rising 10 feet above the ground and was ready to be cut and dried at the time the discovery was made…Marijuana is regarded as a dangerous narcotic. Smoked, it undermines the moral fiber, experts say." Special Investigator Clifford J. West and a squad of patrolmen arrested William Robert Shook and Sidney T. Yarborough on suspicion of violating the Narcotics Act. West and U.S. Bureau of Narcotics inspector D.W. Hoke hoped to discover if the two were involved with a gang peddling marijuana cigarettes across the mid-South. In addition to the 1,225-square-foot crop of marijuana, police also uncovered a shed across from the gardens that appeared to be used for drying and storing the illegal plant.

July 31, 1905

African Americans Protest Segregated Streetcars

At four o'clock on this day, a mass meeting of African Americans was held in Church's Park to protest the Tennessee law that required blacks to sit in segregated seats after boarding trains and city streetcars. According to a reporter for the *Commercial Appeal* newspaper, "The leaders of the race have been studying the law and believe that it is too humiliating to them and that their humiliation is more noticed on street cars than on railroad trains." The opportunity to challenge the Hancock Law came when Mary Morrison, a twenty-one-year-old "wash woman" who lived with her mother at 279 Exchange, refused to sit in the "colored-only" section. Morrison was arrested and later convicted of violating the state's Jim Crow segregation law. After listening to several speeches, those attending the meeting adopted a resolution to raise $5,000 to pay black attorneys Benjamin F. Booth and Josiah T. Settle to challenge the law in court. The two respected lawyers argued that the Jim Crow law violated Morrison's Fourteenth Amendment right to equal protection under the law. The case wound its way to the Tennessee Supreme Court, and in August 1906, it rendered its judgment. Justice John K. Shields upheld the Hancock Law declaring that it "applied equally to both races." The bravery of Mary Morrison may not have ended segregation on Tennessee's street railways, but it did set the stage for later civil rights protests that transformed Memphis and the rest of the American South.

August 1, 1944

Veterans' Service Centers Open

The U.S. Employment Service on this day announced the opening of a center, located on South Second Avenue, to help returning African American servicemen take advantage of benefits guaranteed them by federal law. The manager of the center was World War I veteran John J. Guinozzo, who worked closely with Veterans' Bureau representative and fellow Great War soldier Woodward Morris and his assistant, wounded World War II vet Frank Catino. As reported by the *Commercial Appeal*, "All applicants must bring their honorable discharges. Application blanks and assistance for the various benefits, including vocational training, continuance of education, disability compensation, etc., will be furnished for filling out and mailing to the proper boards and government agencies." A second center for white veterans was also opened at the U.S. Employment Service's office on Union Avenue. A Memphian played an important role in creating the veterans' benefits offered to World War II servicemen. Colonel Roane Waring, World War I veteran and former national commander of the American Legion, was appointed a special consultant to advise the War Department on ways to assist members of the armed forces in returning to civilian life in 1943.

August 2, 1979

B.B. King and Bobby Blue Bland Join Forces

Blues legends B.B. King and Bobby Blue Bland partnered on this day to perform at the Auditorium Dixon Myers Hall. Around 1,800 midsoutherners packed the hall to hear the two masters play what was in effect a graduate course in the blues. In a review in the *Press-Scimitar*, critic Aldore Collier wrote: "Bland, who performed first during the three-hour musical marathon, has a more slow and deliberate style. The native Memphian…gurgled his 49-year-old vocal cords with such tunes as 'I'll Take Care of You,' 'Stay with Me Awhile,' and 'Gonna Make Me Love Somebody Else.' The pace of the music took a 180-degree turn when King strolled onto the stage. The legendary 'King of the Blues' quickly got the audience's adrenalin flowing…Oldies…came booming out of his barrel-like voice with the assistance of his constant companion—his guitar, Lucille. The duo…received a barrage of feedback from the audience because of the humorous, conversational lyrics that took jabs at men, women, religion and adultery."

Bobby Blue Bland was inducted into the Rock and Roll Hall of Fame in 1992 and received the Lifetime Achievement Award from the Grammys in 1997. His partner, B.B. King, was also inducted into the Rock and Roll Hall of Fame and won fourteen Grammys during his storied career. In 2006, President George W. Bush honored King with the Presidential Medal of Freedom.

August 3, 1947

Peabody Head Waiter Served His Last Customer

One of Memphis's most noble citizens passed away on this day. Alonzo Locke, headwaiter at the Peabody Hotel, was beloved for his courtliness, attention to detail and his ability to remember the name of anyone who ever ate in his establishment. The *Press-Scimitar*'s Clark Porteous put it this way:

> *Alonzo of the Peabody, a tradition in his own time, has gone to a heavenly hotel…Alonzo of the flashing smile, the Chesterfieldian courtesy, the humble yet proud demeanor— Alonzo who was a Memphis institution and one of the leading ambassadors of good will not only for the Negro race but for all mankind…all over the nation there are people who will be a bit saddened to learn of his death. For Alonzo and the ducks in the lobby fountains were the two things about the Peabody that persons who met Memphians in distant cities were certain to inquire about.*

Born in Rutherford, Tennessee, Locke came to Memphis in 1905 to serve as headwaiter at the Hotel Gayoso. When the Peabody opened in its new location in 1925, Locke was appointed headwaiter and remained there until his death. On September 2, 1947, St. Paul School was renamed W. Alonzo Locke Elementary School in his honor.

August 4, 1967

Syncopation Heard in Mid-South Coliseum

Over six thousand fans of syncopation attended the Memphis Jazz Festival at the Mid-South Coliseum on this day. Produced by Newport Jazz Festival director George Wein, Memphis was chosen to host a southern festival because of its storied musical heritage and its central location. A few weeks before the festival, Wein explained that ticket "sales have vastly exceeded our expectations. We are receiving ticket requests from Nashville, Little Rock and Jonesboro, Ark., Greenwood, Jackson and Grenada, Miss." Several leading jazz specialists performed, including Julian "Cannonball" Adderley, pianist Ramsey Lewis, vocalist Nina Simone, the Dizzy Gillespie Quintet and Herbie Mann. As reported by the *Commercial Appeal*'s James Cortese, "Mann, recognized as one of the most gifted of the modernists on the flute, soloed like a nightingale on a bridge of sound against a background produced by the unusual combination of lute, xylophone, drum and bass." During an interview, Mann told Cortese that the "Memphis Sound and Ray Charles…have 'influenced me the most.'"

August 5, 1931

Custard Stand Owner Smashes Curb

Charged with violating the city's sidewalk ordinance, attorney and businessman Tom Collier appeared before Judge Lewis Fitzhugh on this day and defiantly exclaimed, "I did it and I'll do it again." Collier was upset with the city for refusing his request for a permit to cut openings in a curb that surrounded his golf driving range and frozen custard stand on Poplar Avenue—so upset that he took a sledgehammer and busted a nine-foot section of the curbing to unblock his driveway. His attorney, J.G. Reasonover, argued that the "city had no right to block a driveway that had been there 50 years—it committed a nuisance." Judge Fitzhugh countered that despite Collier having a sound argument against the city, "that is not the issue in this case. You took the law into your own hands instead of proceeding in the proper manner in chancery court. The only issue is the violation of the ordinance." Fitzhugh found Collier guilty, levying an $11 fine against the disgruntled attorney, who refused to accept the verdict. "I intend to keep on cutting that curbing," Collier declared in open court. However, before he had a chance to raise his hammer, the city attorney's office hauled Collier back into court and placed him under a $250 Peace Bond, which meant if he smashed the concrete, he would forfeit the money. Collier continued to bedevil city officials—he frequently destroyed traffic signs near his property and refused to pay his property taxes—until he dropped dead walking down a city street on May 4, 1944.

August 6, 1936

A Jungle Runs Through Memphis

One of the most unusual eating establishments in Memphis history announced on this day that it would open at 7:00 a.m. and remain in operation until 3:00 a.m because of customer demand. Located at Union Avenue and Waldran Boulevard, Fortune's Jungle Garden drive-in was owned by Harold Fortune and designed by landscape architect John F. Highberger. According to the *Press-Scimitar*, "The tropical planting lends a true jungle effect and with large shady elm trees and the woven cane and moss canopy (suspended on cables between trees) it is cool and delightful in the Jungle even on the hottest days. Parrots, macaws, grizzly bears, Bengal tigers, as well as lions, monkeys and wildcats, many made from metal and concrete, peer at you from the undergrowth." The menu included Jungle barbecue and Jungle golden-brown fried chicken in addition to sandwiches and Fortune's All-Cream Ice Cream. Thomas Fortune and his partner, F.W. Ward, founded a drugstore in 1883, which began offering curbside service to customers in 1906, making Fortune-Ward arguably the first drive-in restaurant in the United States. The Jungle Garden was opened in 1920 and remained a popular attraction until it closed in 1966 to make way for the interstate highway system.

August 7, 1903

Slot Machine Owner Convicted

Shelby County sheriff George W. Blackwell no doubt felt a sense of relief and vindication on this day when a jury found saloon owner L. Faccaro guilty of operating a gambling device. The guilty verdict was handed down even though the prosecution's main piece of evidence, a slot machine found in Faccaro's place, had mysteriously disappeared from the sheriff's office. Faccaro was arrested in his Front Street saloon on June 26 by Deputy Sheriff Joseph P. Hefly, who confiscated the slot machine, which was quickly stolen by parties unknown. Indicted by the grand jury shortly thereafter, Faccaro was brought before Judge John T. Moss, who presided over his trial. The *Commercial Appeal* reported that the "deputy sheriff who made the arrest of the defendant testified that he went to the saloon, where he found both the defendant and the machine at work, the defendant raking in the nickels over the counter and the machine…eating them alive whenever they came its way."

August 8, 1910

New Factory Opens in South Memphis

Construction of a large feed plant was begun on this day on an eight-acre site in South Memphis. The *Commercial Appeal* stated: "[The] International Sugar Feed Company of Memphis and Minneapolis, Minn., will immediately erect an eight-story factory to include an elevator and a hundred and fifty-car capacity warehouse upon a tract of eight acres of land located on Mallory Avenue, the main line of the Illinois Central Railroad and the Union Railway, popularly known as the belt line. The total investment in the Memphis plant will be approximately a quarter of a million dollars…It's [*sic*] capacity will be fifteen cars, or 300 tons of horse and mule, dairy, hog, chicken and special cattle feed per day. Improved machinery, with which it is to be equipped, will make it possible to operate the big plant with from thirty to fifty men."

The company decided to locate in Memphis after intense negotiations with James S. Warren, industrial commissioner for the Business Men's Club. According to the company's southern representative, Will A. Hall, they "chose Memphis simply because this city offered the best advantages. The close proximity to the sugar, grain and cotton seed product markets, the excellent shipping facilities and the splendid freight rates combine to make this city the logical point for the South and Southwest."

August 9, 1962

Monkey Invaded Loeb Estate

The children of William Loeb, president of Loeb's Laundry, squealed with delight as they watched a runaway monkey glide furtively through their backyard. According to the *Commercial Appeal*: "It's a swift animal, and it hides in many trees about the yard. It may be a pet, but it is very shy and spends most of the time in hiding. Mr. Loeb at first doubted if his children knew what they were talking about when they came in Tuesday and calmly said, 'Daddy, there's a monkey in the sycamore tree.' But yesterday Mr. Loeb got a fleeting glance of the spry animal when it leaped form the sycamore onto the bathhouse roof, then scurried up another tree."

The Loeb family owned and operated one of the most successful businesses in Memphis history. The company was founded in 1887 by Henry Loeb, whose son (also named William) grew the concern into one of the largest laundry services in the United States. In 1942, his sons William and Henry took over the business upon his death. A shrewd and ambitious businessman, William Loeb expanded the company's holdings to include a chain of barbecue and fried chicken restaurants and a group of convenience stores. In 1952, William Loeb created a series of advertisements featuring his nine children, which ran in the local newspapers twice a week until 1969 and remains a fondly remembered advertising campaign. The company continues in business to this day as Loeb Properties.

August 10, 1949

Loud Children Spark Mud Island Feud

The quiet of a summer afternoon on Mud Island was disturbed on this day by shotgun blasts when an argument between two neighbors evolved into a violent feud. The day before, August 9, Lillian Curry and her children were visiting Sue Thomas, who lived next door to seventy-five-year-old carpenter Omer Gibson. The sounds of children playing upset Gibson, who walked next door and asked them to hush. "They can make as much noise as they want to," Mrs. Curry defiantly replied. As reported by Roy Jennings of the *Commercial Appeal*, the argument then turned ugly: "Mr. Gibson told police Mrs. Curry struck him with a stick…In retaliation, he knocked her down, he said. Then both went to their island homes and got their shotguns. Hers was a .410, his a 12 gauge. Then they returned for battle. They began firing when they sighted each other across a clearing." Gibson was shot between the eyes while a load of buckshot pierced Curry's abdomen. When the mêlée began, Curry's mother, Susie Allen, dove in front of her child and was shot in the wrist and shoulder. All three were evacuated to the mainland for medical treatment. Mud Island was formed from a sand bar when the Mississippi River changed directions in the wake of the 1913 flood. At least two hundred hardy souls lived on Mud Island until the 1960s.

August 11, 1888

A Walk Down Beale Street

The *Daily Appeal* on this day described what it was like to walk down Beale Street and visit its market on a Saturday night. According to the unknown writer, the first thing you noticed when stepping onto the street was "the peculiar mixed style of its architecture, its crooked topography, and the curious jumble it presents of pretentious buildings looking down in lofty contempt upon the mean shanties that surround them." The majority of those walking with the reporter were African Americans, the "men mostly arrayed in their shirt sleeves, the women carefully arrayed in their showiest garments. Some of the men loiter around the numerous saloons in good humored groups, exchanging merry jests." The writer walked to the entrance to the market where he encountered a "swarthy-hued Italian, with a job lot of bananas…Next to him a crowd is gathered around the man with the lung testing machine, which is operated through a rubber tube at 5 cents a blow." In one corner, patrons lined up to buy "handkerchiefs, soap, buttons, pocketbooks, lead pencils, chromos, tin and crockery ware" while "a step or two further south and you run foul of a lunch stand, where hot fried catfish is served fresh from the pan to eager patrons." The account left by the *Daily Appeal* reporter provides us with a fascinating glimpse of Beale Street in the 1880s.

August 12, 1978

Historic Home Lost to Fast Food

Historic preservationists spent this month trying to save the Frank F. Hill Mansion, a historic fifteen-room home located at 1400 Union Avenue. In July, the trustee for the Hill estate announced he was negotiating with the Arby's Roast Beef Houses fast food restaurant chain to sell the property. Financier Frank Hill built his residential showcase in 1909 and amassed an extensive collection of oriental rugs and paintings. A grassroots effort to save the ornate structure was led by Memphis Heritage Inc., which temporarily halted the sale when a contract was signed and $20,000 in earnest money was raised to purchase the seventy-three-year-old home. The contract required Memphis Heritage to raise $260,000 by November 1. But by mid-August, donations stalled, and in the end, not enough money was raised to save the historic home. In January 1979, demolition began on the mansion, although two life-size stone lions that graced the outside of the home and a stained-glass window were saved and donated to Brooks Memorial Art Gallery.

Historic preservationists were unsuccessful in saving the Hill Mansion from demolition.

August 13, 1928

Our Gang Comedy Filmed in Memphis

Hollywood filmmaker Jack Roach, brother of famed movie director Hal Roach, began filming a local version of an *Our Gang* comedy in Memphis on this day. Scouting for talent, the Hal Roach Studios sent camera crews to several cities, including Memphis. Local children submitted their photographs to the *Evening Appeal*, and readers chose seven to appear in the short film. Roach and his crew—which included chief cameraman Lester Lang, who gained fame as the cinematographer on the silent version of *Ben Hur*—shot most of their scenes at the fairgrounds over a three-day period. Jack Roach was very pleased with his time in Memphis. Commenting to a reporter, he said, "California has nothing on this. Perhaps it's a little cooler but the photographic conditions here are excellent. We have made a good picture, I believe." The completed film, entitled *Pie Eatin' Contest*, was shown at Loew's State Theater in late August 1928. *Pie Eatin' Contest* was not the only Hollywood production filmed in Memphis during that year. Director King Vidor also shot his film *Hallelujah*, the first movie musical with an all-black cast, in and around Memphis in 1928.

August 14, 1917

Soldiers Drill in Overton Park

Spectators fascinated with military formations watched the Second Tennessee Infantry practice close order drill in Overton Park the *Commercial Appeal* reported on this day:

> *The occasion was a battalion drill and inspection by Maj. Roane Waring. Battery A, First Field Artillery, participated in the morning events and passed in review before the major and Capt. Thomas Fauntleroy, Second Tennessee, who acted as adjutant for battalion. It was an all-day affair for the members of the two Memphis units of the Second Tennessee. They assembled at the park at 8 o'clock in the morning, and within a short time were formed in company fronts on the parade ground in front of the casino. A few commands from Capt. Fauntleroy brought the soldiers to attention and then Maj. Waring took charge of the drill work for more than an hour.*

Spectators and soldiers alike enjoyed music played by the second infantry band led by Harry Blix during a luncheon break. In the afternoon, the drilling continued along with vigorous hikes through the park's old forest.

August 15, 1951

Memphis Soldier Wins DFC in Korea

Eighteen-year-old Private Edward Oberon Cleaborn of Company A, Twenty-fourth Regiment, Twenty-fifth Division, was killed in action on this day in Korea. Cleaborn, a Boy Scout, graduate of Florida Street School and a former student at Booker T. Washington High School, grew up in the African American section of southwest Memphis. For his bravery, Private Cleaborn was posthumously awarded the Distinguished Service Cross by General Douglas McArthur and President Harry S. Truman. As reported by *Press-Scimitar* staff writer Clark Porteous, Cleaborn "stood on a ridge and held off the enemy while members of his company, including wounded, withdrew. He fired his weapon so much, the citation said, that his hands were severely burned...Far East Command headquarters said Cleaborn 'single-handedly wiped out Red machine-gun crews threatening his unit.'" At a February 1951 ceremony honoring the fallen soldier, Mayor Watkins Overton said, "No words of mine can add to the glory of Pvt. Cleaborn, who gave his life for his comrades, for his country. Memphis is proud of the sacrifice he made. Memphis is proud that he lived here." In 1955, a housing project was named in honor of this brave Korean War veteran.

August 16, 1978

Elvis Fans Spend Night in Graceland

Thousands of Elvis Presley fans poured into Memphis to honor the singer on the first anniversary of his death. When they arrived, they found a city in chaos and discovered many of the events they planned to attend cancelled because the fire and police departments were on strike. Mayor Wyeth Chandler imposed an 8:00 p.m. curfew that severely hampered the ability of Elvis fans to negotiate through the city. Three hundred devotees of the King of rock 'n' roll were allowed to spend the night just inside the gates of Graceland in order to avoid violating the curfew. Volunteer emergency workers along with twenty-five members of the Tennessee National Guard did their best to help the anguished multitude and maintain order outside Presley's mansion. A memorial concert scheduled for that evening at the Mid-South Coliseum was cancelled when city officials refused to lift the curfew. The show's headliner, Elvis Wade, expressed his disgust when he commented that "we thought the city could do at least this one thing for Elvis. We thought we could donate our show, to show the love and respect we have for the man. This just blows my mind." Outside Graceland, tears sprinkled the face of New Jersey native Mary Horrocks, who cried, "They won't let you grieve in private." Her friend Dolores Treadwell consoled her by saying, "Maybe next time it will be nicer." She was right. The city organized Elvis Tribute Week, and mid-August has become the most popular time for tourists to visit Memphis.

August 17, 1958

Traffic Bottleneck on Lamar Cleared

For years, thousands of Memphis drivers have suffered through a major traffic snarl when they glided through the intersection of Lamar and Park Avenues. This changed when an eight-lane underpass opened on this day. According to city engineer Will Fowler, the $560,000 project, which was delayed for three months due to bad weather and a labor shortage, was needed because over forty-five thousand automobiles used the roadway on a daily basis. As reported by the *Commercial Appeal*, "Cars began streaming under the Illinois Central Railroad bridge spanning Lamar minutes after workmen—without advance notice—removed barricades that had restricted traffic for two lanes since construction was started in September, 1956. To accommodate the heavy traffic, Lamar has been widened from South Parkway East to about 300 feet east of the new underpass." The abrupt opening nearly caused an accident when an eastbound motorist "reached the project site and automatically pulled his car onto the left side of the street…He discovered his mistake when he heard the horns of oncoming cars."

August 18, 1932

Cactus Jack Swooped into Town

An American Airways plane carrying John Nance "Cactus Jack" Garner, Speaker of the U.S. House of Representatives and Democratic vice presidential nominee, landed at the Municipal Airport on this day. A raucous crowd of 350 Memphians, led by Congressman E.H. Crump, Senator Kenneth McKellar and Mayor Watkins Overton, met the plane as it taxied on the runway. When Garner emerged from the aircraft, Crump cut loose with a Rebel yell that electrified the waiting spectators. The *Commercial Appeal* reported that "the nominee was led toward the waiting crowd which pushed at the chains bounding the airport. 'Everywhere I go I find that people want to see what kind of a monkey they have as a nominee,' Mr. Garner declared as he faced the crowd. 'Even the Yankees.' 'I know you're going to be the best vice president we've had,' Mr. Crump declared, slapping Mr. Garner on the back. 'I'll admit that,' Mr. Garner retorted sprightly." Garner spoke highly of his old Tennessee friend: "I admire Mr. Crump very much." Once the nominee was back in the air headed for San Antonio, Crump and Mayor Overton sent a radiogram to his plane. "We are stronger for you than ever and stand ready to serve you and Roosevelt night and day until Nov. 8 and four years thereafter and then some."

August 19, 1966

Device Explodes at Beatles Concert

The Beatles arrived in Memphis to perform two concerts at the Mid-South Coliseum. While screaming teenagers attempted to get close and soldiers gaped at their long hair, an American Airlines Electra Jet landed John Lennon, Paul McCartney, George Harrison and Ringo Starr at the Tennessee Air National Guard runway on Democrat Road. Whisked to the coliseum, the Beatles performed before 7,589 raucous fans who could not hear their music but nonetheless writhed in ecstasy. The Beatles had been nervous about venturing into the American South after Lennon remarked in an interview that they were "more popular than Jesus," but other than a few anti-Beatle demonstrators walking outside the coliseum, no incident marked the four o'clock show. At their seven o'clock press conference, they were asked about the controversy, and Lennon replied, "I don't mind people banning our records or not liking them. That's their right." In the crowd for both concerts was Edwin Howard of the *Press-Scimitar*, who described the pandemonium of their second appearance: "Shortly after the Beatles appeared for the evening show, a firecracker exploded on the main floor and Julie Wilson and Nick Isch, both 16, of Batesville, Miss., were rushed out and to the aid station by police." The explosion rattled the Beatles, who for a moment thought they were being shot at. Nevertheless, they finished their performance and left Memphis at 12:12 a.m. without incident.

August 20, 1942

Black Moses Is Born

Isaac Hayes, the "Black Moses" of soul music, was born on this day thirty-eight miles from Memphis in Covington, Tennessee. In 1948, Hayes moved to Memphis with his grandparents Willie and Rushia Wade. Trapped in extreme poverty, Hayes once said that he "used to dream, just dream about being able to have a warm bed to sleep in and a nice square meal and some decent clothes to wear." Music became his way to achieve these basic comforts of life and a good deal more. Hayes performed at several nightclubs and was later hired to play piano at Stax Records. In 1962, he and lyricist David Porter composed several important soul songs including "Hold On, I'm Coming" and "Soul Man." Hayes was asked by Metro-Goldwyn-Mayer to compose the music for the film *Shaft*, which won Hayes two Grammys and an Academy Award.

Isaac Hayes, seen here with his family, was known as the "Black Moses" of soul music.

August 21, 1961

World's Largest Indoor Putt-Putt Course Opens on Lamar
The Cherokee Bowling Lanes, located at 2930 Lamar Avenue, hummed with the sounds of crashing pins and sliding shoes on this, its opening day. Designed by Windrom, Haglund & Venable Architects, it contained fifty-two lanes—twelve always available for open bowling—a snack bar, free nursery, pro shop and the world's only thirty-six-hole indoor miniature golf course tucked away in the basement. Commenting on the new facility, the *Commercial Appeal* explained: "[The] decoration and color…was planned by Peggy Land Leppert & Associates…The spacious atmosphere is accentuated by using shades of blue, gold and lavender carefully blended and repeated in the carpeting, which was woven especially for Cherokee. The booths in the dining area are upholstered in midday blue naugahyde with solid white Formica tops. The chairs and snack bar stools are of alternating white, gold, turquoise, lavender and blue. The perfectly-planned color arrangement is further enhanced by paneling and the most realistic artificial plantings throughout."

Cherokee Bowling Lanes remained a popular recreational facility for Memphians living in the eastern sections of the city until it ceased operations in 2004. Soon after it closed, bowler James K. Polk explained that he "was really sad to see Cherokee close. I had bowled there for more than 20 years. It was like splitting up a family."

August 22, 1887

Woman's Skin Turned White

A fifty-year-old African American woman named Julia Mitchell suffered from an unknown medical condition that turned her ebony skin a pale white. On this day, she met with a *Daily Appeal* reporter and described the history of her mysterious ailment. Mitchell first noticed her condition after returning from a trip to Iuka Springs in Mississippi in the summer of 1885. While there, she drank liberally of the mineral spring water, which eventually made her ill. Soon after returning to Memphis, small white spots began appearing on her hands, arms and face. These pigmentless spots grew to cover her entire body save for the joints of her hands, arms and legs, and her hair turned completely white as well. Physicians differed on what caused the condition; some believed it was a natural occurrence in some humans while others thought it was a slowly progressing disease. The *Appeal* reporter condescendingly wrote that "Julia says she has been approached by museum agents to become identified with the world of freaks. Her main objection to this, provided an adequate salary is promised, is that she fears her lack of intelligence will be imposed upon and the money wrongfully kept from her." Although unknown at the time, Mitchell was suffering from vitiligo, which was described by the *Merck Manual* as a "loss of skin melanocytes that causes areas of skin depigmentation."

August 23, 1956

Lonesome Rhodes Came to Town

Noted movie director Elia Kazan on this day began filming scenes in downtown Memphis for his motion picture *A Face in the Crowd*. Starring Andy Griffith and Patricia Neal, the film is the fictionalized account of a Memphis TV personality, Lonesome Rhodes, who became a national figure only to be corrupted and destroyed by fame. The first day of shooting began on the rooftop of the Hotel Claridge, which was made up to look like a local restaurant. Filming was set to begin at 10:00 a.m. but was delayed because only forty Memphians had shown up for work as extras. A few more extras arrived after the Front Street Theatre and modeling agencies were contacted; however, Kazan still did not have enough extras, so the sets were reconfigured to accommodate a smaller crowd. One of the extras was Eddie Cooper who "read in the morning paper that a movie crew was in town…so I put on a tie and jacket and took the bus downtown…They lined us up, picked out the dressiest of us and herded us up the elevators to the rooftop where we spent all day pushing tomatoes around with a fork." The movie crew remained in the Bluff City for two more days filming scenes at the Peabody Hotel and Beale Street. *A Face in the Crowd* is considered one of the most important films of the twentieth century and is fondly remembered by many Memphians who were able to watch and participate in the making of a Hollywood classic.

August 24, 1968

Leonard's Sold to Corporation

T.W. "Bill" Hoehn Jr., president of Hoehn Chevrolet, disclosed on this day that he and a group of investors had bought Memphis's legendary restaurant, Leonard's Pit Barbeque located at 1140 South Bellevue Boulevard. Hoehn explained that "Mr. Leonard Heuberger, the owner for 46 years, will continue to head up everything. All the personnel will continue—no changes contemplated." In 1922, Heuberger traded a Model T Ford for a small café on the corner of Trigg and Latham, where he sold a plate of barbecue and beans for ten cents. Ten years later, he moved to Bellevue, where he developed the pulled pork and coleslaw sandwich and the half-barbecue, half-spaghetti plate. Both of these innovations laid the foundation for Memphis to be recognized as the barbecue capital of the world. After the investors bought Leonard's in 1968, the restaurant expanded to other places, but the Bellevue location remained until it closed in June 1991. Cashier Bernice Clark, who worked at Leonard's for twenty-nine years, summed it up for many when she said, "This is breaking my heart. I hate to see the place go, not just for me but for Memphis—it's a landmark."

August 25, 1929

Bottles Thrown at Chicks Game

Violence erupted at Russwood Park on this day during a baseball game between the Memphis Chicks and the Atlanta Crackers. The trouble began when an irate horsehide enthusiast objected to a decision rendered by umpire Gomer James by throwing a bottle at him. Fans in the right field bleachers then cut loose with a volley of glass, which angered the Crackers' bullpen. As Chicks secretary Frank Longinotti joined police captain Hulet Smith, Sergeant Julio Vannuci and several patrolmen in rushing the field, Atlanta first baseman Dick Burrus picked up some of the discarded Coke bottles and threw them back into the stands. The manager of the Chicks, Doc Prothro, then strode onto the field to talk to the opposing team's leader. As described by the *Commercial Appeal*'s Herbert Caldwell, "When Wilber Good, manager of the Crackers threatened to take his team off the field Prothro implored with him not to act so hurriedly. Prothro accused Burrus of prolonging the affair to a state of seriousness. Burrus according to Prothro cursed him a called him a liar. Then like any other man would have done Prothro took a punch at Burrus and the fight was on until stopped by police and other players." Burrus was then arrested for "Assault with a Pop Bottle," but he quickly skulked out of Memphis after posting a fifty-dollar bond. The Atlanta player was also fined forty dollars by Southern Baseball Association president John D. Martin for fighting and throwing bottles at spectators. Prothro got off easier; he was only fined fifteen dollars for fighting.

August 26, 1991

Peabody Duckmaster Makes Final Walk

Edward D. Pembroke, legendary duckmaster for the Peabody Hotel, retired on this day after fifty years of service. Born in Pennsylvania, Pembroke ran away to join a circus when he was nine years old. In 1940, he wandered into Memphis, where he got a job at the Peabody, first as a bell captain and then as caretaker of the hotel's ceremonial ducks. Eight years before Pembroke arrived, in the winter of 1932, hotel manager Frank Schutt and automobile dealer Edward "Chip" Barwick arrived back in town after a duck hunting trip in Arkansas. Warmed and fortified by several sips of whiskey, the two thought it would be funny to place their live duck decoys in the hotel's fountain. The site of live ducks in the lobby of the South's grandest hotel became so popular that the management soon made it a permanent part of the establishment's service. Over time an elaborate ritual was created to escort the ducks to the fountain. Every day at 11:00 a.m., Pembroke marched the ducks from their Royal Duck Palace to the lobby while the music of John Philip Sousa played in the background. When the day was spent, they would again be marched back to their rooftop perch. The Peabody ducks and their African American master were so well known that they appeared on the *Tonight Show* starring Johnny Carson, *Good Morning America* and the *Today* show. On his retirement, Pembroke stated that he'd "rather work with them than have people squalling at me." Duckmaster Edward D. Pembroke died on August 21, 1994.

August 27, 1927

Mayor Turns Sears Crosstown Key

One of the largest Sears, Roebuck & Company stores in the United States was opened on this day in the Crosstown neighborhood. According to the *Evening Appeal*, "Two thousand people stood in a semi-circle around the tower entrance to the 17-story plant at North Cleveland and North Parkway at 9 o'clock and saw Mayor Rowlett Paine turn the key that opened the Sears-Roebuck retail store to business. And thousands more came and continued to come, until the whole ground floor was packed with curious humanity." The ceremonies began with an address by Julius Rosenwald, chairman of the Board of Sears and Roebuck who declared that the "millions we have already spent here will seem as nothing compared to the millions more the establishment of this enterprise will bring into Memphis." This was followed by manager Walter L. Acroyd who read a telegram from Sears president C.M. Little, who praised "the thousands of Memphis workmen who have made possible the completion of our plant in 180 days and set a record in industrial construction." Sears Crosstown remained in operation until the retail center was closed on September 30, 1983.

August 28, 1924

Fake Puppy Racket Exposed

Post office inspector V.V. Sugg ordered the arrest of well-known confidence man T.E. McLendon for defrauding the public through the mail. Picked up in Germantown, McLendon appeared before U.S. commissioner George Poole, who released the alleged grifter on a $10,000 bond. According to the *Commercial Appeal*:

> *Government officials charge that his game is to fake pedigrees for dogs, advertise their aristocratic lineage in the public prints and clean up in the sale of them. The federal grand jury brought two indictments against him on this charge last May. He will face trial on these indictments at the November term of court. In all Inspector Sugg estimates that McLendon has used between 30 and 35 fictitious names to carry on his enterprise, about 12 of which were conceived since the indictments in May. He is no more jealous of his name than his address, according to the inspector. Binghamton, Buntyn and Normal seem to serve better than Memphis, Mr. Sugg declares.*

August 29, 1977

Elvis Grave Robbers Captured in Cemetery

Three men skulking around Forest Hill Cemetery were arrested shortly after midnight on this day for plotting to crack open the Presley family mausoleum and steal the body of Elvis Presley. Police, acting on a tip, had staked out the cemetery for several days when they spotted Ronnie Lee Adkins, Raymond M. Green and Eugene Nelson attempting to open an iron gate at the rear of the mausoleum. Before police could confront them, a passing car's headlights spooked the would-be grave robbers, who rushed to a waiting car and sped away down Hernando Road. Officers caught up with them on Elvis Presley Boulevard, ending their body-snatching career before it really began. According to William Steverson of the *Commercial Appeal*, police director E. Winslow Chapman stated that "he did not know how the suspects planned to open the crypt, which is sealed with two large concrete slabs and covered by a solid sheet of marble." The following day, police revealed that the informant was none other than Ronnie Adkins, who claimed the others planned to hold the singer's body for ransom. The charges against Adkins were dropped, and after a brief trial in October, Green and Nelson were set free because they did not have burglary tools with them at the time of their arrest. A month after the plot was uncovered, Elvis's father, Vernon Presley, had the remains of his son and wife, Gladys, moved to the stately confines of Graceland.

August 30, 1896

Jewish Temple Reopens

Temple Israel, the oldest reform Jewish congregation in Memphis, on this day completed renovations of its synagogue located on Poplar Avenue near Second Street. Although the building was only twelve years old, many improvements were added to the structure, which, in the words of the *Commercial Appeal*, made Temple Israel "one of the handsomest houses of worship in the South." Taken on a tour by choirmaster Professor Winkler, the reporter wrote that on "the chancel and pulpit stand a red Brussels carpet has been placed. Directly in the rear of the altar is located the case in which the Books of the law are preserved...The lighting arrangements of the building are excellent. In the center are five suspended handsome chandeliers, each holding ten incandescent electric lights. These serve to fully reveal the beauty of the interior finishing, which is in gold and blue." In 1916, the Children of Israel moved to a new, larger synagogue at Poplar Avenue and Montgomery Street, and in 1976, it moved to a modern facility on thirty-five acres at East Massey Road.

August 31, 1976

Lucy Opry Preserved Bluegrass Music

Paul Vancil, staff writer for the *Press-Scimitar*, reported on the activities of bluegrass musician Doug Cole, who was known as the Godfather of Memphis bluegrass for his many contributions to local music. As leader of the Dixie Bluegrass Boys, Cole, along with fellow musicians Bill Beck, Carl Collins, Paul Copeland, Mike Kisner and Johnny McDonald, performed all across Memphis and the mid-South and recorded an album. According to Vancil: "Cole is also one of the founders of Lucy Opry, a Friday night show in an old church north of Memphis on Fite Road. The show is free (although they pass the hat), open to the public—and strictly bluegrass. Lucy Opry is perhaps the best illustration of Cole's devotion to his music. He and his group play there every Friday night, with few exceptions. They are joined by many other bands and have hosted such 'grass greats as Vassar Clements, Earl Garner and Merle (Red) Taylor. There is little profit ('Two years ago Lucy cleared $42') and that goes back into the operation. And often the musicians and their wives are also the janitors."

The lack of money meant little to Cole, who explained that for him, bluegrass music was "like eating—you can't do without it." The Lucy Opry continued to provide concerts to those who couldn't do without bluegrass music until it ceased operations in December 2009.

September 1, 1892

Blackmail Plot Uncovered

A blackmail scheme was uncovered involving an elderly man, a comely young woman and her middle-aged husband. For over a year, twenty-six-year-old Lillie King carried on a torrid affair with James Yonge, a sixty-five-year-old wealthy cotton factor. The extortion plot began on the morning of August 23, when Mrs. King sent a note asking Yonge to come to her home at 240 Poplar Street. As the cotton factor began to undress for his assignation, he received an unexpected shock. Bursting from a closet was Lillie's husband, Robert, armed with a cowhide whip in one hand and a navy revolver in the other. The aggrieved husband restrained his violent impulses and instead offered a proposition. Since Yonge had soiled his home, it would be proper for him to pay for an unsoiled one. In exchange for King's silence, Yonge would pay $5,500. According to the *Daily Avalanche*, "He was prepared for business and presented three notes for Mr. Yonge to sign." King also presented him with a deed of trust on a piece of property as collateral for the notes. Yonge signed the papers, but all the documents were dated August 22, which raised the concern of the real estate agent chosen by King to execute the deal. Consequently, Yonge was approached by both the agent and the police, who exposed the illegal scheme and forced King to hand over the notes.

September 2, 1949

New South Memphis School Opens

The board of education on this day opened Longview Heights, a new eight-grade grammar school in South Memphis, to alleviate overcrowding. The one-story building, constructed of fire-resistant concrete, was located near the Pine Hill Golf Course on Alice Avenue. It included an auditorium, twelve classrooms, a cafeteria, a teacher's workroom and a clinic. According to Jack Cooper of the *Commercial Appeal*, the "institution will draw its students from an area bounded roughly by Pine Hill Golf Course on the east, Person on the north, the Illinois Central Railroad on the west, and Mallory at the city limits on the south." Fourteen teachers were selected to staff the school, and the board chose as principal Treadwell High history teacher Margaret McCorkle, a Memphis State College graduate and an eighteen-year veteran of the school system. Superintendent Ball stated that "if a pupil wishes to transfer, he must register at the new school." Despite the fact that Longview Heights opened two years after the U.S. Supreme Court's *Brown v. Board of Education* decision banning segregated schools, African American pupils were not eligible to transfer there. The education board tentatively desegregated its schools in October 1961, but it was not until court-ordered busing was implemented in January 1973 that the Memphis City Schools were fully integrated.

September 3, 1970

Homemade Bombs Found in Overton Park

Police lieutenant Fred Murray was patrolling Overton Park on this day when he discovered three homemade bombs near the golf course clubhouse. Two of the bombs were inside metal strongboxes, and the third was housed in a five-gallon metal jerrycan. As the bomb squad assembled in the park, officers fired shots from a high-powered rifle into the devices to make sure they could be handled. Menno Duerksen of the *Press-Scimitar* wrote that each "bomb had a mechanism attached to it consisting of an alarm clock, a home-made switch mechanism, batteries and what appeared to be an electric blasting cap inside a steel pipe casing…Lt. Charles Moore of the crime scene squad, who has had bomb training, said the detonator boosters have not been opened and he can only assume what is inside. The gasoline-ammonium nitrate mixture, he said, is not dangerous unless set off by a booster detonator and this, presumably, is what is inside the iron pipes attached to the clocks." One of the bombs was later turned over to the Pace Corporation for examination by its explosives experts, while the other two were detonated by the police bomb disposal unit. Police apparently never learned who built the bombs or why they were placed in Overton Park.

September 4, 1971

Jerry Lee Lewis's Wife Remarries

Myra Gale Brown Lewis, cousin and former wife of rock 'n' roll pioneer Jerry Lee Lewis, on this day married the private detective hired to catalogue her estranged husband's infidelities. The wedding ceremony between Myra and Peter A. Malito was held at her parents' home nearly four months after she obtained a divorce from Lewis. They secretly married on December 12, 1957, and Myra quickly found herself adrift in a world she little understood. While accompanying her husband on tour, she wrote to her best friend, Barbara Ann Nance, from Chicago: "Everyone here is still in their winter clothes and in their big coats. You can't imagine how stupid I feel—almost everything I brought is white. I stick out like a sore thumb!" Their union angered Myra's parents and much of the population of the United States and Europe. The marriage, and ensuing scandal, nearly wrecked Lewis's career and took its toll on her as well. She endured years of abuse but finally had enough when, during a phone conversation with her wayward husband, she threatened to kill herself with a pearl-handled pistol, and he replied, "Put the phone close, so I can hear it go off."

September 5, 1969

Memphis Celebrates Its Sesquicentennial

Many Memphians spent the summer of 1969 buying souvenirs related to the city's 150th birthday celebration. Memphis Sesquicentennial Incorporated, the organization created to oversee the many celebratory events, authorized the creation of several keepsakes that were gobbled up by local collectors. These included whiskey decanters and envelopes with the official mural emblazoned on them as well as gold and silver coins with the official emblem on one side and images of Hernando DeSoto, Andrew Jackson and W.C. Handy on the other. Goldsmith's department store sold cuff links, tie tacks and ashtrays, while the Gulf Oil Company offered commemorative glassware with gas sales. Several major events also took place that generated excitement about Memphis's past. These included an award-winning float at the Tournament of Roses Parade, a log cabin in Court Square, the creation of a hiking trail to the city's historic sites, the publishing of a history of the Bluff City and the issuing of a stamp honoring Memphis's birthday, featuring W.C. Handy. According to Memphis Sesquicentennial president Howard Willey, who was elected the same day that Dr. Martin Luther King Jr. was assassinated, "When issues tended to divide our community, the event and work of our 150th Anniversary celebration formed the vehicle that would bring us together."

September 6, 1962

Historian Gets Something Off His Chest

Dr. Gerald Capers, historian and author of *Biography of a River Town*, on this day shared his feelings about his hometown with the *Press-Scimitar*'s Clark Porteous:

> *Since I left here 30 years ago, I have come back usually twice a year. I read the Memphis newspapers, hear the palaver on the buses, streets and at parties, and my mother regularly sends me clippings giving the local news. But there is something I have always wanted to get off my chest…Many a beautiful woman is short on brains and character. This is how Memphis strikes me. It's* [sic] *dominant note is one of pure "dee" country ignorance and prejudice….No large Southern city, in my opinion, so presents in bold relief the intellectual and esthetic poverty of the South as Memphis…in its 140 years of existence, has Memphis ever produced a poet, a novelist, a musician, an artist, a scientist or even a judge of national character? W.C. Handy might be so regarded, but its typical contributions to the national scene are Boss Ed Crump, Clarence Saunders, Richard Halliburton, Memphis Bill Terry, Machine Gun Kelly and now Elvis Presley.*

Capers apparently did not know, or never bothered to find out, the many contributions to science, the arts and industry that are included within the pages of this book.

September 7, 1981

Topless Kingpin Sentenced to Prison

Arthur Wayne Baldwin, Memphis's adult entertainment kingpin, was sentenced to prison on this day for income tax evasion. U.S. district court judge Robert M. McRae sentenced Baldwin to one year in state prison for failing to file an income tax return in 1978. Baldwin operated several topless dance clubs that spread prostitution and drugs into many parts of Memphis. In September 1979, the Internal Revenue Service began investigating Baldwin's finances after his home was burglarized and over $100,000 in cash was recovered from the break-in. While his finances were being looked into, Baldwin laid plans to firebomb the Follies Lounge, owned by rival vice lord Danny Owens. Indicted in September 1980, Baldwin was found guilty of conspiracy and sentenced to ten years in a federal penitentiary shortly before his income tax conviction. Baldwin pleaded guilty to conspiring to blow up the Classic Cat nightclub in Nashville, owned by his former wife. Shortly after his guilty plea, Baldwin announced he had become a Jehovah's Witness and was studying accounting. Released in 1987, Baldwin spent his remaining years attempting to overcome his criminal past. In the mid-1990s, he opened Chariots of Fire Christian School with his father and sister in nearby Earle, Arkansas. Upon his death in September 1997, his sister Martha Love stated that it was "sad that the public will never know the sweet and caring man who spent his last years lecturing young adults."

September 8, 1954

Integrated Shopping Center Opens

Plans for the grand opening of the Lamar-Airways Shopping Center were finalized on this day by owners Nathan and Herbert Shainberg and Ben Goldstein. Billed as the "South's largest integrated shopping center" a three-day extravaganza began at 9:00 a.m. on Thursday, September 9, when WMC radio and television personalities cut entrance ribbons to open Pic-Pac grocery, Katz Drug, Three Sister's women's clothing and nine other stores. Lamar Avenue was located on what had once been an American Indian trail, so the events included appearances by the Choctaw Ramblers and Chief Wishackchihumma and Princess Hushihumma of the Choctaw tribe. At seven o'clock that night, Mayor Frank Tobey formally dedicated the shopping center as thousands gathered in the parking lot. Afterward, they were introduced to a new singer named Elvis Presley. Unlike most mainstream white businesses, the Lamar-Airways Shopping Center did not ignore the African American community. On Friday evening, the main event was a music program hosted by WDIA's Rufus Thomas, Nat D. Williams and Theo "Bless My Bones" Wade. Coming four months after the Supreme Court outlawed school segregation, the opening of the Lamar-Airways center showed that Memphians could gather together peacefully in spite of the disabling legacy of racism.

September 9, 1977

Memphian Crowned Miss Black America

A Memphis State University sophomore was on this day crowned Miss Black America during a nationally televised competition at the Santa Monica, California Civic Auditorium. Claire D. Ford, daughter of Mr. and Mrs. Henry Claxton Ford, had previously won the Miss Black Memphis and Miss Black Tennessee titles before winning the national crown. The show was hosted by actor Billy Dee Williams, while singer Pearl Bailey, Lawrence Hilton-Jacobs of TV's *Welcome Back Kotter*, Dr. Joyce Brothers and football star Jim Brown served as judges. During the talent portion of the competition, Ford impressed the judges with her rendition of Quincy Jones's "Everything Must Change." In addition to the crown and title, Ford also won $10,000 and screen tests at Universal Pictures and NBC Television. Once her reign was completed, Ford graduated from Memphis State University in 1981 with a bachelor's degree in communication arts. For many years, she worked as the public relations manager for a local advertising agency, where she served as publicity director for *Today's Black Woman*, a nationally syndicated television program.

September 10, 1978

Fourth TV Station Begins Broadcasting

Memphis's fourth commercial television station, and the city's first to broadcast in ultra-high frequency, began its first day of programming at 7:00 a.m. with a show hosted by evangelist Jimmy Swaggart. Located at 2225 Union Avenue, WPTY channel 24 was owned by Delta Television Corporation, a subsidiary of New York's Petry Television. In addition to several religious programs, the station broadcast Popeye cartoons, the Three Stooges, an Elvis movie, Mississippi State football highlights and a half-hour introduction to the new station entitled *Hello Memphis*. The *Commercial Appeal* reported that to "pick up WPTY, first turn the set's tuning knob to the position labeled UHF, between channels 2 and 13. That position puts a separate UHF tuning dial—usually on the side or top of a set—into active use. The UHF tuners on late model TV sets click into place at each channel number between 18 and 83. On these sets, simply turn the tuner to 24." WPTY remained an independent television station until December 1, 1995, when it became an American Broadcasting Company affiliate after the Fox Network purchased Memphis's longtime ABC station WHBQ.

September 11, 1982

Medicine Man Returns from Spiritual Quest

Sam Bielich, described by the *Commercial Appeal*'s Al Dunning as a "career sophomore, part-time model and full-time wacko at Memphis sporting events," returned to the Bluff City after an alleged spiritual quest to "get his head straight." In the summer of 1981, Bielich was attending a Memphis Chicks baseball game when, after drinking a snootful of beer, he wandered onto the field and "started spelling out C-H-I-C-K-S. It was amazing. The crowd really gets into spelling out Chicks," Bielich later explained. Shortly thereafter, he donned an American Indian costume and began cheering at many sporting events. Calling himself "the Medicine Man," he quickly became a fixture at Memphis State University football contests and Chicks baseball games until he briefly disappeared in the summer of 1982. The new Medicine Man debuted during the Vanderbilt–Memphis State football game, and he soon began appearing in local car commercials. Bielich continued his sporting appearances until early 1984, when both the Chicks and Memphis State refused to pay him for his antics. He eventually left Memphis, changed his name to Sam Ayers and became a professional actor. Bielich/Ayers appeared in several soap operas and had a recurring role in the NBC television series *The Pretender*, which ran from 1996 to 2000.

September 12, 1921

Chicks Win Southern League Pennant

The Chickasaw baseball club won the Southern League championship by defeating the Birmingham Barons three runs to two on this day. Herbert Caldwell of the *Commercial Appeal* reported that "Spencer Arthur Abbott, Chief of the Chickasaws, making his debut as a manager in the Southern League, and his gallant tribe, established Southern League history when they won for Memphis its first championship since 1904." In that championship season, the Chicks led the league from their opening-day victory against Little Rock on April 14 until the final contest against Birmingham. The Tribe finished the season having won 101 games and lost a mere 46. Barons pitcher Phil Morrison stymied the Tribe for most of the game, but Birmingham's fortunes changed in the bottom of the ninth when Morrison walked Rhino Williams and gave up three singles to Chicks McLarry, Brown and Camp, which put the Tribe over the top for the game and the championship. In addition to the 1904 and 1921 pennants, the Memphis Chickasaws also won Southern League championships in 1924, 1930, 1953 and 1955.

September 13, 1976

Disc Jockey Fired from WMPS Radio

Popular radio entertainer Rick Dees, whom *People* magazine called the "Confederate Woody Allen," was fired for promoting his hit record "Disco Duck" on his morning program. Known for his imitation of Elvis Presley singing the praises of jelly donuts, announcing the hourly temperature in "Dees-grees" and playing a recording of Mayor Wyeth Chandler saying in a thick southern drawl, "Yes, suh, Mistuh Dees" in answer to any outlandish question that popped in his head. At the time of his firing, WMPS was the number-one radio station in Memphis, and "Disco Duck" was number eight on *Billboard* magazine's Top 40 record charts. The song reached number one on October 16, soon after WMPS's main competitor, WHBQ, signed Dees to a lucrative contract. "Disco Duck" appeared in the film *Saturday Night Fever*, and in February 1977, it won a People's Choice Award for favorite new song. Dees continued to broadcast over WHBQ until April 1979, when he was hired by KHL Radio in Los Angeles. Rick Dees's career not only influenced the culture of the Bluff City but also, in a small way, fused Memphis-style rhythm with disco music to create one of the most successful novelty songs in the history of American popular culture.

September 14, 1953

Biblemobile Slides through Memphis

The Memphis Union Mission's mobile chapel pulled up in front of Memphis Technical High School at 8:02 a.m. and conducted a brief Bible lesson and gospel singing for any student who wished Christian fortification before classes began. In addition to Tech, the Biblemobile parked in front of Central, South Side, Humes, East and Treadwell High Schools each week. Union Mission superintendent Jimmy Stroud stated that the services were "a singing and inspirational session, designed for youth. The Memphis Union Mission was founded by Stroud on June 17, 1945, at 107–11 Poplar Avenue. Jimmy Stroud came to Memphis after serving as assistant superintendent at the Charleston, West Virginia Union Mission. The *Press-Scimitar*'s Eldon Roark stated that "few people have led a more sacrificial life than Jimmy. He has done great work in keeping Union Mission going, helping people in all walks of life, but especially down-and-outers."

September 15, 1956

States Rights' Party Convenes in Memphis

The National States' Rights Party concluded its conference at the Chisca Hotel on this day. The 325 delegates from across the country excoriated the two major parties and selected its presidential and vice presidential nominees. For president, the group chose T. Coleman Andrews of Richmond, Virginia, and Thomas H. Werdell of Bakersfield, California, received the nod for the second spot. Included in the delegation were Tennesseans Ed Worthington of the Memphis White Citizens' Council and Tennessee Federation for Constitutional Government member Sims Crownover, who declared Governor Frank Clement a "traitor" for sending the National Guard to enforce school desegregation in the town of Clinton. The delegates also adopted a platform that called for restricting the power of the federal government, especially its authority to levy taxes. Several speakers echoed this fear of the central government, including conservative candy manufacturer Robert H.W. Welch. Thomas Michael of the *Commercial Appeal* reported that "all took the same general text—that America is headed for socialism, or worse, and will not be turned from that course by either the Republicans or the Democrats."

September 16, 1915

Nervous Deputy Given Pistol

Fritz Aehle, former sales executive for a local brewery, on this day was appointed a courtroom deputy by Sheriff John Reichman. Once the oath was administered, Reichman informed Aehle that he would have to secure a pistol to carry while on duty. The former salesman protested that he didn't know how to use firearms and consequently refused to secure one. Amused by Aehle's refusal, the sheriff and some of his deputies conspired with criminal court judge William Bacon to pull a joke on the nervous deputy. Judge Bacon ordered Aehle to join him in the criminal court clerk's office where a group of deputies and court officials were waiting. When Aehle arrived, Bacon said, "I have a little present for you." As reported by the *Commercial Appeal*: "The others took off their hats and stood around Fritz in a solemn manner. Fritz was somewhat abashed but stood his ground…'We are going to present you a pistol,' continued the judge, 'as it is incumbent upon you to tote one. Out of respect to your nationality we have ordered one of the latest improved German weapons.' Then Judge Bacon reached into his desk and pulled out an old flint-lock, single-barrel pistol about two feet long…Fritz is not a gun expert, but he saw in a moment that the weapon belonged to some curio shop. His face reddened. 'The drinks are on me,' he blushed."

September 17, 1930

Tributes Paid to Bishop Gailor

On this day, 230 people attended a banquet at the Hotel Peabody to honor Memphian Thomas F. Gailor, Episcopal bishop for the state of Tennessee. The highlight of the evening came when Bishop Gailor outlined the course of his life. The *Commercial Appeal* reported that the prelate began his address by saying, "My memory carries me back to the days when Main Street was mud, and when carriages were often stuck in the mire at the corner of Main and Adams Street. I have lived through the Civil War and the conditions which followed in its wake. We must remember that the Civil War was the greatest in all history and we must not be disturbed by the unsettled conditions now." Gailor graduated from Memphis High School and attended the General Theological Seminary in New York. While there, a church in Chicago recruited him for its pulpit. Unsure of what to do, Gailor wrote to Bishop Charles Todd Quintard, who replied, "The devil's after you; come home." Taking Quintard's advice, Gailor returned to the Volunteer State, where he preached at a small church in Pulaski. In 1883, he became chaplain for the University of the South in Sewanee and later was appointed chancellor. When Quintard died in 1898, Gailor was named as his successor. For the rest of his, life Bishop Gailor divided his time between Memphis and Sewanee until he died on October 3, 1935.

September 18, 1908

Jefferson Theater Opens

A new theater opened at 293 Madison Avenue. Named for Joseph Jefferson, the venue was managed by well-known impresario A.B. Morrison. The first play performed was Francois Villon's *If I Were King*, starring Sidney Toler, who later portrayed Chinese detective Charlie Chan in a series of popular films. As movies became more popular than stage plays, the Jefferson changed its name to the Lyric and was forced to offer vaudeville productions as well as boxing and wrestling matches to keep its doors open. These attractions, however, were not enough to keep the theater profitable, so in 1928, it closed. Three years later, the building was purchased by the Junior Order of American Mechanics. The organization defaulted on its contract, which led to its foreclosure in April 1940. The city purchased the abandoned theater for $12,958, but before it could decide what to do with the building, it was destroyed during a winter lightning storm. The *Press-Scimitar*'s Clark Porteous wrote: "There have been some great shows at the 33-year-old Lyric Theater…Ben Hur with real horses on the stage running on a turntable, Shakespearean plays and the like. But probably the most spectacular show ever seen was the tragic grand finale of the old yellow brick playhouse last night—the five alarm blaze that gutted the theater where Memphis and the Mid-South in bygone years applauded the great and near-great of the entertainment world.

September 19, 1969

Rufus Thomas Bridges the Generation Gap

An aide to President Richard Nixon on this day asked WDIA disc jockey and Stax recording artist Rufus Thomas to join a committee of radio personalities charged with drafting an antinarcotics program for the United States. Thomas was one of nine disc jockeys chosen by presidential aide Bud Wilkinson to serve on the antidrug task force. "I am one of two black men selected for the position, and the only one from the Mid-South states," Thomas explained. The soul singer further stated that "music is the basic thing that kids like...Somewhere, disk jockeys can get down there and talk their language and show it to them. Communications is the only way to bridge the generation gap. We hope to get the message across with posters, book covers, book markers, bumper stickers and many other visual aids." Rufus Thomas was one of the most significant performers in the history of Memphis music. In 1953, his song "Bear Cat" was Sun Records first major hit months before Sam Phillips recorded Elvis. With his daughter Carla, he recorded "'Cause I Love You" for Satellite Records, which later changed its name to Stax. At Stax, he recorded many important soul songs, including "Walking the Dog." Seven months before he died on December 15, 2001, the eighty-four-year-old Thomas told an audience at Memphis in May's Beale Street Music Festival that "W.C. Handy wrote the blues a long time ago. He passed them on to me, and now I'm passing them on to you."

September 20, 1886

Higbee School's New Term Begins

Classes began on this day at the Higbee School for Young Ladies located in the Robertson Topp mansion on Beale Street near the intersection of Lauderdale. The students returned to find the schools' main building completely renovated. The *Daily Appeal* explained that the "double story building, containing seven commodious, light and airy apartments, has been added for the use of the boarders, and the space heretofore reserved for their occupancy will hereafter be used for classrooms." Jenny M. Higbee came to Memphis in 1865 and was hired as principal of the Memphis High School. A decade later, she was appointed principal of the Presbyterian Grammar School, and she later founded her own private institution. Higbee died in 1903, but two of her teachers, Hattie L. White and Mary E. Pimm, kept the school open until 1914. Robertson Topp, a lawyer and real estate promoter, arrived in Memphis in 1831. He purchased a section of land near the city and developed the Town of South Memphis, which was absorbed by Memphis in 1850. Topp also built the Gayoso House Hotel and served as president of the Memphis & Ohio Railroad. Robertson Topp died in 1876, and his home became the Higbee School for Young Ladies the following year.

September 21, 1963

Tigers Smash Ole Miss Offense

For seventeen straight years, the University of Mississippi Rebels defeated the Memphis State Tigers in the mid-South's most popular football rivalry. But on this day, fortune favored Memphis over the Southeastern Conference champion Ole Miss Rebels. According to the *Commercial Appeal*'s Charles Gillespie, the two rivals "pounded one another for four quarters, with no quarter offered, and the result was a 0–0 standoff, the first great shock of the 1963 intercollegiate football season." Over the course of the game, the Tigers' defensive line successfully kept the Rebels' offense from gaining sufficient ground to score. When it was all said and done Ole Miss was only able to move fifty-seven yards down the field. During the first half, the Rebels were stopped cold one yard from the Memphis State goal line, and later, Ole Miss players were stunned to watch Tigers sophomore halfback Bob Sherlag intercept a pass, which again prevented them from scoring. The upset did not prevent Ole Miss from capturing the 1963 SEC crown, but it did keep them from achieving a national championship.

September 22, 1880

Thugs Terrorize Church

The *Daily Appeal* reported that the Alabama Street Presbyterian Church has been harassed by a gang of ruffians on Sunday mornings. They began by stretching wire across the sidewalk near the church, which tripped and seriously injured several parishioners, many of them women, but on September 19, they graduated to a more outrageous form of harassment. According to the newspaper, "The scoundrels last Sunday smeared the steps of the church, and even the windows, with human excrement, to the disgust of worshipers, many of whom have been made sick by the stench thus raised. Anything more brutal and infamous than this has seldom fallen under our notice. A church dedicated to the worship of God should always be held sacred—sacred especially from defilement." The editorial writer went on to describe the perpetrators as "filthy young beasts who degrade human nature" who should be punished by having "forty lashes well laid on by an experienced hand." The Alabama Street Presbyterian Church was organized on July 23, 1868, by Dr. J.O. Stedman. In 1925, the congregation moved to a new building at the corner of Claybrook Street and Poplar Avenue and was renamed Grace Covenant Church. Eleven years later, in 1936, Grace merged with First Presbyterian Church, located at Third Street and Poplar Avenue, which was first organized in 1828.

September 23, 1926

Prohibition Agents Raid Mississippi River Islands

When the sale and manufacture of alcohol was prohibited in the United States, enterprising moonshiners and bootleggers used many of the isolated Mississippi River islands to pour booze into Memphis. This was a constant problem for federal Prohibition agent Alvin J. Howe, who joined forces with the U.S. Coast Guard to enforce the Prohibition statute. Prohibition Bureau supervisor Hiram Sutterfield joined Howe, Captain C.C. Lee and six handpicked men and boarded U.S. Patrol Boat AB8 to cruise down the river searching for illegal activity. At Josie Harris Island, located twelve miles south of Memphis, they found a 2,000-gallon still, 7,000 gallons of mash and 610 gallons of whiskey, all of which they destroyed with dynamite. A similar setup was also found and destroyed on Centennial Island. The *Commercial Appeal* reported: "[The] prohibition agents are investigating a war between moonshiners of the upper end of Island 40 where a recent raid was staged. Following the destruction of [a] 1,000-gallon still several days ago, the agents returned this week and got another outfit, presumably erected by the same owners."

Howe hoped that the increased number of raids against the river island moonshiners would "make Memphis a dry city in which to live." Despite Howe's best efforts, however, the Mississippi bootleggers bedeviled the Prohibition Bureau until the federal anti-liquor amendment was repealed in 1933.

September 24, 1937

Police Ban on Private Dicks Lifted

Police commissioner Clifford Davis announced on this day that the police department had reversed its yearlong policy of refusing to issue special commissions to operatives from the Fox-Pelletier International Detective Agency, which allowed them to legally carry firearms while on duty. Davis stated to the press that the "rules which we are issuing commissions to special officers does not permit a concern to mix detective work with night patrol work." So Fox-Pelletier agreed to abandon private detective work and offer only night patrol services to its clients. The agency was formed by George L. Pelletier and his partner, John Fox, in 1928, after both had worked for the Memphis Police Department for several years. Born in Indianapolis, Pelletier spent twenty-one years working as a stage comedian in vaudeville before becoming a private detective in 1921. Three years later, he married the stepdaughter of Memphis police inspector Will Griffin and joined the city's detective bureau. Rising to the rank of lieutenant, Pelletier worked in the auto theft bureau until his resignation. When he died in July 1939, the *Press-Scimitar* recounted that in "1927 he worked on the case of a man suspected of having stolen Birmingham bonds. The man would tell detectives nothing, so Mr. Pelletier, remembering an attorney role he had once played on the stage, got some glasses with a ribbon, a brief case and a 'phony' card, and introduced himself to the man as 'No. 1 mouthpiece.' The suspect told him everything."

September 25, 1970

Ed Sullivan Show *Broadcasted from Memphis*

Ed Sullivan, host of the most popular variety program in the history of network television, taped his weekly show at Blues Stadium as part of the Mid-South Fair. Recording began at 3:30 p.m. after three days of rehearsals. Several well-known entertainers appeared on the show, including Loretta Lynn, Arthur Godfrey, former Miss America Judi Ford and Archie Campbell of TV's *Hee-Haw*. During the taping, there was an anxious moment when a helium truck, used to fill balloons for the opening segment, caught fire. It quickly was brought under control and the show continued without further problems. After the Blues Stadium show, a film crew recorded Sullivan and his wife walking through the fairgrounds and talking with people. Associate producer Jack McGeehan said that they decided to film a show at a fair and "Memphis came highly recommended...We've gotten more cooperation and more general feeling of welcome in Memphis than anywhere we've taken the show in 11 years. Everyone keeps thanking us, asking if they can help." During an interview in his dressing room, Sullivan echoed his producer when he said, "We're having a wonderful time in Memphis."

September 26, 1943

Women's Army Corps Volunteers Called to Duty

The War Department on this day ordered 12 members of the Women's Army Corps, all from Memphis or the mid-South, to report to the Second WAC Training Center in Daytona Beach, Florida. Alma Acuragi, Elece Williams, May Overton, Olivia Rowland, Willie McNutt, Claire E. Long, Ruth E. Taylor, Nancy B. Robertson, Agnes Lyon, Grace A. Hicks, Marguerite Snyder and Louise H. Webb were some of the many Memphians who served in the Women's Army Corps during World War II. One such Memphian was Lina Farley Rhodes, who gave up her position as Mayor Walter Chandler's secretary to enlist in the WACs on March 20, 1943. After her training, she was assigned to the combat crew orderly room at Dyersburg Army Air Field, where she served until her discharge on April 12, 1945. These brave women were among the 150,000 females who served honorably doing essential work in the Women's Army Corps during the Second World War.

September 27, 1918

Memphian Awarded Distinguished Service Cross

Near Bellicourt, France, Memphian Orvil L. Cotten, a corporal with Company C, 105th Signal Battalion, exhibited bravery in the face of the enemy, which led to President Woodrow Wilson awarding him the Distinguished Service Cross. According to his citation, "In order to maintain communications between two regiments of infantry and, after an assisting detachment had suffered severe causalities, Corporal Cotten alone kept the line in repair, working under constant shellfire. Although badly gassed, he refused evacuation, requesting and obtaining permission to continue his work." Impressed with his heroism, King George V and the British High Command also decorated Cotten with the military medal. Born in Falkner, Mississippi, on March 27, 1896, as a young man, Cotten moved to Memphis, where he took a job as a cable man for the Cumberland Telephone Company. After the war, he continued his communications career by becoming a repairman with the Southern Bell Telephone and Telegraph Company. Cotten later was promoted to foreman and supervisor before retiring after forty-five years of service. Cotten died on April 6, 1992, at the age of ninety-six. Twenty other Memphians also were awarded the Distinguished Service Cross during the First World War.

September 28, 1938

Memphis Yugoslavian Remembered for His Parade Floats
While Memphians followed the negotiations between Great Britain and Nazi Germany over the fate of ethnic Germans living in Czechoslovakia, the *Press-Scimitar* interviewed Yugoslavian immigrant Mike Abt about his views on the European crisis: "It's been a long time since I was there and I'm not absolutely in touch with the situation. But I will say this, the Czech people are mild, peaceful and home-loving, but they will fight…They are patriotic and fearless. If they ever take up arms, it will be a war of annihilation. They will never surrender." Abt immigrated to the United States in 1910, when he was thirteen years old. An honors graduate of the Cleveland School of Art, in 1920, Abt and a group of fellow artists bought a boat and floated down the Mississippi River to sketch the countryside. When they arrived in Memphis, Abt decided to stay, and two years later, he was hired to be an art teacher at Tech High School. Although a talented artist and teacher, Abt was beloved for the beautiful and intricate floats he created for the Cotton Carnival and Spirit of Christmas parades. When he died in 1952, columnist Eldon Roark said that Abt "had a wonderful sense of humor, and he got a kick out of life's little absurdities as well as out of its beauty."

September 29, 1962

Fantastic Features Debuts on WHBQ-TV

At 6:00 p.m. on this day, many Memphians turned their TV dials to channel 13 to watch *The Giant Behemoth*, a B-grade horror movie. In addition to the film's "giant radioactive sea creature," the audience was also introduced to the show's "monster of ceremonies," who quickly became one of the most beloved characters in Memphis history. For the first time on that Saturday evening, viewers heard the menacing theme from the science fiction movie *Destination Moon* as they watched a man wearing a top hat drive a horse-drawn hearse through a tree-lined road in Overton Park. The scene then cut to a close-up that revealed the man's long fangs as he pulled a casket from the hearse. The casket was then opened, and as smoke whirled out of the wooden box, the scene faded to the blood-dripped words "Fantastic Features." "Gooooood eeevening, I am Sivad," the host intoned as he introduced the movie. For a generation of Memphians, those opening scenes were indelibly etched on their minds as the scariest thing they ever saw when young. The show was created by WHBQ program director Lance Russell, who "came up with the idea of…running a series that would draw…the younger audience, with some kind of science fiction and horror movies." Russell chose Malco Movie Theatre advertising executive Watson Davis to host the show, and Davis adopted the stage name of Sivad, his last name spelled backwards. The show ran until February 5, 1972.

September 30, 1988

Attorney General Resigns Post

Mike Cody was appointed U.S. attorney by President Jimmy Carter in 1977.

Memphian W.J. Michael Cody ended his term as Tennessee's attorney general on this day after serving four years. Born in Memphis in 1936, Cody attended Rhodes College and the University of Virginia Law School. The following year, he returned to Memphis, where he practiced law with noted attorney Lucius Burch. In 1968, he represented Dr. Martin Luther King Jr. when the city blocked a proposed march during the sanitation strike. Elected to the Memphis City Council in 1975, he was appointed U.S. attorney by President Jimmy Carter in 1977. As attorney general for Tennessee, Cody stopped a North Carolina paper mill from discharging waste into a Tennessee River and reformed state prisons. According to Richard Locker of the *Commercial Appeal*, "It was Cody's adherence, sometimes courageous adherence, to principles of ethics in government that will remain the hallmark of his service."

October 1, 1978

Mud Boy and the Neutrons Calls It Quits

One of the city's most influential musical groups, Mud Boy and the Neutrons, ended its ill-starred career with a concert at the Orpheum Theatre. Mud Boy was founded by guitarist Lee Baker, washboard player Jimmy Crosthwait, pianist Jim Dickinson and guitarist Sid Selvidge in 1972. According to the *Commercial Appeal*'s Walter Dawson, the "group wanted to bring attention to the area's blues legacy and to see that the surviving bluesmen were able to work and get at least part of what was coming to them." Selvidge stated that they had "been promoting old black folks for years and never taken a nickel from 'em and at great expense to ourselves…We've been knocking city hall over the head since nineteen sixty-whatever, and all of a sudden…it's in their own, lily-white, East-Memphis interest to be downtown and the old bluesmen can help 'em sell it… now it's finally come down to where they say, 'Well, we can't control them (Mud Boy). They're white boys, and we don't want 'em.'" Despite these hard feelings, Baker, Crosthwait, Dickinson and Selvidge continued to promote the blues and make important contributions to Memphis music for decades after Mud Boy and the Neutrons came to an end.

October 2, 1920

Lawlessness on the Decline

For eight months, chief of police Joe Burney dodged questions about the operation of his department, preferring, in his words, to "carry out the duties of my office." Burney reported that the "law abiding people of Memphis are taking an interest in the conduct of the city and are co-operating as never before with this department in an effort to make Memphis a good place in which decent men and women can make their homes and raise their families." As a result of this improvement in "moral conditions," gambling, illegal liquor sales and prostitution were in decline since the beginning of 1920. The police chief also reported that morale among police officers had improved because of a promise by police commissioner John B. Edgar to raise salaries and the elimination of the requirement that officers had to actively campaign for the faction in power during election season. "The commissioner doesn't know how the men are going to vote in the November election. Neither do I—and we don't want to know. But we both know they will play no part in seeking votes or interfering with voters on one side or the other," the police chief explained. Despite Burney's assurances, political campaigning remained a requirement of some city workers until Memphis voters forbade the practice in 1966.

October 3, 1927

Lucky Lindy Lands in Memphis

Charles Lindbergh, the famed aviator whose daring flight across the Atlantic from New York to Paris had electrified the world, landed in Memphis during a nationwide tour designed to promote the growth of American aviation. Lindy's Spirit of St. Louis plane touched down at Armstrong Field at 2:00 p.m. after spending several minutes circling the downtown business district. Those watching from the Columbian Mutual Tower received a special thrill when Lindbergh came within one hundred yards of the structure. After landing, the Lone Eagle was whisked to Overton Park, where thousands watched as Mayor Rowlett Paine welcomed him. Lindbergh spoke on the importance of aviation and the need for modern airports. With his speech concluded, Lindbergh introduced Captain H.E. Lackey, commanding officer of the USS *Memphis*, which brought the famed aviator back from France after his epic flight. The citizens of Memphis donated funds for a silver tea service, which was presented to Captain Lackey by a group of local Boy Scouts. A parade and banquet followed, and then Lindbergh spent the night in the Peabody Hotel before continuing his nationwide tour. His visit had a profound effect on the Bluff City. The need for an airport was made apparent, and in 1928, the Memphis Municipal Airport was opened.

October 4, 1911

Rain Dampens Final Day of Tri-State Fair

A heavy downpour marred the final day of the 1911 Tri-State Fair. According to the *Commercial Appeal*, the last day was "to end in one big flare of glory, unexcelled in the history of Memphis. The Marine Band had been secured at an enormous cost." A vaudeville troupe was scheduled to conduct midair acrobatics, but they were the first to cancel when the rain began. The marine band, however, was made of sterner stuff. It performed under the clouds until the rain became too heavy and then retreated to the covered stands, where it finished its concert. For a century and a half, Memphians embraced the Tri-State Fair, which began in 1856. In 1929, the name was changed to the Mid-South Fair, and in 2008, it left Memphis for north Mississippi.

Begun in 1856, the Tri-State Fair became the Mid-South Fair in 1929.

October 5, 1931

Nine-Year-Old Girl Loses Job

The youngest person ever chosen to select members of the Shelby County Grand Jury lost her position when the Tennessee General Assembly repealed the law requiring "a child under 12 years of age draw the names of the grand jury from a box." The law pressing children into this service was passed by the legislature in 1929, after Tennessee governor Henry Horton appointed Edgar Webster judge of the first Shelby County criminal court. Both Horton and Webster were enemies of Memphis political boss E.H. Crump, who feared the judge would select grand juries hostile to his organization. So the Shelby delegation to the general assembly, which owed its allegiance to Crump, passed a bill eliminating the judge's power to select grand juries. Webster chose Josephine Hicks, nine-year-old daughter of Deputy C.L. Hicks, to make the selections, and she remained at her post even after Webster was defeated by Crump candidate Phil Wallace in 1930. The following year, the legislature repealed the law, leaving Josephine without a job. The *Evening Appeal* reported on this day that Judge Wallace was so impressed with his young selector that he presented her with a gold wristwatch for her service.

October 6, 1946

Jewish Community Honors War Sacrifice

The congregation of Baron Hirsch synagogue unveiled a monument on this day to their fellow members who died serving the Allied cause in World War II. The ceremony, overseen by Shelby County attorney general Will Gerber, began when a navy color guard removed an American flag draped over the monument while a firing squad discharged a salute and the sound of "Taps" drifted through the cemetery. After Reverend M. Levin chanted the Al Morahmin, Baron Hirsch rabbi Dr. Isadore Goodman read the names of Sergeant Paul Goldstein, Master Sergeant Eugene Klibanoff, Lieutenant Leo Malkin, Petty Officer Paul Policha, Sergeant Charles N. Rosenblum, Private Charles Strauch, Corporal Harry Washer and Private Ervin Weis. In dedicating the monument, Major General Arthur A. White declared that the sacrifice made by these Jewish Memphians "was a demonstration of courage, character and manhood that will forever reflect credit upon American youth...it is a fitting thing that there should be some such tangible symbol of the love and respect we bear them. In a deeper sense, however, that memorial must be engraved in our hearts...We must not fail them in safeguarding the principles for which they fought and died."

October 7, 1981

Grand Opening of the Mall of Memphis

The mid-South's largest enclosed shopping mall opened on this day in southeastern Memphis near Parkway Village. Thousands of Memphians flocked to the grand opening of the one-million-square-foot, $85 million shopping facility. Development of the facility began in 1972, when Stanley Trezevant and James Bridger purchased thirty acres of land at Interstate 240 and Perkins Road, and construction began in September 1979. With its movie theater, ice skating rink, restaurant, food court, video arcade, department stores and specialty shops, the Mall of Memphis became, in effect, the city's new main street, where Memphians of diverse backgrounds mingled with their rural neighbors as both shopped and looked for amusement. By the 1990s, a series of crimes at and near the shopping center earned it the nickname "Mall of Murder," which, along with declining sales and the loss of several important tenants, forced the mall to close on December 24, 2003.

October 8, 1942

Seven People Allowed to Buy New Cars

The Shelby County Rationing Board on this day gave permission for seven new automobiles to be purchased in Memphis. According to the *Commercial Appeal*, three companies—Mid-South Concrete Pipe, S. K. Jones Construction and the Southern Cotton Oil—were issued permits along with the Naval Reserve Aviation Base. Also receiving the new car nod was heavy equipment operator L.A. Green; John C. Ryall, supervisor at the National Fireworks Company; and motor patrol operator Harry A. Sinclair." Not long after the Japanese attack on Pearl Harbor and America's entry into World War II, the Office of Price Administration rationed the sale and use of rubber tires, which also restricted consumers' abilities to purchase automobiles. In May 1942, gasoline was rationed, which further inhibited car sales as well as driving. The *Commercial Appeal* reported that in October 1943, the local rationing board sanctioned Memphians Roy Appling, Ruby F. Nelson, H.H. Splawn and Edgar Lee Wynne for "misusing supplemental gasoline ration coupons to go to night clubs near the Mississippi-Tennessee state line."

October 9, 1977

Noted Artist Dewitt Jordan Shot

An argument exploded into gunfire on this day, killing forty-four-year-old Dewitt Jordan, one of the most celebrated artists to ever reside in Memphis. Arrested for murder was Jimmy Richard Edwards, who admitted to firing the fatal bullet but claimed self-defense. The police report explained: "Jordan and Edwards' sister, Ms. Connie Gidwani, were engaged…. An argument developed after Jordan said he wanted Ms. Gidwani to go to East Tennessee with him…Edwards told officers the argument became heated and Jordan picked up a small hammer from a nearby table and threatened him. Edwards pulled a pistol…and the gun discharged, striking Jordan."

Chesley Monroe Edwards, the shooter's father, confirmed his son's version of the events, but his daughter disagreed. Contacted by the *Commercial Appeal*'s Jerome Wright, Gidwani stated that the gun was brought to the house to protect her from prowlers, and it accidently went off when Edwards was showing her and Jordan how to use it. Ranked one of the top-ten artists in the United States by *Time* magazine, Jordan painted several important works, including his masterpiece *Birth of the Blues*. In 1968, he explained that he liked "to paint all of God's children…Negroes say I degrade them because I do pictures of the old stereotype. Whites say I'm trying to use my art to get the Negroes to rise up…But that's my heritage. Hell, man, that's the South."

October 10, 1979

Beloved Memphian Killed by Reckless Driver

Anthony "Monk" Cassata was immortalized in Carroll Cloar's 1964 painting *Historic Encounter Between E. H. Crump and W.C. Handy on Beale Street.*

Anthony Cassata, known affectionately to generations of Memphians as "Monk," died after being run down by a careless driver. Monk was crossing Madison Avenue when an automobile ran into Cassata, throwing him several feet into the air. Rushed to Baptist Hospital on Union Avenue, he was pronounced dead at 1:00 a.m. on this day. Monk was a beloved figure in Memphis. In 1964, he was immortalized in Carroll Cloar's painting *Historic Encounter between E.H. Crump and W.C. Handy on Beale Street.* Cloar stated that he "included Monk in the painting along with Crump, Shifty Logan and others famous in the 1930s and '40s because he was a part of Memphis." Monsignor Paul Clunan of St. Louis Catholic Church echoed Cloar when he said Monk "was as much a part of Memphis as the Mississippi River—a simple person who had the purity of a child."

October 11, 1954

African American Physician Honored

The *Commercial Appeal* reported on this day that the African American Tri-State Fair honored Dr. Miles Vanderhorst Lynk for his sixty-three years of service to the medical profession. Thousands watched as Dr. B.F. McCleave, president of the Bluff City Medical Society, delivered a moving tribute to the famed black physician. Lynk began his medical practice in Jackson, Tennessee, where he also started a medical school for African Americans called the University of West Tennessee. In order to expand and attract more students, Lynk moved his college to Memphis in 1907. The leading black physicians in Memphis served on the faculty, including one of the first women to practice medicine in the city, Dr. Fanny M. Kneeland. The school issued 216 medical degrees before it closed in 1924, which greatly improved health care for African Americans in Memphis. Dr. Miles V. Lynk continued to practice medicine until his death in 1948. A historical marker honoring his life was erected in Memphis by the Tennessee Historical Commission in 1996.

October 12, 1950

Juror Protests Light Sentence

Jesse D. O'Dell on this day appeared before Judge Sam D. Campbell and pleaded guilty to a charge of drunk driving. With the guilty plea in hand, Assistant Attorney General Marvin Goff, Jr. outlined the case against Dell and then recommended to the jury a fine of seventy-five dollars and court costs. Judge Campbell then asked the jury to be sworn in if it agreed with Goff's recommendation. Instead, one juror, radio announcer Paul Dorman, asked a question: "Is that all he's going to get?" The judge said, yes, and Dorman replied, "Then he's going to walk out of here and drive again?" The judge answered this second question by ordering the broadcaster out of the courtroom. Speaking to reporters, Dorman stated he thought a small fine was little more than a slap on the wrist: "I think they should take away his license for six months at least." The newsmen explained to Dorman that anyone convicted of driving under the influence automatically lost their driving privileges. "I wasn't told that by the judge," he explained. Paul Dorman began his broadcasting career at WREC radio in December 1943. He made the transition to television, anchoring the weekend evening news on WREG-TV until his retirement in 1984.

October 13, 1971

Police Raid Whirlaway Club

Police officials organized a raid on the Whirlaway Club at 3092 Lamar on this day. When police arrived the following night, they discovered two scantily clad dancers in the middle of a striptease routine. Shirley Ann McDaniel had just finished stripping and was "bumping and grinding" while wearing pasties and sheer black panties when vice detectives arrived on the scene. The detectives also witnessed Mary Kathleen Selph, wearing a Confederate flag cape and blue see-through costume, strip to pasties and a G-string. The two dancers were arrested and charged with indecent exposure. The owner of the club, John Jones Ogden, was also arrested and was charged with allowing a lewd act. The three defendants appeared before city court judge Ray W. Churchill on October 27. After hearing testimony, Churchill dismissed the charges against McDaniel and Selph because the city ordinance defined indecendent exposure as "appearing nude in public" and since they were not in public, nor completely nude, the law did not apply. "As long as they have some clothes on they are not nude," the judge declared. Churchill also dismissed the charge against Ogden since the dancers were not guilty of committing a lewd act. Billed as Memphis's oldest nightclub, the Whirlaway was opened in 1947 by Ogden and his wife, Jean, and closed in 1976. The Whirlaway was one of the first nightclubs in Memphis to offer topless dancers, strobe lights and a full floorshow.

October 14, 1987

Gospel Composer Moves on Up

One of the most prolific composers in the history of Gospel music died in Memphis. Dr. William Herbert Brewster, pastor of East Trigg Avenue Baptist Church, was internationally recognized for his songwriting abilities but only wanted to be known as "God's sharecropper." Born in rural West Tennessee in 1897 to the son of a slave, Brewster became a minister while still a teenager, giving his first sermon at Smith Chapel Baptist Church on September 30, 1914. In January 1925, he moved to Memphis to preside over Pilgrim Baptist Church. In 1930, he also became pastor of East Trigg Baptist Church, and while serving both congregations, he began to write gospel songs for his parishioners to perform. Inspired by the music of W.C. Handy, Brewster incorporated Memphis-style blues into his compositions, making them very popular beyond the confines of his churches. Performing at a church convention in Chicago in 1946, his song "Move on up a Little Higher" was heard by gospel singer Mahalia Jackson, who later recorded it. "Move on up a Little Higher" was the first gospel recording to sell over one million copies, and it solidified Brewster's place as a leading gospel composer. He would go on to write over two hundred songs and inspire many musicians, including a young Elvis Presley, who often visited East Trigg church. Noted musicologist David Evans declared that Brewster was "a giant among gospel composers."

October 15, 1933

"Memphis Bill" Terry Welcomed Home

Guy Newbern of the *Commercial Appeal* described the extravagant homecoming ceremonies for Memphian William Harold Terry: "Mighty man of baseball came home yesterday to receive the acclaim of the homefolks for piloting the New York Giants to the world's baseball championship." The festivities began with a parade down Main Street where thousands cheered the World Series champion as he rode by on a flag-draped car. The parade ended at city hall, where Mayor Watkins Overton officially welcomed him home. Overwhelmed by the 100,000 laughing and screaming fans, especially the many children who crowded around him begging for an autograph, "Memphis Bill" said that seeing his fellow Memphians was the "greatest thrill I ever experienced off the playing field." That evening, a banquet was held at the Hotel Devoy, where Terry explained that "just before I prepared to leave for home, Alan Gould, Associated Press sports editor, asked me why I didn't live in New York. Because I would rather live in Memphis was my answer." Born in Atlanta, Terry moved to Memphis as a young boy, and in 1930, he joined the New York Giants, where he spent fourteen years in the Major Leagues with a lifetime batting average of .341. Elected to the Baseball Hall of Fame, Memphis Bill died on October 9, 1989, in Jacksonville, Florida.

October 16, 1919

Soldier Slaps Wife; Gets Shot

Violence erupted on Second Street when World War I veteran, national guardsman and former police officer Frank P. Foglesong accosted his estranged wife and received a bullet in the leg for his trouble. Mrs. Foglesong had recently sued for divorce after her husband beat her. A peace warrant was issued by Squire John J. McNamara to prevent further violence, but it did little good on this day. When Foglesong saw his wife coming out of a café on Second Street near Madison Avenue, he began verbally threatening her. Walking nearby was Captain Parker, who happened to be an officer in Foglesong's unit, the Fourth Tennessee Infantry. Parker approached the two and tried to make peace, but Foglesong lunged for his wife, striking her hard on the cheek. Parker grabbed the soldier and attempted to detain him until police arrived, but Foglesong slapped the captain on the jaw and broke free. Watching the altercation was sixty-five-year-old night watchman J.P. Hendrix, who shot Foglesong in the leg as he ran from Parker. Taken to Baptist Hospital, Foglesong was treated and released while Hendrix was briefly arrested before being bailed out by his employer, the Burns Night Patrol Company.

October 17, 1930

John Philip Sousa Phones Memphis

One of the nation's most celebrated composers and bandleaders, John Philip Sousa, placed a long-distance telephone call to Memphis on this day. Sousa called Charles A. McElravy, manager of the city auditorium, to discuss plans for two concerts scheduled for October 18. When Sousa and his band arrived by train at Union Station, they were met by fire and police commissioner Clifford Davis, who presented the "March King" with a key to the city. Following this brief ceremony, the American Legion's drum and bugle corps joined Sousa's musicians and the Memphis Rotary Club's Boy's Band in a parade down Main Street. In addition to his own compositions, Sousa also performed the *Thirty-Second Division March* written by Memphian Theodore A. Steinmetz. His 1930 appearance was something of a homecoming for Sousa, who began his career as a conductor in Memphis on October 25, 1875. According to Sousa, he was "first violinist in Ford's Theater in Washington when Milton Nobles came there to play his drama called 'Bohemians and Detectives.' Later when the organization traveled south the orchestra leader became ill and I was engaged to lead the orchestra. I assumed the position at Memphis." From this brief beginning, Sousa went on to lead the U.S. Marine Band from 1880 to 1892 and compose many songs, including the official march of the United States, *Stars and Stripes Forever.*

October 18, 1974

Hot Grits Poured on Soul Singer

A former girlfriend of Memphis soul singer Al Green on this day committed suicide after pouring a pan of hot grits on the award-winning performer. Green told sheriff's deputies that Mary Woodson of Madison, New Jersey, whom he had met in New York in 1973, had unexpectedly appeared at a recording session, and afterward, he asked Woodson to join him and his companion Carlotta Williams at his home in northwest Shelby County. Green and Woodson had a long conversation during which Woodson asked him to marry her. Green refused and left her to go take a bath. As reported by the *Commercial Appeal*'s James Cole, "At about 1:15 a.m. Mrs. Woodson appeared at the doorway holding a pot of boiling grits and threw them on the singer. While he was attempting to wash off the grits, he and Williams heard two shots and later found Woodson lying on the floor near a bedroom." When sheriff's deputies arrived, they found the .38-caliber revolver, which belonged to Green, and a note that said, "All I wanted was to be with you and love you until I die. I love you, Al." After the forensic evidence was analyzed, Green was cleared of any involvement, but the event had a profound effect on him. In 1976, he was ordained as a minister and founded the nondenominational Full Gospel Tabernacle in Whitehaven. Commenting on his faith, Green said, "I try to help others. If the Lord blesses you, you must try to help someone else…That's why I got a license to practice 'the ministry.' I am going to be an evangelist. Everybody can realize they are blessed."

October 19, 1956

Elvis Arrested

Elvis Presley, who recently arrived back home after appearing on the Ed Sullivan TV show and filming a movie in Hollywood, was driving down Gayoso on this day when the air conditioner on his Continental Mark II automobile malfunctioned. Hoping to get it fixed, he pulled into the Gulf station at the corner of Second Street. Soon after arriving, a small group of teenage girls surrounded the singing star. Not liking his gas pumps blocked, manager Edd Hopper ordered Presley to move. According to the King of rock 'n' roll, he said, "Yes sir, I will. I was writing my name, and trying to hurry when Mr. Hopper asked me to move again…I signed the autographs and was turning on my key when he reached in the window and hit me on the head with his hand. I was more or less stunned because I wasn't expecting that. I started to get out of the car and he pushed me back. Then I jumped out and hit him and he pulled a knife on me." Attendant Aubrey Brown then swung at Presley, who punched him as well. Police broke up the fight, and all three were charged with assault and disorderly conduct. In a courtroom packed with Elvis fans, acting judge Sam Friedman heard testimony, dismissed the charges against Presley and found Hopper and Brown guilty of assault. However, Friedman suggested to Elvis that "in the future try to be considerate and co-operate with businessmen. Avoid crowds where business will be interrupted."

October 20, 1971

Historic Building Damaged by Fire

The historic Rogers building, home to Sardou's Steak and Lobster House, was damaged on this day when two separate fires, one in the basement and the other in the ladies' restroom, quickly engulfed the building. Acting Fire Marshal C.E. Torian explained that the fire in the basement was started by transients burning trash. As reported by the *Press-Scimitar*, "The history-laced, four-story brick Rogers Building...was extensively damaged as firemen battled the blaze, using eleven hand ladders, three machine ladders and more than 20 pieces of motorized equipment." The building was constructed in 1904 by Dr. William B. Rogers, who had been president of the board of health in 1890 and was the resident surgeon at Saint Joseph Hospital. In 1916, entrepreneur Clarence Saunders opened his first Piggly Wiggly grocery store on the first floor of the Rogers Building. Saunders offered his own unique system of self-service, which transformed the grocery industry and the buying habits of the American consumer. After the First World War, the building was converted into a hotel, and the Piggly Wiggly storefront became a series of restaurants. The building survived the 1971 fire, but a second conflagration in 1983 led to its demolition in 1984.

October 21, 1939

Pick Cotton or Go to Jail

Welfare Commission chairman Aubrey Clapp ordered the arrest of unemployed carpenter Elmer Winton for vagrancy when he refused to take a job picking cotton in Missouri. As reported by the *Commercial Appeal*, "In City Court, he pleaded he was unfitted for cotton picking and felt 75 cents a 100 pounds would not be sufficient to support his wife and eight children." Clapp told the press that "all in the world I was trying to do was to help him solve his problems. A Tipton, Mo., man had promised him a house and food during the picking season in addition to the 75 cents a 100." Faced with jail time if he refused, Winton agreed to move but changed his mind before travel arrangements were completed. While hiding out from the police, Winton secured a part-time job with the DeSoto Fish Market on North Main Street for $5 a week. He then was able to rent a small house near South Highland, where a *Commercial Appeal* reporter visited them on this day. Without an ounce of compassion, the correspondent wrote, "Bare-footed and holding an 18-month-old-son in her arms, Mrs. Winton highlighted the Winton family history. 'We were burned out twice in Arkansas. The last time was in 1937…and we came to Memphis. I hadn't gotten over the first fire scare when the second one came along. We had to throw the children out the windows like bales of hay to save them.'"

October 22, 1965

Combo Man Dies of Brain Tumor

Funeral arrangements were announced on this day for musician Bill Black, who rocketed to fame as Elvis Presley's bassist and later sold millions of records with his instrumental combo. Black died on October 21 from a brain tumor that surgery failed to remove. In 1954, Black, guitarist Scotty Moore and Presley recorded Arthur "Big Boy" Crudup's song "That's All Right" for Sun Records owner Sam Phillips, which was largely responsible for the development of Memphis-style rock 'n' roll music that spread across the globe in the 1950s. Elvis, Scotty and Bill went on to record some of the most important music of the twentieth century before the three parted company in September 1957. Two years later, in 1959, Black formed Bill Black's Combo with drummer Jerry Arnold, saxophonist Ace Cannon, organist and pianist Bobby Emmons and guitarist Reggie Young. The group recorded instrumentals for Hi Records that sold millions of copies and made Bill Black's Combo one of the most popular groups in Europe and the United States. The group performed on the Ed Sullivan and American Bandstand television shows, and in 1964 it toured with the Beatles during their American tour. When Elvis learned of his friend's death, he stated that Black was "a great man and a person that everyone loved...We were longtime friends and Bill was very pleasant to work with. This comes as such a shock to me that I can hardly explain how much I loved Bill."

October 23, 1924

Dames Mark Local History

The early history of Memphis was celebrated on this day with the dedication of a granite boulder and bronze plaque in Auction Square. The marker was donated by Mrs. Olivia Hall Grosvenor of the Memphis chapter of the National Society of Colonial Dames, and in honor of the gift, the square was renamed Colonial Park. The event began with the raising of the American flag by a troop of Boy Scouts followed by the reading of poet Walter Malone's epic *DeSoto's Vision*. Mayor Rowlett Paine then accepted the gift as descendants of the city's founders placed wreaths on the boulder. Included on the plaque were two Memphis history events they mistakenly claimed took place on or near the spot: Hernando DeSoto first observing the Mississippi and Andrew Jackson, John Overton and James Winchester meeting at Bell Tavern to lay out the city. The plaque disappeared during World War II, but the boulder remains in Colonial Park, shorn of its significance. Although the bronze plaque contained some inaccuracies, its disappearance sparked one of the most persistent myths in Memphis history. With the plaque gone, and the park once being called Auction Square, many jumped to the conclusion that the granite block was used to auction slaves. To be sure, slavery flourished in Memphis with dealers operating throughout much of downtown, but not in Auction Square. Despite information to the contrary, many still choose to believe that the granite boulder constructed in 1924 had something to do with the evils of slavery.

October 24, 1961

Historic Homes Saved from Destruction

The Memphis City Commission on this day agreed to lease two historic homes to the Association for the Preservation of Tennessee Antiquities in order to save the buildings from destruction. The James Lee and Noland Fontaine homes were slated for demolition but the agreement spared the historic structures. The group planned to restore the two homes and a small carriage house. Built in 1847 by C.W. Goyer, the James Lee home was purchased in 1890. Amos Woodruff built a mansion on a lot next to the Lee home in 1870. Noland Fontaine bought the home in 1880, and it remained a residence until 1930, when Rosa Lee gave it and her father's home to the City of Memphis. The Memphis Academy of Art was housed in the Lee home until it moved its operation to Overton Park in 1959.

The James Lee house was saved from destruction by the Memphis chapter of the Association for the Preservation of Tennessee Antiquities.

October 25, 1862

President Commutes Memphian's Death Sentence

President Abraham Lincoln on this day lifted a death sentence imposed by a military commission on a Confederate smuggler operating out of Memphis. On August 18, 1862, Memphian Sely Lewis attempted to pass through Union lines with boots, chloroform, morphine and snuff, which he allegedly planned to pass on to Confederate forces. Arrested by Federal soldiers, Lewis was charged with smuggling and violating the fifty-seventh article of war, which forbade sharing intelligence with the enemy and was punishable by death. On August 26, a military trial was held, and after hearing testimony and examining the evidence, the tribunal found Lewis guilty of both charges and formally declared him a spy. The commissioners then recommended that the "prisoner be hanged as a spy until he is dead." The military commander of Memphis, Major General William T. Sherman, forwarded the commission's decision to President Lincoln, who reviewed the case and drew a different conclusion. In his order, Lincoln declared that "so far as the sentence in the case relates to the accused as a spy it is disapproved, the commission not having jurisdiction of the offense. The sentence of death is mitigated to imprisonment for a term of six months."

October 26, 1968

Television Star Attends Homecoming

Barbara Anderson, Emmy-winning star of the NBC television series *Ironside* and former Miss Memphis, returned home to the Bluff City to attend the homecoming festivities of Memphis State University. In an interview with Woodrow Paige Jr., the former Memphis State student and Front Street Theatre actress was asked if she missed life in the Bluff City. Anderson replied, "No, I don't really miss Memphis. I like to come back, but my parents moved recently to San Diego, so I don't get much chance." Homecoming activities began on this day with a parade down Highland Avenue with Anderson sharing a float with 1968 homecoming queen, Christie Brown. The parade was temporarily halted by a train when the Southern Railroad reneged on its promise of suspending locomotive traffic during the event. The parade quickly continued once the train had passed, and afterward, Anderson attended a luncheon in the newly built University Center with Tennessee governor Buford Ellington. Once the meal was completed, Anderson was reacquainted with the Memphis State campus, which boasted a new library along with recently constructed biology, chemistry and English buildings. That evening, the television star watched the Memphis State football team defeat the University of Southern Mississippi, 29 to 7. Anderson finished her own personal homecoming by attending an alumni dance at the Holiday Inn–Rivermont.

October 27, 1983

Beale Street Historian Dies

One of the most celebrated residents of Beale Street, historian, newspaper columnist and disc jockey Nat D. Williams, succumbed to a stroke. Born on Beale in 1907, Williams was fascinated by the culture and history of the famed avenue. Earning a master's degree from Tennessee State University, Williams taught history at Booker T. Washington for forty-three years; in 1948, he became the South's first African American disc jockey when he began broadcasting on radio station WDIA. In addition, for many years he served as master of ceremonies at the Palace Theater's amateur night programs. In 1932, he began writing a newspaper column for the *Memphis World* and *Pittsburgh Courier* entitled "Down on Beale," chronicling the culture of Memphis's most famous thoroughfare while also discussing the experiences of African Americans in a segregated society. In an editorial printed at the time of his death, the *Press-Scimitar* stated that Williams was "Beale Street's unofficial ambassador and it's [*sic*] most ardent advocate, he surpassed even the immortal W.C. Handy in making Beale known around the world as the Home of the Blues and the main street of Black America."

October 28, 1878

Health Department Asks Memphians to Come Home

The Memphis Board of Health on this day announced that the yellow fever epidemic that killed five thousand people and devastated the city was over. In its resolution, the board declared that "the thermometer having fallen three degrees below freezing point, it is entirely safe for refugees to return to the city, providing their premises have been thoroughly ventilated and fumigated." The *Daily Memphis Avalanche* urged those who had fled to "come home. These words have a talismanic sound. They tell us we are to meet the dear friends from whom we have been separated for more than two long sad weary months; two months of sickness and sorrow that have almost engulfed us. We thank God, the hour has come. The epidemic is at an end. Health takes the place of where but a few short weeks ago death reigned supreme." Despite the pleas of the newspapers, thousands who escaped Memphis during the summer of 1878 did not return.

October 29, 1894

Memphians Pour through the Doors of Cossitt Library
Every day, at least 250 Memphians walked through the doors of the Cossitt Library to use its reading materials. Opened on April 12, 1893, the first free public library in Memphis was paid for by a $75,000 gift from the estate of Frederick Cossitt. According to the *Commercial Appeal*, the library had available twenty-two daily and fifty-two weekly newspapers, forty-eight magazines and seven thousand reference books. The library also had an extensive collection of biographies, volumes on American and world history and 2,500 fiction books. The library was open from 8:00 a.m. to 10:00 p.m. on Monday through Saturday and 2:00 to 6:00 p.m. on Sundays. Both the men's and ladies' reading rooms were often filled with inquiring Memphis residents. To meet the needs of its users, the library board was in the process of adding an additional four thousand titles to Cossitt's shelves. "The enormous demand for books keeps the librarian Mr. [Mel] Nunnally, busy all day. As fast as he can, however, he is making a register of the books, and as soon as he has them all on his list in regular order, the library will become a circulating one," explained the newspaper. Cossitt Library was a very significant institution in Memphis history, and the large public library system it spawned remains an important part of the city's social fabric.

October 30, 1947

First Female Magistrate Dies

Alma Hogshead Law, first woman in Memphis history to be elected a magistrate and serve on the Shelby County Quarterly Court, died on this day at the home of her son W.H. Law. Born near Holly Springs, Mississippi, Alma Hogshead attended Hudsonville School with Edward Hull Crump, who, like Law, moved to Memphis and became involved in politics. Before moving to the Bluff City, she earned a teaching certificate and taught school in Water Valley, Mississippi. Moving to Memphis, Hogshead taught at the Lauderdale School and, in 1909, married Illinois Central Railroad engineer Al Law. In addition to teaching, Law was a member of the Ladies Auxiliary of the Brotherhood of Locomotive Engineers and First Methodist Church. As a teacher and civic leader, Law was well respected, and in 1929, she was elected the county's first female magistrate by a vote of 990 to 45. As magistrate, she acted as a judge hearing cases and as a member of the quarterly court, which acted as the executive branch of Shelby County government. In 1936, she was elected first vice-chairman of the court, and she remained a county official until her death in 1947.

October 31, 1964

Memphis State Crushes Wake Forest

The Deacons of Wake Forest swept into town with their star fullback Brian Piccolo with hopes of destroying the Memphis State Tigers football team. The Deacons failed to defeat the stalwart Tigers, who scored an impressive 23 points to Wake Forest's 14. Early in the game, Wake Forest's Piccolo ran eighty yards for a touchdown, but the Tigers soon gained possession of the ball, and fullback David Brown drove to the end zone for their first touchdown. Just before halftime, Billy Fletcher kicked a fifty-five-yard field goal, which gave Memphis State the lead. According to the *Commercial Appeal*'s Charles Gillespie, in the second half, with the Tigers up 9–7, Memphis wingback Bob Sherlag "turned in a tremendous 55-yard punt return that Wake Forest did not overcome, and when the Deacons were still threatening to overcome it he intercepted a John Mackovic pass on the Tiger three-yard line and ran it back 63 yards to throttle Wake Forest's gallant effort."

Memphis State coach Billy "Spook" Murphy was gracious in victory when he stated after the game that "Wake Forest played a fine football game. Both Piccolo and Mackovic are fine athletes and they kept the heat on us."

November 1, 1940

Bing Crosby's Birth of the Blues Premieres in Memphis
In the pages of the *Commercial Appeal* newspaper on this day, reporter Harry Martin described the first night's showing of a Hollywood movie with a local connection at the Malco Theatre.

> *They unveiled Bing Crosby's "Birth of the Blues" last night at the very spot where the white man's Memphis intersects that of the Negro—Beale and Main. At a cloud-drenched corner of the same thoroughfare where William Christopher Handy first put those immortal indigo laments of his race into written sharps and flats, with the venerable Negro composer himself a happy witness and participant, Paramount staked the world premiere of its studio's newest musical production.*

The film starred Crosby as a New Orleans clarinet player, who, along with singer Mary Martin and a character named "Memphis" played by Brian Donlevy, assembles a jazz band and "discovers" the blues. Martin and other local critics agreed that the film was very entertaining but woefully inaccurate in its portrayal of the origins of blues music: "Nowhere in the picture is W.C. Handy given credit for his great contribution to jazz, and the picture is more about the discovery of the musical form by white men than about the actual birth of the blues."

November 2, 1965

Mrs. Montesi Murdered

Wearing pink pajamas, Evelyn Brunner Montesi was shot dead in her home at 311 South Perkins on this day. According to her husband, Louis Francis Montesi, at 9:45 p.m., they heard a knock on the door, and Mrs. Montesi got out of bed to answer it. Hearing a scuffle and then a shot, Montesi ran to the front door, where he was attacked by an unknown assailant while his wife bled from a single bullet to the chest. Police were called, and they found Evelyn Montesi lying near the northwest corner of the house, not by the front door. "There are some unexplained aspects of this that will require a lot of investigation," reported assistant police chief Henry Lux, who also explained that there were signs of a struggle in many parts of the house and that several shell casings were found but no weapon. The police didn't accept Montesi's version of the shooting, and he was indicted for first-degree murder. A trial was held in April 1966, and Montesi was found guilty of voluntary manslaughter and sentenced to ten years in prison. However, the conviction was overturned, and two years later, he was tried again and found guilty of involuntary manslaughter. This conviction was also overturned on appeal. Montesi was the oldest son of Fred Montesi, the owner of a chain of local grocery stores. When the family sold the stores in 1955, Louis became an executive with Liberty Cash Grocers Inc., through which he reopened a new chain of Fred Montesi stores in 1960.

November 3, 1976

Hungry Bandit Robs Bank

An unknown man on this day walked into Yiftos Restaurant near the intersection of Madison Avenue and Morrison Street, looked over the menu and realized he was a little short. He told the waitress, "I'll be back; I don't have enough money" and then ran out of the restaurant clutching the menu in his hand. A short time later, wearing a black and red ski mask, he walked into the First National Bank on Union Avenue and stole over $12,000. The *Commercial Appeal*'s Michael Clark reported: "Jim Roper, a bank public relations official said the man entered the branch's west door, 'leaped over tellers' row and took money from the cash drawer of the drive-in teller before moving down the row and taking money from another teller. He then jumped over the counter and fled. Yumie Kirk, branch manager, followed the robber out the west door. The robber fled behind houses, crossed Diana and went to the rear of the apartment building at 40 South Morrison. Kirk said he saw the man approach the steps at the back of the apartment building and, assuming he was headed for an apartment there, went back to meet police officers."

As the bandit entered the apartment, a red-dye bomb exploded in the bag, smearing some of the ill-gotten money with scarlet paint. The robber threw the damaged cash outside the apartment building but escaped with enough of the bank's money to buy several meals in the city's most expensive restaurants.

November 4, 1901

Toll Charged to Cross Nonconnah Creek

The *Commercial Appeal* reported on this day: "[The] county allowed Nonconnah bridge to become so run down that abandonment for a time was unavoidable. At a recent meeting the court appropriated money for repairing the bridge. It was necessary to tear it up to such an extent that it could not be used as a part of the highway. Hence the people who used this road in reaching Memphis had to select some other route into the city. To enter by the Horn Lake Road meant to many of them a distance of ten to twelve miles greater than by following the Hernando Road. When travel over the bridge was suspended the people had to find some other way."

Travelers found this other way on the property of African American justice of the peace N.L. Edwards. With the bridge closed, a group of white farmers asked Edwards to cut a road through his place, and in exchange, they offered to pay a modest toll when crossing his land. Edwards "cut the bank down to the south side of the creek, blazed a road through a thicket to a point where the creek was fordable and allowed wagons to pass through their cotton field for a distance of about a quarter of a mile before re-entering the public road again. For this they have charged a toll of 10 cents each way." Traversing Nonconnah Creek was problematic for much of the twentieth century. In 1937 and 1955, the creek flooded, and on March 16, 1980, the Perkins Bridge over Nonconnah Creek collapsed, killing one motorist and injuring two others.

November 5, 1916

Integrated Political Meeting Held in Peabody Hotel

The Shelby County Republican Party held a closed-door meeting at the Peabody Hotel that was attended by chairman of the Tennessee Republican Executive Committee J. Will Taylor and African American GOP leader Robert Church Jr. According to the *Commercial Appeal*: "Mr. Taylor was accompanied by James S. Beasley, who was chairman of the state board of prison commissioners…As soon as Will Taylor had registered more than a dozen went up to the conference. John W. Farley, the white Republican candidate for congress, arrived 20 minutes late. Bob Church came into the hotel by the parlor entrance at 11:30 o'clock… He entered the elevator at once and was whisked up to the third floor and entered the conference chamber without the formality of knocking."

The purpose of the meeting was to secure the support of Church and his powerful Lincoln League organization for Farley. It is not known precisely what was discussed in the meeting; however, an agreement may have been reached, for the *Commercial Appeal* declared that at "12:30 o'clock cigars were ordered up and at 1 o'clock the conference broke up, its members leaving in parties of twos and threes."

November 6, 1980

Memphis Singers Return Home

A party was held on this day at the Germantown home of Eugene Phillips to celebrate the homecoming of two of Memphis's most celebrated singers. According to the *Press-Scimitar*, "Anita Ward, whose disco hit record 'Ring My Bell,' earned her a Grammy nomination earlier this year, and Carla Thomas, who had her first hit records at age 17, were guests of honor at the dinner party." Thomas had just returned from Washington, D.C., where she performed at a local nightclub. Before her engagement in the nation's capital, Carla toured Europe for three weeks with her father, Rufus Thomas. "I love working with daddy. It cuts down on the pressure when he's with me, and it means less time on stage, so it's less demanding," Carla said. Ward, who had been teaching elementary school before her song hit number one on the *Billboard* charts in the summer of 1979, had recently toured Chile, Ecuador and France. Speaking of France, Ward explained that "a lot of people are surprised at the following I have over there. The reception was beautiful. The clubs were packed every night." In 1960, Carla Thomas recorded "'Cause I Love You" with her father, Rufus, for Stax Records, and in 1961, her song "Gee Whiz" made it to number ten on the *Billboard* charts. "Gee Whiz" was Stax's first major hit and was largely responsible for Atlantic Records distributing Memphis soul music across the nation.

November 7, 1922

Memphis Boxer Smashes Opponent

Well-regarded Memphis pugilist Kid Dugan spent eight rounds on this day severely beating Sailor Henessey before being awarded the match at the Southern Athletic Club. According to *Commercial Appeal* correspondent Herbert Caldwell, "Throughout the seventh and eighth rounds Hennessey, with the crimson trickling from his open mouth, lolled about the ring upon unsteady legs, tottering and reeling under the impact of Dugan's pile driving rights to body and gamely, but helplessly and feebly, trying to fight back." Surveying the bloody scene, referee Billy Haack stopped the fight and awarded the decision to Kid Dugan at the end of the eighth round. Although not as popular as professional wrestling, boxing matches were well attended, especially at the Fairgrounds Boxing Arena. The Golden Gloves held matches there, and the Park Commission conducted summer clinics in the facility. Thousands of young Memphians participated in these programs, and while they may not have been as successful as Kid Dugan, they did learn the art of self-defense like seventeen-year-old Golden Gloves champion Calvin McKinney, who became interested in boxing after being bullied in school. "Nobody picks on me anymore," he said in 1981.

November 8, 1899

Gangster Acquitted of Murder

A sigh of relief was no doubt uttered by Mike Shanley when a jury of his peers acquitted him of killing streetcar conductor C.H. Clark at Montgomery Park in April 1899. Shanley was aiming his pistol at rival gangster Ed Ryan when Clark accidently found himself in the line of fire. Both Clark and Ryan were felled as a large crowd, gathered to watch horse racing, fled in panic. The notorious gangster was defended by Ralph Davis and William Fitzgerald, while the prosecution rested in the hands of West Tennessee attorney general Malcolm Patterson. The defense argued that Ryan threatened Shanley and that he had little choice but to defend himself. Davis and Fitzgerald also declared that Clark's death was a tragic accident, but the prosecution painted a far different picture. According to Patterson, the two underworld figures argued violently, and later, Shanley ducked behind the bleachers and started firing his pistol. Despite Patterson's impassioned plea, the jury found Shanley not guilty, which quashed the state's hope of convicting him of Ryan's murder. Flush with victory, Shanley opened a saloon and then seized control of Ryan's criminal enterprises and territory. Although he escaped the hangman, Shanley was himself shot and killed by police for resisting arrest in 1908.

November 9, 1972

Hungry Fisherman Serves Hungry Memphians

Shoney's South on this day opened its first Hungry Fisherman restaurant in Memphis. Located at Interstate 40 and Macon Road, the establishment sat on eleven acres near the edge of a five-acre lake. According to the *Press-Scimitar*'s Robert Johnson: "You enter the restaurant on a slightly inclined wooden ramp, and the rails at the sides are big oars, authentic even to not having been painted...The restaurant itself, a vast room, has a beautiful chandelier...windows on all sides giving a view of the lake, seats 425...Salad bars, from which patrons serve themselves, are in three lifeboats, with stainless steel receptacles for salad, dressings...On the far wall is the captain's bridge, and an entrance leads to an outside bridge with rail, from which children, and adults, can feed some of the 50,000 fish which the lake will be stocked. The menus are on boards, shaped like a fish. As is to be expected, the emphasis is on fresh fish and seafood...It is difficult to give an idea of what the average check will be, because it ranges from free perch for children under 6 to live Maine lobster, chosen from a live lobster tank, at $6.95."

Like the Luau, the Hungry Fisherman was one of the most popular high-concept restaurants to open in Memphis, and it remained so until it closed in 1993.

November 10, 1958

Shelby Foote Fights the Civil War

Random House on this day published the first volume of novelist Shelby Foote's masterpiece *The Civil War: A Narrative*. Covering the beginning of the war through the Battle of Perryville, the book was followed by volume two, *Fredericksburg to Meridan*, in 1963 and the final book, *Red River to Appomattox*, was published in 1974. Writing in the *New York Times*, noted historian Frank Vandiver declared that

Shelby Foote was perhaps the most important writer to call Memphis home.

the first volume "is good history and finely wrought." In addition to his *Narrative*, Foote published six novels. Four of these were set in the Mississippi Delta, one in Memphis and the sixth, *Shiloh*, was set during that pivotal Civil War battle. In 1990, he was a central figure in filmmaker Ken Burns's seminal documentary *The Civil War*. When Shelby Foote died on June 27, 2005, he was revered as one of America's greatest writers.

November 11, 1921

Ford Plant Murderers Convicted

The four bandits who attempted to rob the Ford Motor Company payroll office in August 1921 were on this day found guilty of first-degree murder and sentenced to life imprisonment. The jury deliberated for twenty-four hours before convicting Thomas Taylor Harriss, Jesse Carl Jones, Orville Taylor Jones and Edwin Von Steinkirch. On the morning of August 10, the four men pulled up to the Ford plant in a dark blue Cadillac just as the weekly payroll was being delivered by clerk Edgar McHenry, agent Howard Gamble and patrolmen Polk Carraway and W.S. Harris. The trigger-happy bandits opened fire, killing Carraway and Gamble and wounding Harris. Unharmed, McHenry grabbed the money satchel, ran under fire into the payroll office and slammed the payroll into the office safe. The dark blue Cadillac sped off toward the eastern edge of the city. Meanwhile, Lieutenant Vincent Lucarini grabbed patrolmen C.L. Bonds and Al Rodgers and mechanic Eddie Heckinger and commandeered another dark blue Cadillac owned by grocer Joe Robilio. As the five men sped east down Poplar Avenue, Deputy Sheriff Morris Irby gathered a forty-man posse, which hid in bushes near Poplar Avenue while he stood in the middle of the road, looking for a dark blue Cadillac. When one appeared and refused to stop, Irby and his posse opened fire. Unfortunately, it was the Robilio Cadillac rather than the one used by the bandits. The hail of mistaken bullets killed Lucarini and wounded Bonds, Heckinger and Robilio.

November 12, 1931

Trackless Trolley Line Proved Popular

A.D. McWhorter, superintendent of the Memphis Street Railway Company, announced on this day that since November 8, the number of riders on the new electric coaches operating on the Lamar Avenue line had far exceeded the company's expectations: "Volume of business has surprised us all. We are pleased with the smooth working of the new vehicle and service on the Lamar line is the best given anywhere." According to the *Evening Appeal*, the "number of passengers using the coaches is nearly one-third more than the number that rode the trolley cars." On the same day as this announcement, a truck filled with ten tons of batteries ran a red light at Vance Avenue and Third Street and crashed into the back of a trackless trolley, causing $1,000 worth of damage. No one riding in the coach was injured, but Ed Wilmsen, brother of truck driver Henry Wilmsen, was thrown from the vehicle and landed atop an open manhole where three Memphis Power & Light employees were busy working. Wilmsen was not hurt, but one of the workers "was shaken and bruised by his fall." Electric coaches remained in operation in Memphis until the street railway company converted to diesel engine coaches in 1960. The last electric line was canceled on April 22, 1960, and in December, the city created the Metropolitan Transit Authority, which purchased the street railway company for $2,333,546.

November 13, 1980

Blues Can't Be Found in Memphis

In honor of the first annual Handy Awards, the city of Memphis declared the week of November 10–16 Memphis Blues Week. Although Memphians in 1980 could attend the awards show and hear blues music in some clubs, it was nearly impossible to find the seminal recordings that made Memphis the "home of the blues." The *Commercial Appeal*'s music critic Walter Dawson wrote on this day: "Earlier this year, Yazoo Records…issued an album called, The Memphis Jug Band, a collection of tracks from the '20s and '30s by one of the most successful Memphis music artists from that era. The record has shown up on the ballot for the Blues Foundation's National Blues Music Awards Show coming up Sunday, but that is about the only place the record has shown up around here…What is intriguing about that is that there are a number of labels like Yazoo throughout the world that reissue Memphis blues, but those records never seem to find their way home. Thus, while Memphis music is available worldwide, it's seldom found here."

As Dawson's comments suggest, throughout much of its history, Memphis was ambivalent about its musical heritage while the rest of the world lovingly celebrated it.

November 14, 1927

"King of the Underworld" Returns to Memphis

Henry Diggs Nolen, reputed "king" of the Memphis underworld, on this day snuck into his hometown even though the visit was a violation of his parole. Nolen was convicted of forgery and sentenced to fifteen years in the state penitentiary, but he was paroled after four years with the condition he stay out of Memphis. Before his forgery conviction, Nolen spent time in federal prison for selling illegal narcotics and was released from Fort Leavenworth shortly before he skulked back into Memphis. Police commissioner Thomas Allen ordered Chief Joe Burney to arrest Nolen, who was picked up at his brother's drugstore. Released on bond, Nolen's parole was revoked by Judge Ben L. Capell, who ordered him to serve the rest of his term in prison. However, he didn't stay behind bars for long. A heavy drinker, Nolen died on September 3, 1928, while being treated for chronic alcoholism at St. Joseph Hospital. Nolen's criminal exploits lived far beyond the forty-one years he spent on this earth. On July 23, 1939, the *Commercial Appeal* took note of the twenty-fifth anniversary of his first prison break: "He nailed himself in coffin boxes, dug under prison walls or simply walked away, but he always managed to escape."

November 15, 1863

Memphians Impressed into Union Army during Civil War

The commander of the Union army's Sixteenth Corps, Major General S.A. Hurlbut, on this day issued General Orders No. 157, which prevented all goods save firewood and food from entering or leaving the military district and forced eligible Memphians to join the Federal army: "The people in the district of West Tennessee and the northern counties of Mississippi, having shown no disposition and made no attempt to protect themselves from marauders and guerrilla bands, but having submitted themselves without organized resistance to the domination of these petty tyrants…have proved themselves unworthy of the indulgence shown them by the Government. It is therefore ordered that the lines of pickets around the several military posts of this command in Tennessee and Mississippi be closed… All persons residing under the protection of the United States, and physically capable of military duty, are liable to perform the same in a country under martial law. Especially in the City of Memphis, where it is known that many have fled to escape liability to military service at home, this rule will be strictly applied…In pursuance, therefore…all officers commanding district, division, and detached brigades of this corps, will immediately proceed to impress into the service of the United States such able-bodied persons liable to military duty as may be required to fill up the existing regiments and batteries to their maximum."

November 16, 1982

Blues Awards Handed Out

The third-annual Blues Music Awards was held on this day in the Memphis Ballroom of the Peabody Hotel. According to the *Commercial Appeal*'s Walter Dawson, the "awards program is sponsored by the Blues Foundation, a nonprofit group dedicated to preserving and fostering the blues, and its awards are called the 'Handys' after W.C. Handy." The biggest winner of the evening was Bobby "Blue" Bland who received the Blues Vocalist of the Year award and was honored for the Vintage or Reissue Album of the Year for *Woke Up Screaming*. Memphian George Jackson also received a Handy for his song "Down Home Blues" recorded by Z.Z. Hill. Koko Taylor was named female blues artist of the year and Johnny Copeland was given the award for male blues artist of the year. Traditional blues album of the year was given to *Going Back* by Buddy Guy and Junior Wells, Larry Davis's "Since I Been Loving You" was named blues single of the year and the blues instrumentalist of the year was presented to Gatemouth Brown. *Living Blues* magazine also received a Handy and special awards were given to radio stations WEVL and KWAM. In addition, Little Laura Dukes, Grandma Dixie Davis, Ma Rainey II and Harry Godwin were designated Memphis Blues Treasures. Founded in 1980, the Blues Foundation continues to host the Handy Awards each year and promote the rich legacy of the blues and the Memphis sound.

November 17, 1961

Famed Church Leader Dies

Charles Harrison Mason, the ninety-nine-year-old founder and presiding bishop of the Church of God in Christ, died on this day while visiting his two daughters in Detroit. Born a slave in rural Shelby County on September 8, 1862, Mason moved with his family to Plumersville, Arkansas, in 1878. As a child, Mason suffered from ill health and bad dreams until he experienced a religious conversion in 1880. He was ordained a minister and later enrolled at Arkansas Baptist College, but according to historian Perre Magness Mason, he "dropped out after three months, expounding what the teachers considered a radical definition of holiness. He said the way the schools were conducted grieved his soul. He was ordered out of town, tossed into jail and beaten by outraged churchgoers." Mason founded a church in Lexington, Mississippi, and in 1907, he attended the Azuza Street Pentecostal revival in Los Angeles. Bringing the Pentecostal faith back to the South, Mason relocated to Memphis and founded the Church of God in Christ. Within a decade, Mason had established COGIC congregations in Chicago, Detroit, Philadelphia and St. Louis, and by the 1920s, the church had expanded into Africa, Haiti, Mexico and the Virgin Islands. In 1956, Mayor Edmund Orgill officially honored Bishop Mason and his church for their many contributions to the spiritual life of Memphis.

November 18, 1944

Memphian Invades Philippines

In October 1944, navy lieutenant commander John W. Cross participated in the liberation of the Japanese-held Philippine Islands, and on October 24, he wrote a letter to his brother, Richard M. Cross Jr., describing what he had seen. On this day, Richard shared his brother's letter with the *Commercial Appeal*, which published it the following morning. In his letter, Cross wrote: "At 10 o'clock the landing craft loaded with troops set out for the beach. The landing parties ran into some opposition on the beach, especially pill boxes of dirt and log construction, but were soon across it and through the coconut plantation which was as far as I could follow with my glasses…Yesterday in the afternoon, I watched for an hour as planes from one of our carriers dropped bombs on a hillside facing us. They came one by one, every half minute or so, dived at the…positions, zoomed and circled back to carriers for another load. They kept this up all afternoon, just like a string of dump trucks working on a highway."

Lieutenant Commander Cross ended his correspondence by praising those who landed on the Philippines: "It's a tough, dirty, sweaty war for our foot soldiers and they really deserve all of the credit in the world. I wonder how they manage to keep going, they work and fight all day and then they fight all night. When they sleep and eat I don't know. I give all of the credit to that guy called 'G. I. Joe.'"

November 19, 1974

Harriet the Spy *Author Dies*

Noted Memphis artist and children's book author Louise Perkins Fitzhugh died today in New Milford, Connecticut. The daughter of Republican political leader Milsaps Fitzhugh, she graduated from Miss Hutchinson's School and Barnard College. In 1961, Fitzhugh illustrated Sandra Scoppettone's children's book *Suzuki Beane*. She wrote and illustrated her first children's book, *Harriet the Spy*, in 1964. Published by Harper and Row, the book was immediately acclaimed as a classic of children's literature. A review in the *Chicago Tribune* declared that *Harriet the Spy* "is a brilliantly written, unsparingly realistic story, a superb portrait of an extraordinary child." The Gesell Institute of Child Development recommended the book by stating that "in our opinion it shows quite as much understanding of child behavior as Salinger's *Catcher in the Rye* and is equally amusing." A sequel to *Harriet the Spy*, *The Long Secret*, was published the following year, and Fitzhugh also cowrote with Scoppettone the antiwar novel *Bang, Bang You're Dead*. In its obituary of Fitzhugh, the *New York Times* explained that *Harriet the Spy* "helped introduce a new realism to children's fiction and has been widely imitated."

November 20, 1917

Reverend T.J. Searcy Laid to Rest

A funeral service was held on this day at Robert Church's Beale Street auditorium for the African American pastor of Metropolitan Baptist Church, Reverend T.J. Searcy. Four thousand black and white Memphians packed the auditorium while over one thousand stood outside the building to pay their respects to the well-known Memphis leader. A reporter for the *Commercial Appeal* described the scene:

> *Men and women, white and colored, representing every walk of life were present and sat patiently through a funeral service that will never be forgotten in the history of the colored people of Memphis. Following the processional…Scripture reading and prayer, and a selection by the Howe Institute Quartette, more than 50 telegrams of condolence from friends throughout the country were read…The funeral sermon was preached by Dr. T.O. Fuller of Howe Institute with closing remarks by Dr. Sutton E. Griggs. Masonic and other secret orders took part in the services and the remains were laid to rest in Elmwood Cemetery. Probably no man in this country was more thoroughly loved by those who knew him than was Rev. Searcy. He held the esteem, respect and good will of white and colored alike, and he was one of the most progressive leaders of his people. Truly it could be said of him that—"He lived in a house by the side of the road and was a friend to man."*

November 21, 1960

Catholic Church Celebrates One Hundred Years of Service

A Pontifical High Mass and dinner was held on this day to mark the centennial of St. Mary's Catholic Church. The Reverend William L. Adrian led the 6:00 p.m. celebratory Mass, and afterward, a dinner was held for members of the congregation, former pastors and city officials. The current pastor of St. Mary's Catholic, Reverend Elstan Coghill, presided over the dinner, which was attended by over fifty people. The church was founded in November 1860, when Reverend Wenceslaus J. Repis began holding services for German Catholics in a house at the corner of Market and Second Streets. In 1864, the home was torn down, and the present church building was constructed on the site. Completed in 1870, the structure was built using a gothic architectural style. The *Commercial Appeal* reported that "during the Yellow Fever epidemics of 1873, 1878 and 1879 St. Mary's gave six martyrs in the fight against the disease." The parish was instrumental in establishing St. Joseph Hospital in 1899, and it operated a night school and kindergarten from 1889 to 1960. St. Mary's Catholic remains to this day one of the most important churches in Memphis.

November 22, 1989

Cookie Priest Introduces the President

President George Herbert Walker Bush arrived in Memphis on this day to honor a group of volunteers who, in the words of the chief executive, were "great American success stories. And they're powerful reminders that everyone can do something for somebody else." Meeting with volunteers at St. Jude Children's Research Hospital, Bush was moved by their spirit, exclaiming, "I just can't help but think of all those children and be thankful for you all." The president then spoke to a large crowd on the lawn of the *Commercial Appeal* building. A cold rain fell as the president was introduced by Reverend Donald Mowery, executive director of Youth Service USA. Bush was well acquainted with Mowery and had even given the Episcopal priest his nickname. While Bush was serving as vice president, Mowery presented him with homemade chocolate chip cookies while briefing him on his organization's job training, drug rehabilitation and truancy programs. While munching on the snack, Bush said, "from now on you'll be known as the 'cookie priest' in the White House."

November 23, 1954

Mayor Snores Too Loud

Lucille Adams Tobey, wife of Mayor Frank Tobey, on this day revealed many intimate details about her husband while appearing on the WMCT television program *Interesting Persons*, sponsored by the *Press-Scimitar* newspaper. According to Mrs. Tobey her husband "snores. Not just a gentle snore, but a real he-man snore—long and loud." The mayor's wife also revealed that his favorite pie was lemon. Devoted to each other, the couple met downtown for lunch at the Little Tea Shop, Gerber's or Lowenstein's regardless of the executive's schedule. During her interview with the *Press-Scimitar*'s Null Adams, Mrs. Tobey explained that the story of their standing lunch date had been published in many newspapers. "And as a result of that little story I now get invited to many official luncheons when Frank is invited to speak. Sometimes I am the only woman there."

Frank Tobey (right), seen here in a humorous pose with entertainer Danny Thomas (left), was instrumental in bringing St. Jude Children's Research Hospital to Memphis.

November 24, 1971

Fred Davis Kept the Government Train from Jumping the Track

On this day, Fred Davis took pride in his election as the first African American chair of the Memphis City Council. The *Press-Scimitar*'s Clark Porteous wrote that as "a councilman for the past four years, Davis has become known as one of the most effective bridges between the black and white communities. He is considered a racial moderate." First elected in 1967, Davis was one of the first African Americans elected to the Memphis City Council in the twentieth century. He accomplished a great deal while a member of the council, including the adoption of a fair housing policy and reduced bus fares for senior citizens. However, all was not easy for the first black chairman. When he retired from the council in 1979, Davis explained that the "white folks were looking to see how a black would handle a position of high responsibility and prestige. I did well enough to gain the confidence of the white community. They saw that the train was not going to jump the track." When his term as chairman ended in December 1972, white city council member Tom Todd stated that "we are proud of you and I mean this from the bottom of my heart. Not many people could have done the job you have. I think the whole council joins me in this."

November 25, 1986

African American Neighborhood Sells Out

Residents of the McKinney-Truse neighborhood received welcome news on this day when the city council approved a redevelopment study that was the first step in their plan to sell their properties as one unit rather than individually so they could secure a higher selling price. Located behind the Eastgate Shopping Center at Poplar and Mt. Moriah, the Truse subdivision was developed in 1900 to provide affordable housing for African Americans. In 1942, the McKinney neighborhood was built nearby, creating a black enclave in the middle of white East Memphis. According to the *Commercial Appeal*'s Peggy McCollough, "McKinney-Truse is like a dilapidated pocket on a pair of Brooks Brother's pants, and residents complain that real estate businesses have been trying to pick that pocket for years—offering low prices for the choice land, then attempting to get it rezoned piece by piece from residential to commercial." In 1985, the residents banded together to create the McKinney-Truse Neighborhood Association and worked with an attorney to get the redevelopment study approved by the council. Although in 1986 it appeared that the sale was imminent, it would take another decade before the owners were able to sell their property. In October 1997, the homes were demolished to make way for a Home Depot store, which opened the following year.

November 26, 1969

Entertainment District Planned for Madison and Cooper

A new entertainment district for Memphis was announced one day after Shelby County voters cast 74,758 ballots to approve the sale of liquor by the drink. Located near the intersection of Madison Avenue and Cooper Street extending to Trimble and Florence Streets, the district was named Overton Square for its proximity to the park of the same name. According to *Commercial Appeal* reporter Louis Silver, Overton Square was "patterned after the mood of such spots as New York City's Upper East Side and San Francisco's Ghirardeli Square." The district opened in May 1970 with its flagship restaurant TGI Friday's, a New York City–based chain. The *Press-Scimitar*'s Robert Johnson wrote that Friday's opened by "putting a sign in the window, and by 7 that night they had about 200 people inside. It's been like that ever since." Other popular businesses included the restaurants Bombay Bicycle Club and Paulette's, Lafayette's Music Room and Burkle's Bakery. The district continued to grow in popularity throughout the 1970s; however, by the mid-1980s, many Memphians began returning to downtown, and Overton Square suffered. In 1985, it was sold to two New York companies, and in 1990, it filed for bankruptcy. Attempts were made in the early 2000s to raze the historic buildings in the square, but preservationists were successful in saving the buildings. In 2011, Loeb Properties bought Overton Square and transformed it into a theater arts district.

November 27, 1950

Convicts Bust Out of County Big House

Alarms rang out on this day when eight prisoners escaped from the Shelby County Penal Farm. The escape was planned by Norman Eugene Carter, who conspired with Ralph A. Hartsell, John S. Johnston, Lealand Mullins, Daniel Thomas Perkins, James L. Rape, Woodrow L. Sanders and Albert Xiques to break free of the prison farm. According to *Commercial Appeal* reporter Bob Marks: "When three of a large group of prisoners awaiting their turn to get haircuts stepped out of a large cell on the main corridor, Carter rushed at the nearest guard. He grabbed him; snatched his pistol from its holster, slugged him to the ground. Then he took the guard's blackjack and keys. The other six escapees slugged another guard and forced a third unarmed guard to walk into the cell they had just occupied. The other two guards were carried into the cell and Carter locked the door from the outside."

Two of the escapees boarded a prison dump truck, which, fortunately for them, had its key in the ignition. They crashed through the locked prison gate while the other six ran through the opening and into the woods. Carter and five others were captured the next morning but Perkins and Johnston eluded capture for an additional day. Opened in 1929, the Shelby County Penal Farm was one of the nation's leading agricultural prisons until it ceased operation in 1964.

November 28, 1963

Thanksgiving Day Riot in North Memphis

Two members of one of the most violence-prone families in the history of Memphis had little to be grateful for on this Thanksgiving Day because they were in jail. Albert and George Tiller were arrested for assault and battery after a street fight erupted in front of Albert's home in North Memphis. The ruckus began after Russell Moore, who lived a few doors down, barred Albert from entering his steakhouse on North Watkins. Taking umbrage at this, Albert attacked Moore while his brothers George and Michael joined in the fun. The fight soon spread from the street to Albert's apartment, where he pulled a shotgun and pistol. When patrolmen B.B. Viar and Leonard Wright arrived on the scene, they attempted to break up the fight but were quickly overpowered by the Tiller bothers. Given that George held the mid-South amateur heavyweight boxing title and Albert was the novice boxing champion of North Memphis, it was not surprising that Viar suffered a broken nose and jaw while Wright was injured about the face during the scuffle. It took twenty-five squad cars to quell the disturbance and cart the Tillers to jail. Albert and George were convicted of three counts of assault and battery and spent twenty months in the county penal farm. When released Albert told the press that "people think we're Jesse James and his brother because we've gotten so much bad publicity. It's gotten to where we can't go in a place now because the owner is scared we'll tear it up. It's hard to enjoy a beer nowadays."

November 29, 1942

Program Honors Miss Lucie

Teacher and gospel music composer Lucie E. Campbell was honored on this day at the Booker T. Washington High School auditorium. The program consisted of the Southern Male Chorus, Booker T. Washington band and a one-hundred-voice singing group performing her many gospel songs. Known to her students as Miss Lucie, Campbell taught English and history at Booker T. Washington High School for forty-three years. A nationally recognized educator, Campbell was invited by President Franklin D. Roosevelt in 1934 to attend a White House conference on Negro Child Welfare, and she was a member of the National Education Association's Policy Planning Commission. Campbell began writing songs as the music director of the National Baptist Convention. Her many songs included "Touch Me, Lord Jesus," "Hold my Hand, Precious Lord" and "He'll Understand and Say Well Done," which was recorded by Pat Boone and Lawrence Welk. Campbell said her songs "come from conditions, from the hope of getting out from under handicaps and depressions. They're inspired by seeing through a cloud, by seeing the sunshine beyond." Summing up her career, the *Press-Scimitar* declared, "What W.C. Handy is to the blues, Lucie E. Campbell is to religious songs."

November 30, 1964

Largest Barbecue Sandwich Shop in Nation Opens in Memphis
William Loeb announced on this day that his company had opened the largest barbecue pork sandwich shop in the United States at 1055 South Bellevue. Founded in June of 1963, Loeb's Barbeque was owned by Amelia Company, which was a partnership between Jack Scharff and Loeb. The owner of a large laundry business, William Loeb became interested in pork when he met A.B. Coleman, a former manager of the Tops barbecue sandwich chain. Hiring Coleman as general manager, Loeb and Scharff opened their first shop at 3178 Summer Avenue, five blocks west of Highland. According to the *Commercial Appeal*, "The shop on Bellevue is the 18th in the Loeb chain, now 17 months old, and is twice as large as any of the others." In June 1965, Loeb formed the LoBo Corporation with singer Pat Boone to franchise the barbecue shops across the nation under the name Loeb's Tennessee Pit Bar-B-Q. Claiming to be "the South's largest home-owned Bar-B-Q chain," by early 1966, there were twenty-four shops in Memphis, two in Arkansas, eight in Mississippi and one in Alabama. Although it never became a national chain, it was one of the most popular barbecue restaurants in Memphis until it closed in the 1980s.

December 1, 1949

Lumber Inspectors' School Dedicated

The National Hardwood Lumber Association and the Lumbermen's Club of Memphis opened a new school to train hardwood lumber inspectors on this day. According to instructor L.C. Nicely, the students "were taught hardwood lumber grading from textbook to actual yard experience so when they finish the course they have correct and definite knowledge." During the dedication ceremonies, Mayor Watkins Overton stated: "The National Hardwood Lumber Association has helped to raise the standard of ethics of the hardwood industry and we are appreciative that it selected Memphis for the site of the training school."

The school quickly became well known, and in 1951, the *Commercial Appeal*'s Irvine H. Anderson wrote that the school was so successful that "students have enrolled from every part of the United States and Canada, and a number have come from as far as Britain, Holland, Sweden, Switzerland, Mexico and British Honduras." Located at Nickey Bros. Inc. on Summer Avenue, the school was the only one of its kind in the United States and further enhanced Memphis's reputation as the hardwood capital of the world.

December 2, 1929

Chinese Restaurant Opens in Memphis

One of the most well-regarded restaurants in Memphis during the 1920s and 1930s was the Shanghai Café, owned and operated by Wong Kop, who was recognized as the leader of the Memphis Chinese community. The *Commercial Appeal* reported on this day that "Connoisseurs of Chow Mein, Chop Suey or any of the other hundred and one tasty Chinese dishes will find their palates pleased to the ultimate with the foods prepared by the Shangai Café at 160–162 Hernando Street…Wong Kop, with many years of cafe operation in Memphis to his credit, makes a trip to China each year to learn the latest improvements in the culinary arts and the preparation of new Chinese dishes." The restaurant closed around 1934 when Wong Kop was convicted of peddling narcotics and sentenced to ten years in federal prison. Since the mid-nineteenth century, Memphis has been home to a vibrant Chinese community. Chinese groceries, laundries and restaurants dotted the Memphis landscape and added much to the economic life of the city. By 1961, there were at least three hundred Chinese Americans living in Memphis, including two architects, several physicians, two college professors and many businessmen like Jack Wong, owner of Joy Young restaurant. Although they have proudly clung to their Chinese heritage, they also embraced the culture of the Bluff City. As Memphis restaurateur Bernard Chang explained, "I am very Americanized, a regular redneck."

December 3, 1937

World's Largest Santa Erected in Memphis

Thousands of excited children visited the fifteen-foot-tall Santa Claus seated on an eight-foot platform in Court Square during the 1937 holiday season. Purported to be the world's largest St. Nick, the statue was erected in Court Square after appearing in the Spirit of Christmas Parade held on November 26. Twenty-three floats and seventeen marching bands snaked down Main Street as 200,000 people watched from crowded sidewalks. According to police commissioner Clifford Davis, this was "the largest crowd I have ever seen in Memphis." The floats, which included displays of Old King Cole, the Three Little Pigs, Little Miss Muffet and a toy circus, were constructed by National Youth Administration workers. According to the *Commercial Appeal*, "The Spirit of Christmas Parade was unquestionably the finest and most elaborate ever staged. The beauty of the floats… and the number of bands, raised last night's display to a position of eminence that the future will find hard to sustain." The Santa Claus was a popular attraction during the 1937 Christmas season. Not only could one marvel at its large size, but boys and girls were also able to talk directly to St. Nick through a hidden sound system located in the base of the statue.

December 4, 1956

Birth of the Million-Dollar Quartet

Elvis Presley visited Sam Phillips's Sun Records studio on this day as Carl Perkins and Jerry Lee Lewis were finishing a recording session. After hearing stories of Elvis's recent visits to Hollywood and Las Vegas, the three began to play music. Phillips, sensing this might be a historic moment, told producer Jack Clement, "Man, let's record this. This is the type of feel, and probably an occasion that—who knows?—we may never have these people together again." As the tape machine whirred, Phillips called his newest recording star, Johnny Cash, to come down and then phoned *Press-Scimitar* columnist Robert Johnson, who rushed to the studio to report on one of the most important recording sessions in Memphis history. Describing the event as "a barrel-house of fun," Johnson wrote, "If Sam Phillips had been on his toes, he'd have turned the recorder on when that very unrehearsed but talented bunch got to cutting up on 'Blueberry Hill' and a lot of other songs. That quartet could sell a million." Thus Elvis Presley, Carl Perkins, Jerry Lee Lewis and Johnny Cash became known as the Million-Dollar Quartet. As his fellow musicians began to drift out of the studio, Elvis said wistfully, "That's why I hate to get started in these jam sessions. I'm always the last one to leave."

December 5, 1977

Enchanted Forest Spreads Christmas Cheer

Goldsmith's department store spent its fourteenth Christmas season delighting the children of Memphis with its Enchanted Forest display. For many Memphis children, a trip to the downtown Goldsmith's store to walk through a snowy trail filled with elves, reindeer, dolls and Santa Claus was an integral part of Christmas in the Bluff City. A *Commercial Appeal* reporter on this day described a visit to the store: "'I liked Ernie and Big Bird and the orange guy and reindeer sticking his tongue out,' said Joshua Grieswell, 6. Joshua, who lives at 1400 Peabody, came to the Enchanted Forest at Goldsmith's downtown on a recent night with his upstairs neighbors, Mr. and Mrs. Mitchell Brackin and their 10 year-old foster daughter Rita Golden. 'I liked the whole thing, especially the little doll with whiskers and the little doll that's breathing,' said Rita….Hester Shipp, 3, daughter of Mr. and Mrs. Charles Shipp of 1611 Vinton, seemed too awed by her journey through the Enchanted Forest to say much…Joshua Grieswell wasn't satisfied. 'Can we go back and see it again?'"

The exhibit was created in 1963 by display director George Hettinger, who based the Enchanted Forest on Walt Disney's "It's a Small World" exhibit at the New York World's Fair. When the downtown Goldsmith's store was closed in 1990, the exhibit was first moved to the Agricenter and later to the Pink Palace Museum, where it continues to delight Memphis children during the Christmas season.

December 6, 1969

Radio and TV Mogul Signs Off

Hoyt B. Wooten, founder of TV and radio stations WREC, died on this day. Born in Coldwater Mississippi, he graduated from Mississippi State University and served in World War I. In 1922, he received a license from the Federal Communications Commission to operate KFNG, a ten-watt radio station. Wooten also sold radio equipment, and in 1925, he opened Wooten's Radio Electric Service Company in Memphis's Peabody Hotel. The following year, he moved his radio station to the outskirts of Memphis and changed its call letters to the initials of his radio equipment company. In 1929, the station was relocated to the Peabody Hotel, and WREC became an affiliate of the Columbia Broadcasting System. According to the *Press-Scimitar*, Wooten "became interested in television long before the general public was aware pictures could be transmitted through the air and, on July 19, 1928 he received one of the first six permits issued in the country to build and operate television stations." Despite this early interest, WREC was the third TV station to operate in Memphis when it began broadcasting on January 1, 1956. In addition to his radio and television work, Wooten was also known for the elaborate bomb shelter he built near his home in the suburb of Whitehaven. Powered by two diesel engines, the structure boasted an extensive communications system, large dormitories for men and women, a lounge and large bathrooms.

December 7, 1938

Memphis Jews Plan Colony in Palestine

A group of prominent Memphians laid plans this month to fund a Jewish colony in Palestine. According to the *Commercial Appeal*, a committee was formed "to set up as an everlasting memorial to Hardwig Peres the Peres Memphis Colony, where the oppressed may find sanctuary." Born in Philadelphia, Peres came to Memphis when he was but two months old. His father, Jacob, was appointed the first rabbi of Temple Israel, and he also established a brokerage business, which Hardwig entered when he finished the eighth grade. In addition to his spiritual and financial work, Jacob was also very involved in civic affairs. He was elected president of the Memphis Board of Education in 1868, and Hardwig followed in his footsteps, becoming school board president in 1917. On January 5, 1939, Temple Israel held a birthday celebration for Peres at which 1,500 people attended. During the festivities, a check for $15,000 was presented to Peres to fund the Palestinian colony. Rabbi Stephen Wise, president of the World Jewish Congress and keynote speaker for the celebration, exclaimed, "Imagine Hardwig getting a check! All his life he's been writing and distributing checks. Now he's going to get a check." Overwhelmed by the generosity of his neighbors, Peres said, "You have been making an investment in Palestine. The land belongs to you."

December 8, 1978

Democratic Party Conference Opens in the Bluff City

Democratic Party delegates arrived in Memphis for a three-day national conference to outline goals and debate President Jimmy Carter's proposal to curb inflation by cutting social service programs. The president, Mrs. Carter, Vice President Walter Mondale and Massachusetts senator Edward Kennedy also arrived in Memphis to participate in the conference. At the opening session, Carter declared, "As president, I have no alternative except to bring inflation under control." The *Commercial Appeal* reported that "Carter said no American family should be reduced to poverty, or bankruptcy, or go without needed health care because they can't keep up with the costs of living." As freezing rain fell on the streets of Memphis, liberal delegates attacked the president's anti-inflation plan by calling for a resolution condemning them. Vice President Mondale chided the liberals by reminding them that "nothing will sour a progressive nation more quickly than runaway inflation," while Massachusetts senator Edward Kennedy cheered them on by calling for a national healthcare system. Despite Kennedy's enthusiasm, the liberals were defeated in a roll call vote. As the *Commercial Appeal*'s John Bennett observed, "Democrats ended their three-day party conference…by defeating a challenge to President Carter's inflation-fighting plan to slash spending for social services."

December 9, 1927

Lil Hardin Struts with Some Barbecue

In Chicago, Louis Armstrong and His Hot Fives recorded "Struttin' with Some Barbeque," composed by his wife, Memphian Lil Hardin. Born in the Bluff City on February 3, 1898, Hardin soaked up the blues music drifting through her neighborhood from Beale Street. She played piano and organ in her church, but it was the music of W.C. Handy that influenced Hardin's musical style. Studying music at Fisk University in Nashville, she moved with her family to Chicago in 1917. Hardin joined the New Orleans Creole Jazz Band, and it was there she met Armstrong, whom she married in 1924. After playing with King Oliver's orchestra, Armstrong formed his own band, the Hot Fives (and later the Hot Sevens) with his wife on piano. Hardin had a strong musical influence on her husband, composing many songs that blended Memphis blues with New Orleans jazz to produce some of the most important recordings in the history of American music. Hardin divorced Armstrong in 1938, but she remained a respected jazz musician for the rest of her life. Lil Hardin died in 1971 while performing Handy's "St. Louis Blues" at a memorial concert for her former husband, who had died six weeks earlier.

December 10, 1972

Opera Singer Comes Home

Ruth Welting, coloratura singer with the New York City Opera, returned to her hometown on this day to perform with the Memphis Symphony Orchestra. According to the *Press-Scimitar*'s Louise N. Ahrens, "Miss Welting's performance...was a revelation to the near-capacity

Memphian Ruth Welting, seen here with famed conductor Pablo Casals, performed regularly with New York's Metropolitan Opera until her death in 1999.

audience which rewarded her with palm-stinging applause and a well-deserved standing ovation. It is also a source of pride to the community to be able to add her name to the growing list of fine artists who hail from Memphis." In 1968, Welting won the Metropolitan Opera's Mid-South Regional Audition while a sophomore at Memphis State University. She later joined the Julliard School of Music's American Opera Center company, and in 1976, she debuted at the Met. That same year, she appeared in the first Metropolitan Opera production to be performed live on public television. Ruth Welting died on December 16, 1999.

December 11, 1953

Gospel Group Buys Airplane

The *Press-Scimitar*'s aviation editor Hilmon Pinegar reported on this day that the famed gospel quartet the Blackwood Brothers of Memphis were using an airplane to make

The Blackwood Brothers gospel quartet logged over 200,000 miles while performing across the South in 1953.

traveling to their many engagements easier. In 1953, the quartet—James and R.W. Blackwood, Bill Lyles and Bill Shaw—traveled 200,000 miles to concerts across the South. Founded in Ackerman, Mississippi, in 1934 by James, R.W., Doyle and Roy Blackwood, the lineup changed over the years, but not their commitment to gospel ministry. The quartet reached the pinnacle of its fame in 1954, when it won first place on the Arthur Godfrey Talent Scout TV program. Two weeks later, Bill Lyles and R.W. Blackwood died in a plane crash. Despite this loss, the quartet continued to perform well into the twenty-first century, was honored with eight Grammy Awards and was inducted into the Gospel Music Hall of Fame in 1998.

December 12, 1977

Beale Street Entertainer Beaten

Robert "Bones" Couch, who performed in Hollywood's first all–African American musical, was severely beaten with an ashtray by an acquaintance who also robbed him of ninety dollars before fleeing the entertainer's home on St. Paul Avenue. In 1928, Couch and his partner, Milton Dixon, were dancing in the lobby of the Peabody Hotel when they were noticed by Robert Golden, assistant to director King Vidor, in Memphis to film his epic musical *Hallelujah!* Impressed by the youngsters' dancing prowess, Vidor hired them for thirty-five dollars per week and room and board. According to Couch's guardian, Mrs. Jessie B. Anderson, "Hal Roach Studios wanted him to replace someone in Our Gang, but I decided we should come on back home because by that time, Milton Dixon, who was 13, was too old to work in Our Gang and he told me he would run off if we stayed." Couch performed whenever he got the chance after returning to Memphis. In 1942, he partnered with entertainer Rufus Thomas, performing at the Flamingo Club, Beale Street Palace and the annual WDIA Goodwill Revue. In the 1950s, he co-hosted, with Thomas, WMCT's groundbreaking and all-black television program *Handy Theater*. Six days after being attacked, Robert "Bones" Couch died.

December 13, 1917

Men Rush to Join Armed forces

At the Memphis recruiting station on this day, 165 men joined the nation's armed forces, which brought the total number of the week's enlistees to 547 men. Eighty recruits joined the army, including 24 men selected to serve in the nonflying mechanic squadron at Park Air Field in nearby Millington. The Naval Aviation Office received 12 recruits for its flying service, and 10 entered the marine corps. The *Commercial Appeal* praised those who joined up:

> *From Arkansas, Mississippi, Tennessee, Kentucky, Alabama, North Carolina, Missouri and Indiana came applicants who—remembering the tragedy of Belgium, the sinking of the Lusitania, the murder of Edith Cavell and the thousands of acts of cowardice and inhumanity committed by the Huns—sought enlistment at the local offices yesterday…Examinations of the lists of men accepted in the present week show that, judging from the names, men of English, Irish, Jewish, Russian and German extraction proved that they are first and foremost Americans by joining some branch of the service.*

December 14, 1980

Memorial Held for Slain Beatle

A memorial was held on this day at Halle Stadium for former Beatle John Lennon, who was murdered in New York on December 8. Three thousand Memphians stood in the mid-December sunshine and listened to eulogies by musician Larry Raspberry and St. Elizabeth's Episcopal Church associate rector John L. Abraham. Lennon was "a person who lived fully…a man who liked his privacy, a fighter, rebellious, an advocate of love and understanding, an artist but not a martyr…Don't write his name on rocks and on bathroom walls. Don't be a part of his name being used for commercial purposes, such as T-shirts and trinkets," Raspberry said. Reverend Abraham reminded the audience that "peace, freedom and love are the things he sang of. He also sang for the broken-hearted." According to the *Press-Scimitar*'s Orville Hancock: "There were no tears, as when Elvis Presley died. But there was solemn concern and a serious contemplation of Lennon's music with the Beatles. The tunes made famous by the legendary British rock group were played for the young crowd…Although the age of those who came ranged from the teens to the 70s or more, the majority of persons in the crowd appeared to be in their 20s, 30s and 40s. They remembered the Beatles, the Sixties; days of rage, confusion and concern…A quiet fell over the stadium, punctuated occasionally by a cough, a baby's cry and the distant echo of an airplane's engine. Then it was over, except for individual memories of the passing of a musician and an era."

December 15, 1929

Clarence Saunders's Tigers Maul Packers

One of the most important football games ever played in Memphis took place on this day at Hodges Stadium, where the Clarence Saunders's Sole Owner Tigers battled the Green Bay Packers. Eight thousand Memphians watched in rapt attention as the Tigers prevented the national champions from scoring during the first half of the game. In the third quarter, Austin Applewhite ran thirty yards for the Tigers' first touchdown. Stunned, the Packers watched in dismay as Tigers Bucky Moore and Tiny Drouilhet intercepted passes to score two more touchdowns. The Packers broke through the Tigers line to score one touchdown, but it was not enough to overcome Saunders's team, which crushed Green Bay 20–6. Clarence Saunders was one of the most important Memphians of the twentieth century. In 1916, he opened his first Piggly Wiggly grocery store, which introduced Saunders's patented version of self-service and transformed the way Americans shopped. In 1924, he lost control of Piggly Wiggly and then founded a rival food store chain, Clarence Saunders Sole Owner of my Name Stores to distance himself from his famous creation. After his team defeated both the Chicago Bears and the Green Bay Packers during the 1929 season, the National Football League asked Saunders to add his franchise to its roster. The grocery store magnate refused because he did not want to play away games. Unfortunately for Memphis, the team folded when Saunders declared bankruptcy in 1931.

December 16, 1975

Grizzlies Telethon Sells Forty Thousand Season Tickets

A telethon was held at the Mid-South Coliseum on this day to secure season ticket pledges for the Memphis Grizzlies football team. It was hoped that the pledges would convince the National Football League's expansion committee to accept the former World Football League team's application to join the NFL. Thousands attended the free three-hour NFL-A-Thon, and many more watched it live on WMC-TV. Crowds lined up at ticket booths to buy season tickets, while WMC's Dick Hawley introduced performers Rufus Thomas, Charlie Rich, Isaac Hayes and George Jones and Tammy Wynette. When he learned that 40,688 pledges were collected, Grizzlies owner John Bassett declared that the NFL-A-Thon was "a great victory for everyone concerned." The victory was short-lived, however. In March 1976, the NFL rejected Memphis's bid for an expansion team.

The World Football League's Grizzlies played two seasons in Memphis during the mid-1970s.

December 17, 1928

Political Violence Erupts in Courthouse

Republican attorney Millsaps Fitzhugh, father of novelist Louise Fitzhugh, was recuperating on this day from a savage beating inflicted on him by Assistant Attorney General Will Gerber. Fitzhugh represented *Evening Appeal* reporter Billy Sisson, who sued Gerber for assault when the attorney general attacked him during the August Democratic Primary. At the trial, Fitzhugh suddenly filed a nonsuit, and after the proceedings came to a close, Gerber shouted at the attorney, "Anyone who'll do a trick like that is a crooked ——." According to Fitzhugh: "I turned and Gerber was glaring at me. I dropped my overcoat and hit him. He struck me in the face. There were several men around and Joe Boyles yelled, 'Kill him!' Some others yelled, 'Stomp him to death' and 'Beat his brains out' or something like that. Several of them were hitting me. They were hitting me so fast I quit trying to fight and put my arms over my face."

Gerber was arrested and put on trial for contempt of court for the beating. Judge A.B. Pittman found Gerber guilty of contempt and fined him $100. Gerber's attorney, L.D. Bejach, filed a motion for a new trial and Judge Pittman heard the evidence again and reduced the fine to $50. However, the judge also sentenced Gerber to five days in jail. Appealing to the Tennessee Supreme Court, the five-day jail sentence was overturned and Gerber was forced to pay only a $25 fine.

December 18, 1985

Berretta's Barbeque Closes

Louis Berretta Jr., owner of one of the most popular barbecue restaurants in Memphis, announced this day he was closing at the end of the year after fifty-three years of operation. To the dismay of many Memphians who fondly remembered eating and hanging out there, Berretta sold the property to a South Carolina developer, who quickly built a convenience store, gas station and laundry at the location. In 1933, Louis Berreta Sr. added a small restaurant to his combination grocery store and filling station at the corner of Park and Highland Avenues. "It was just fields, a few houses, just out in the country. There were no other nearby businesses, and farmers driving wagons into town often stopped to get food and beer." According to the *Commercial Appeal*: "In 1951 the restaurant was remodeled to offer curb service, a major part of its business during the 1950s and early 1960s. At one time Berretta's employed half a dozen car hops, and security guards were kept busy overseeing the crowded parking lot. In addition to thousands of Memphians who just wanted a good barbeque, customers included such notables as Elvis Presley, actress Stella Stevens, Jerry Lee Lewis, Ed Bruce and Wink Martindale. Their autographed pictures hang near the bar."

December 19, 1941

Earth, Wind and Fire Founder Born

Maurice White, composer and musician, was born on this day in South Memphis. Growing up in LeMoyne Gardens, White attended Porter Junior High and Booker T. Washington High School, where he played drums in the band. In addition, he soaked up many musical influences in church. "Everything goes back to Memphis in terms of my music. My grandmother took me around to the churches there, and I heard people singing and playing. The church was my laboratory, the place where everything came together," White remembered. With David Porter, who would cowrite many hit records for Stax, White sang in a quartet at Rose Hill Baptist Church. While playing in the high school band, White said that he "wanted to be the world's best drummer." Moving to Chicago, White was the house drummer for Chess and Okeh records, and in 1970, he founded the group Earth, Wind and Fire. During his career, White won seven Grammy awards and produced seven double-platinum albums for Earth, Wind and Fire; the Emotions; Neil Diamond; and Barbra Streisand. In 1978, Earth, Wind and Fire performed at the Mid-South Coliseum, where a large crowd enthusiastically welcomed home the fellow Memphian. After the show, White explained that the concert was "one of the most gratifying moments of my life. To come home, to know that people care, that people dig what you're doing out there, it's beautiful, simply beautiful, and I love it, and I love them, and I love Memphis."

December 20, 1933

Convicted Attorney Drops Appeal

Disbarred attorney Langford Ramsey on this day decided not to appeal his conviction for helping George "Machine Gun Kelly" Barnes, his former brother-in-law and wanted kidnaper, evade authorities. In abandoning his appeal, Ramsey reported to the Shelby County jail where he served a six-month sentence for harboring a fugitive. After completing that term, Ramsey spent two years in the Atlanta Federal Prison for conspiracy to harbor a fugitive. Ramsey began his brief life of crime when Barnes knocked on his door looking for a place to stay after he and his wife, Kathryn, collected a $200,000 ransom for kidnaping Oklahoma oil millionaire Charles Urschel. Unable to put him up, Ramsey arranged for them to stay with a friend. Captured on September 22, 1933, Memphians were shocked to learn that "Machine Gun Kelly" was in reality George F. Barnes, son of a local businessman and former Central High School student. Barnes had been a petty criminal and bootlegger while a student, but no one who knew him in Memphis thought him capable of becoming Public Enemy Number One. Convicted and sentenced to life in prison, Barnes died on July 17, 1954. When released from prison, Ramsey returned to Memphis and became a door-to-door salesman.

December 21, 1935

Scientist Dies from X-Ray Exposure

Dr. William G. Krauss died on this day due to prolonged exposure to X-rays, which caused the cancer that killed him. Born in Bavaria in 1861, Krauss came to the United States as a young man and settled in Memphis with his parents. He entered the Memphis Hospital Medical College in 1887 and finished his medical degree at St. Louis Medical College. After graduate work in Germany, Krauss returned to Memphis, where he eventually became professor of tropical medicine at the University of Tennessee Medical College and director of laboratories for the city health department. According to the *Commercial Appeal*, Krauss "established the first bacteriological laboratory in Memphis, was the first to use an oil immersion microscopic lens in this city, and the first to equip himself with an X-ray machine." An expert on yellow fever, he treated the sick during the 1897 and 1905 outbreaks. When Mayor Watkins Overton removed Dr. Louis W. Haskell from his post as chief surgeon at the city hospital, Krauss publicly criticized the decision. In reply, Overton demanded his resignation. At a testimonial dinner held in March 1929, Krauss was praised by his colleagues as "one of the world's greatest authorities on tropical diseases, a bacteriologist and chemist of first rank." Although largely forgotten today, Dr. William G. Krauss was one of the most important physicians ever to practice in Memphis.

December 22, 1960

Recluse Returns to Poplar Viaduct

Beloved recluse Jim Kennedy returned on this day to his shack under the Poplar Avenue viaduct after spending two weeks at the Shelby County Penal Farm. Judge Beverly Boushe had sentenced Kennedy to the correctional facility "for his own welfare." Kennedy had lived under the viaduct since 1946, and for the past ten years, Boushe required him to spend time at the penal farm every fall and spring to improve his health. When he was set free, Silvio Robilio, owner of Robilio's Liquor Store, drove Kennedy to the Humane Society Shelter to pick up his dog, Brownie. While they were running that errand, Judge Boushe, Patrolmen W.R. Looney and R.W. Robinson and National Food Store manager Charles Collum were under the viaduct preparing for Kennedy's homecoming. Looney and Robinson set up a kerosene stove donated by florist Jack Jackson, and Collum brought a thirty-pound box of food. Shocked when he arrived on the scene, Kennedy exclaimed, "It's the first time anyone ever did anything like this for me." Judge Boushe discussed with Kennedy the possibility of giving up his shack and moving to the county hospital, but the friendly recluse wouldn't hear of it. "He's happy here," Boushe said.

December 23, 1896

Christmas Food Baskets Distributed

For the tenth holiday season, the Christmas club provided baskets for needy families across the Bluff City. Volunteers spent this day on the first floor of the Neely Building, located at the corner of Main and McCall Streets, packing baskets for those in need. According to the *Commercial Appeal*: "[The] baskets are for the poor of the city who will call and get them…In each basket there will be a turkey or, where a family is very small, a chicken or duck, but each basket will have a fowl of some sort. Then there will be bread, rice, sugar, coffee, cakes, candies, fruits, such as bananas, oranges and apples. Where there is not enough of any one article to fill all the baskets it will be divided as far as it will go. Delicacies will be reserved for the sick and there are many on the list."

Memphis has a long history of helping the needy during the Christmas season. In 1917, the Goodfellows was organized when Bill Shaler of the *News Scimitar* asked his co-workers for money to provide clothing and toys for needy Memphis children. The newspaper adopted the program as its official holiday charity, and this continued when the newspaper changed its name to the *Press-Scimitar*. The Goodfellows program continued until 1983 when the *Press-Scimitar* ceased publication. Other popular Memphis Christmas charities included the *Commercial Appeal*'s Mile-O'-Dimes fundraising drive and Disc Jockey George Klein's annual Christmas Charity Show.

December 24, 1971

Actress Visits for Christmas

Aspiring actress Kathy "Bobo" Bates was in Memphis on this day visiting her parents, Bertye and Langdon Bates, at their East Memphis home. Bates had recently finished performing in her first feature film, *Taking Off*, directed by Czechoslovakian Milos Forman. In the film, she portrayed a singer and performed her own song, "And Even the Horses had Wings." A graduate of White Station High School, she became interested in acting after performing in a school production of *The King and I*. Bates moved to New York after completing a drama degree at Southern Methodist University. There, she went to work for the Museum of Modern Art but was dissatisfied with many of the exhibitions. "One of the exhibits was just some painted cloths hanging from the ceiling. I kept thinking I should have saved some of my dirty cloths from painting scenes and I could have been an artist." One of Bates's most thrilling moments as an actress came when she met Barbra Streisand. I was shaking all over, I was so nervous. I was with Milos Forman, who is Czechoslovakian. He introduced me to her as 'your new competition.' We all laughed about that, but then she said to me, 'What is your accent? Are you Czechoslovakian?' I had to explain, 'No, it's Tennessee.'" Bates would go on to star in many well-known films including *Fried Green Tomatoes* and *Titanic*, and she won an Academy Award for her work in *Misery*.

December 25, 1861

Peace and Violence Served on Christmas Day

Memphians celebrated Christmas with gifts, songs, prayers, reckless driving and homicide. Many of the exchanged gifts came from several well-regarded local establishments. For example, R.A Fagan's Southern Emporium of Fashion at 329 Main Street provided dresses, bonnets, caps and hats for the well-dressed women of Memphis. Items for children's stockings were available at Joseph Specht, a confectioner that supplied "a splendid assortment of candies and cakes…and a large assortment of toys." At St. Peter's, parishioners were treated to a choir accompanied by an orchestra led by Professor J.G. Handwerker. Others engaged in more earthy pursuits. Wagon drivers William Hughes and James Sullivan were stopped by police for speeding and charged with disorderly conduct when they resisted arrest. Early on Christmas morning, John Needam, suffering from a night of heavy drinking, ordered his wife, Bridget, to fix his breakfast. Bridget didn't move as fast as John wanted, so he grabbed a cane and smashed it over her shoulder blade. John then picked up a heavy wooden board and killed her. Needam was soon arrested and spent the rest of Christmas in jail, where presumably they fed him his breakfast.

December 26, 1958

Sale of Pistols Banned in Memphis

Police chief James C. McDonald responded on this day to a citizen complaint regarding the city's strict enforcement of the state law prohibiting the buying and selling of handguns. An anonymous Memphian sent a letter to the *Commercial Appeal* arguing that "every citizen ought to have the right to defend himself and his home from muggers, robbers and perverts who understand only the language of force." The law technically allowed Memphians to own a handgun, but it was illegal to carry one on your person. Chief McDonald stated that "this is far from harsh. If the law wasn't written like this, we would have more armed robberies and murders than we could handle...You can buy all the pistols you want, over the counter, in West Memphis [Arkansas]. You can imagine what we would have to contend with if the same thing was true over here." The *Commercial Appeal*'s Wesley Pruden Jr. further explained that "many newcomers don't remember when Memphis was the so-called murder capital of the world, police officials pointed out. These officers insist the firearms law has done more than any one thing to clean up the reputation of Beale Street, where once gunfire was common punctuation for jazz tunes born there."

December 27, 1964

State Legislator Outlines Plan

The first African American elected to the Tennessee General Assembly in the twentieth century, A.W. Willis, on this day appeared on WHBQ-TV's *Press Conference*, where he outlined his legislative goals for the 1965 session. Willis pledged to implement President Lyndon Johnson's War on Poverty program across the state. The freshman representative also stated he would propose a minimum wage law for Tennessee. True to his word, when Willis arrived in Nashville in January 1965, he introduced a measure to increase the state's antipoverty initiative by $3 million. Although the amount was eventually reduced, Willis's bill passed, and an additional $1 million was added to the state's poverty program. His minimum wage law did not fare so well. Governor Frank Clement supported the measure, but the bill went down to defeat largely because of the opposition of manufacturers and the hotel and restaurant industries. A.W. Willis served in the General Assembly through 1968, but he remained active in civic and political affairs until his death in 1988.

December 28, 1942

War Worker Stripped of Gas Rations

The Memphis Rationing Board held a hearing on this day to investigate W.R. Evans, a worker at the Memphis Naval Air Station at Millington, who was caught speeding on his way to his job. According to police, Evans was driving eighty miles an hour down Jackson Avenue when a traffic officer pulled him over for speeding. City Judge Kinkle fined him $102 and referred the case to the Office of Price Administration, which scheduled the hearing. Rationing Board 2A then revoked all of Evans's gas rationing books. Because of his war work, Evans was given a C gas ration book by Board 2A, which allowed him unlimited access to fuel. In addition, Evans had an A book issued by a South Carolina board and was allowed one grade 3 tire and three recaps. In revoking his books, the chairman of Memphis Rationing Board 2A stated that "we are of the opinion that war workers have been given special preference and that they should appreciate it more than anyone else. We believe that his waste of rubber and violation of OPA rationing regulations was more harmful to the war effort than his work is worth."

December 29, 1934

Clyde Parke Circus Debuts

When Clyde W. Parke lost his office manager position due to the economic ravages of the Great Depression, he took up wood-carving to pass the time. Deciding to build a miniature circus, Parke devoted over a year of his life to making the intricate carvings. By late December 1934, the project was far enough along for Parke to show off his creation to an eager *Commercial Appeal* reporter, who wrote, "The circus is set up on a 'lot' which takes in all of a large room at the Parke home." After Parke completed his massive carving project in April 1935, he explained that "every part of the circus—canvas top, poles, seats, wagons, people and animals—I made myself. All the figures are hand-carved and in perfect proportion. There are 250 wood carvings in the set. There are 36 wagons, 38 animals in cages, 70 horses, 128 people, including actors, drivers, workmen and the like and a complete sideshow full of working model people." For many years, Parke showed his circus at local events such as the Cotton Carnival, but in 1970, he donated it to the Pink Palace Museum, where it continues to amuse Memphians of all ages.

December 30, 1922

Veteran Scout Group Organized

The problem of keeping Boy Scouts active once they have completed the program was addressed by the Memphis Chamber of Commerce on this day. To that end, the chamber organized the Veteran Scout Club to provide trained leadership for the local Boy Scout council and to "interest and keep the boys in line with the organization during that period when he drops from active work with a troop until he is older and eligible to become a scoutmaster or assistant scoutmaster." All officers in the new organization had served on the staff of the summer camp Kia Kima, and many of them were Eagle Scouts. They included chairman Pat B. Barcroft, secretary Jeff Hicks, treasurer Merrill Schwartz and vice-chairman Floyd Kay. Only those who had given five years of faithful service to Scouting were eligible to join. Individual members were required to "live up to his scout obligations for life…keep the local scout authorities in the community in which he lives informed as to his availability for service to the community in case of emergency [and]…take an active part in the promotion of the cause of scouting as the circumstances and conditions in his case permit."

December 31, 1902

Tomahawk Murder on Main Street

George Milliard was murdered by an American Indian named Creeping Bear in front of Fire House No. Four on Main Street. Creeping Bear had appeared in a Wild West show at Olympic Park earlier in the day, and he was waiting to board a train when he decided to take a walk. As Creeping Bear strolled by the firehouse, George Milliard, who lived nearby and was often drunk, saw the Indian still dressed in his Wild West costume and began to taunt him. At first, Creeping Bear ignored him, but when Milliard called him an "Indian Son-of-a-Bitch," he had enough. Pulling his steel tomahawk from his belt, Creeping Bear swiftly delivered a blow to Milliard's head, nearly cleaving it in two. Milliard collapsed, and two men placed him on a chair and put a bucket beside him to catch the flowing blood. According to one eyewitness, "I can close my eyes… and see him sitting there near the side door into the alley, head between his hands, a wide gash in his scalp and blood dripping into the bucket." Lingering for two weeks, Milliard died on January 16, 1903. Creeping Bear was arrested, convicted of first-degree murder and sentenced to fifteen years in prison, but his conviction was overturned by the Tennessee Supreme Court. Creeping Bear was also convicted a second time for voluntary manslaughter, but it too was overturned. A third trial was scheduled but the prosecution abandoned the case, and Creeping Bear was finally allowed to leave Memphis.

SELECTED BIBLIOGRAPHY

Books

Bowman, Rob. *Soulsville, U.S.A: The Story of Stax Records.* New York: Schirmer Trade Books, 1997.

Capers, Gerald M., Jr. *The Biography of a River Town: Memphis, Its Heroic Age.* New Orleans, LA: Tulane University Press, 1966.

Cordell, Gina, and Patrick W. O'Daniel. *Historic Photos of Memphis.* Nashville, TN: Turner Publishing Company, 2006.

Cunningham, Laura. *Lost Memphis.* Charleston, SC: The History Press, 2010.

Dowdy, G. Wayne. *A Brief History of Memphis.* Charleston, SC: The History Press, 2011.

Gordon, Robert. *Respect Yourself: Stax Records and the Soul Explosion.* New York: Bloomsbury, 2013.

Green, Laurie B. *Battling the Plantation Mentality: Memphis and the Black Freedom Struggle.* Chapel Hill: University of North Carolina Press, 2007.

Jones, James B., Jr., ed. *A List of General and Special Orders Issued by Confederate and Federal Authorities Relative to Memphis and West Tennessee, 1861–1865.* Nashville: Tennessee Historical Commission, 1999.

Lauderdale, Vance. *Ask Vance Book Two.* Memphis, TN: Contemporary Media Inc., 2011.

Primary Sources

Memphis Information File, Memphis and Shelby County Room, Memphis Public Library and Information Center.

Newspapers

Memphis Bulletin
Memphis Commercial Appeal
Memphis Daily Appeal
Memphis Daily Avalanche
Memphis Evening Appeal
Memphis Press-Scimitar
Memphis Public Ledger

ABOUT THE AUTHOR

G. Wayne Dowdy is the agency manager of the Memphis Public Library and Information Center's history department and Memphis and Shelby County Room. He holds a master's degree in history from the University of Arkansas and is a certified archives manager. He is the author of *A Brief History of Memphis*; *Mayor Crump Don't Like It: Machine Politics in Memphis*; *Hidden History of Memphis*; and *Crusades for Freedom: Memphis and the Political Transformation of the American South*. Dowdy is the host of the WYPL-TV 18 program *The Memphis Room* and a member of the Tennessee Historical Records Advisory Board, has served as a consultant for the NBC-TV series *Who Do You Think You Are?* and PBS's *History Detectives* and has appeared on C-Span, NOS Dutch Public Radio and in the documentaries *Overton Park: A Century of Change*, *Memphis Memoirs: Downtown* and *Citizens Not Subjects: Reawakening Democracy in Memphis*.